Ruthie,
enjoy our Story!
Best from Louis
Drue 4/2017

Reflections & Recipes

Southern Supreme's
Berta Lou Scott
Shares Memories
& Recipes

SOUTHERN SUPREME

The recipes in **Reflections and Recipes** were submitted by the wonderful customers, employees and family members of Southern Supreme. Although every precaution has been taken to ensure the accuracy of published materials, Southern Supreme, Inc., cannot be held responsible for opinions expressed or facts supplied by its contributors. All recipes are correct to the best of our knowledge and offered without guarantee on the part of the author, Berta Lou Scott, or Southern Supreme, Inc.

Berta Lou Scott
Southern Supreme, Inc
1699 Hoyt Scott Rd
Bear Creek, NC 27207

Distributed by Southern Supreme Gourmet Specialties
Bear Creek, NC 27207
Printed in China

ISBN# 978-0-615-21228-9

Acknowledgements

I would like to thank so many people for their help in creating this book. First, I would like to thank my family for standing by me and encouraging me in this endeavor. I would also like to thank all the people who sent in recipes for me to use.

To my daughters-in-law Gail and Lisa for all the responsibilities that they took over while Belinda, Deborah and I worked on this book.

To my sister Ethelda, who collaborated and edited all the recipes for content. Her knowledge of cooking is one of the reasons we have reached this level of success.

To Reverend Bob Wachs of Pittsboro, North Carolina, Thank you for the time it took you to edit this story and the helpful bits of information that you gave us to make this book possible.

To Darrell Howard for his expertise in photography and his patience in working with me.

To Greg and Tamara Lamb from Lamb Designs for their design and layout abilities (and other avenues about publishing a book in which they guided us) which made this book possible.

To Joe Burke for providing the old photos of the train and Siler City for my Mother's story.

To Deborah Stephenson, I could never begin to express the thanks for her constant drive to push me to capture all the aspects of my life that I wanted to portray. She contributed in so many ways with not only her computer skills, and her photography abilities, but also the ability to make this a fun and unforgettable experience.

To my daughter Belinda, the one person who always said "Whatever you want to do Mama", who stepped up to the plate from the beginning. She has walked diligently beside Deborah and me to get this book to the printer, using her skills of organization and keeping us all on track. Belinda conveyed the memories of happenings and employees that have meant much to me throughout the years.

To my son Randy and son-in-law Wayne for all their hard work behind the scenes that included building, planning, and making space, all for the sake of making a fruitcake.

To my son Ricky and my daughter Sandra. Thank you for always being ready to help when you were needed.

To all my children, all of you are so different yet alike. My love will be with you forever.

To my husband, "Teet" who has been my partner through the years. He helped beyond the call of duty in all aspects of this business. Without him, success would have come a lot harder and much more slowly. May we continue to be thankful to the Lord for our families, friends and customers.

Dedication

*I would like to dedicate my book to my Mama and
Daddy, Burkett P. and Nannie E. Phillips.
Their memory never fades.*

Table of Contents

*H*ello, my name is Berta Lou Phillips Scott and I am the founder of The Southern Supreme Nutty Fruitcake Business.

The fruitcake that I had been baking for years had gotten so popular that I thought I could possibly market it.

Twenty-two years ago, I told my husband Hoyt that the fruitcake business could be a possible answer to a prayer. I related to him the thoughts and encouragements that were inspired by the compliments from the friends that enjoyed my fruitcake.

We decided to take the challenge, but it took hold of us, as well as our family.

The small beginning and the part time jobs it supplied our family have developed into something that I never dreamed possible.

Therefore, I begin my story...

It's impossible for me to tell it, unless I start at the beginning...

The Phillips: Berta Growing Up

*T*he beginning would start with my Mother and Father.

Mama was born in 1905 in Forsyth County to J. P. and Bertha Southern Grubbs. My Mother Nannie, was the third child of six children. Mama's childhood was filled with some difficult events. She often spoke of these times and I recall some of what she told. One of her sisters, Alfie at the age of three, fell into a tub of water and drowned. That was a devastating time for the family. In 1917 when the flu epidemic came to Forsyth County, so many people took sick. My Grandmother Bertha was one of those. She lived about three days after contacting this deadly virus. Grandma is laid to rest in Providence Moravian Church Cemetery in Forsyth County, beside her three-year-old daughter Alfie.

After Grandma passed away, Grandfather decided to make a change in his life. He purchased a tobacco farm in Chatham County, North Carolina. I remember my mother telling the story of how her father and her brother Ray loaded the family wagon with everything they owned and drove to Chatham County, a trip of two days. They slept under the wagon. They cooked by the side of

Johnnycake

2 cups corn meal
2 teaspoons salt
4 cups boiling water
1 tablespoon of shortening

Mix corn meal and salt add boiling water and shortening and beat well. Spread ½ inch thick on a greased baking pan. Bake in a moderate oven (350°) until crisp for 35 to 45 minutes. In traveling days they fried in a greased skillet over an open fire or poured onto a board plank and set beside the fire to cook.

the road; they would fry out some side-meat, cook some beans and make fried cornbread.

FRIED CORNBREAD WAS REFERRED TO AS "JOHNNYCAKES" MANY YEARS AGO

Johnnycake is always a simple bread, originally called a 'Journey Cake'. Circuit riders and other travelers frequently made it, as it was quickly prepared. They mixed cornmeal with water or even snow and baked before an open fire.

Mama, her sisters, Clevie and Ethel and her brother Reeve came down on the train. It stopped at Wells Depot not far from the farm that Grandfather had purchased. Grandpa came to the station and picked them up to carry them to their new home. Of course, Wells Depot has since long gone. The railroad tracks are the only reminder of days gone by.

When we were young, we walked those tracks many, many times. I remember thinking these were the tracks that brought my mother to Chatham County.

After getting established on the tobacco farm, Mama and her sisters enrolled in a one-room schoolhouse called Blue Rock. Soon Ethel, Mama's oldest sister, decided farm life was not for her and returned to Forsyth County. At that time, Mama was only 12 years old. Being the oldest female in the home, she had the job as "Woman of the House." She was not allowed to return to school, but had to stay home and help with the younger children, Clevie and Reeve. She had the burden of all the cooking and cleaning as well as her chores on the tobacco farm.

This is the train my Mama rode to Chatham County.

Mama told us often how they would travel by wagon to Siler City, a growing town in 1918, to buy their necessary supplies.

Bonlee & Western: From 1908 – 1930's transported freight and passengers.

She told of the trip to town; the rough ride in the wagon, and the dusty dirt road that led straight to the heart of Siler City where an old well stood.

Mama made this trip many times over the years as she struggled to help raise her siblings and help her father.

As time passed by Grandpa lost the farm during the "depression era" and he and Uncle Ray returned to Forsyth County. Mama and her sister Clevie did not. They remained in Chatham County where they married and raised their children.

Mama and Aunt Clevie remained very close; they lived within five miles of one another for the rest of their lives. The sister and friendship bond that they developed never faded or diminished over the years.

Siler City- circa 1905 North up Chatham Avenue the Old Well in the center (with roof) is at the intersection of Chatham Avenue and Raleigh Street.

Ruth Richardson, Mama's half sister, Mama and her sister Clevie at Mama's birthday party.

Mama's role as surrogate mother prepared her for a life as a country wife, mother, and grandmother.

After marrying my Father, the hard work didn't stop. Just doing the washing was a two-day ordeal that started every Monday morning. Mama would go in the washhouse Daddy had built for her and build a fire under the cast iron wash pot. Daddy had constructed a brick dais that held the pot above ground so a fire could be under it. The clothes were boiled in hot soapy water until they were clean. She would put the clothes through the ringer to rinse the water, then once again when they were soap free. With this done she would carry the clothes to a mile long clothesline and hang them to dry.

When they dried, Mama would bring the clothes in and prepare them for ironing. Tuesdays were ironing days. She ironed everything and I mean everything including her sheets and pillowcases.

This is the washhouse Daddy built for Mama.

You haven't lived unless you have crawled into a bed made up with freshly laundered and ironed bed linen. One of the things I remember most was Mama's ironed aprons. Mama did not start the day until she had on a freshly starched apron.

Summertime meant garden planting. There was always a garden to maintain. There was canning that had to be done, not to mention preparing three meals a day.

Housework was a never-ending chore with eight children. There were floors to sweep, beds to make, and dishes to wash.

Mama always had an imaginary maid, whose name was Hannah. Mama would come in from doing work outside and proclaim "I'm going to have to fire Hannah; she hasn't done her job". Hannah became a mystical legend to even the grandchildren in the later years. Mama would occasionally ask the grandchildren to do a chore and they would reply, "Grandma, let Hannah do it".

When Mama did have leisure time, she loved to plant and care for her flowers. She had many beautiful flowerbeds. She loved to read; the county bookmobile stopped by our house at least once a week. Every night when she would finally sit down in her favorite chair she would do needlepoint or crewel. Mama's handiwork is framed and graces many of our family members' homes.

Mama always cooked on a wood-burning stove; so there

This is a picture Mama did for me in 1965 for my birthday.

was always wood to bring into the house. I still remember the smells that came from her kitchen when she was cooking her favorite food, pinto beans. In her later years she hung a little plaque in her kitchen that stated; "Kitchen Closed Due To Retirement". Still, on occasion she would cook her pinto beans.

Mama had two vices that I know of. One was "Tube Rose" snuff, which she dipped for 86 years and the other was her favorite movie "Gone With the Wind", which she would watch at least once a year.

My Mother was a soft-spoken, warm-hearted caring individual. I do not recall her ever speaking a harsh or unkind word about any human being. Mama would have been proud being remembered as the good Christian woman that she was.

She lived in a time that was extremely hard, compared to the modern conveniences of today. She was devoted to being a hard worker and trying to keep her family together. Although she never complained, I imagine it was a rough time for one so young.

Mama passed away on May 31, 2002 at the age of 97. Her devotion to Daddy, her kindness to all she met and her love for family is the inspiration for everything I do and am.

Pinto Beans

1 pound pinto beans (always wash and pick out the bad beans and any rocks)

In a 2 or 3 quart pot, add a 1 inch by 3 inch slice of Side meat or fat back. Add pintos and enough water to cover to an inch above the beans.

Bring to a full boil, cover and reduce heat. Cook beans slowly. Stir occasionally, and add water if needed. Add salt, pepper and sugar to taste.

Beans are done when tender and standing in a thick juice

How My Parents Raised Me

Daddy was born in Chatham County in 1901 to Fannie Harper Phillips and Alexander Phillips.

Daddy's name was Burkett. He was one of eight children, five boys and three girls.

He attended school in a one-room schoolhouse at Hickory Grove. When his primary schooling was completed, he went to Bonlee School and stayed in the dormitory at the school. One of his teachers was Ina Andrews. At the time, he was unaware of the impact she would have on the family. Miss Ina taught his children and his grandchildren, as well, before she retired.

Sometimes during the summer months, he cooked for workers at a sawmill. That was where he learned to cook those wonderful melt-in-your-mouth biscuits. He wanted all us girls to learn how to make them but we never did master his technique. I've heard it more than once "Bert, you play with your dough too much."

Mama and Daddy.

Old Fashioned Buttermilk Biscuits

½ cup of lard
2 cups flour (plain)
2 ¼ teaspoon baking soda
1 teaspoon salt
¾ cup buttermilk

Preheat oven to 475°. Cut lard into flour until particles are as fine as course corn meal. Add soda and salt to buttermilk and quickly stir into flour mixture. Turn dough out to floured board knead very little and pinch off the size of biscuit you want. Shape by palm rolling and place on a greased pan. Dot with a pat of butter if desired.

At twenty-two, Daddy passed a Civil Service test to become a mail carrier for Mt. Vernon Springs in a community called Ore Hill, now known as Bear Creek. He started carrying the mail in 1923 and continued doing so until he retired after 42 years of service.

Mama and Daddy were married May 30, 1924. Mama was 19 and Daddy was 24. They had their first child Russell in 1925. They lived on the farm of his father Alexander in a small house called the "John A. House". In 1926, they bought the "Old Hilliard Place" about a mile away on the Mt. Vernon Springs Road. This property consisted of approximately

200 acres of mostly woodland. The remaining 7 children were born in the farmhouse. There were five girls and three boys Allene, Bill Joe, Ethelda, Sue Ann, Jane, Gary, and me. Daddy's mother was a Mid-wife. She attended Mama for the births of most her babies.

Daddy believed that we children should be busy at all times so we would not grow up to be lazy. He kept us busy picking up trash in our huge yard or gathering acorns for the hogs or even picking up rocks on new ground to make it ready for cultivation.

We got an allowance to go to the movies. We all had our own chicken houses as we got older and we got the money from them.

Life was different then from now with children; we always had work to do and we did it. Growing up we all did farm work, gardening, milking the cows and raising chickens. Because the land was mostly wood, clearing and fencing the land was essential. From these experiences, we learned from an early age the value of hard work.

Every morning Mama and Daddy cooked breakfast together while we children did the milking and taking care of the chickens. Mama would make the biscuits and gravy; Daddy would fry up the ham or bacon and cook the oatmeal. If we wanted an egg we told Daddy and he would cook it for us special and we had to eat it, that is if we had time after our chores. We still had to catch the bus and go to school at Bonlee.

The house I was born and raised in.

In the afternoons when we came home from school, our evening chores were waiting to be done. Of course, the cows were milked again and the animals had to be fed.

It's amazing what we remember, and I have a vivid memory of being afraid of milking the cow. I would get my cow in the stable, and when I finished milking her and was ready to leave; the cow would occasionally block the door. I couldn't get her to move. I kept a wooden block at the stable window to climb out if needed. I would climb out that window with the milk still in the bucket but sometimes not. As I got older, that window doesn't look as high. .

The wood boxes for the kitchen cook stove and the living room heater had to be filled every day. Mama was always cooking. We did our homework by a fuel burning Aladdin lamp. Electricity for our farm was late getting to us due to disputes over right-of-ways on other farms.

Dried Apple Fried Pies

2 pounds dried apples (sliced)
3 cups boiling water
1 cup sugar
1 tablespoon butter
1 teaspoon cinnamon
¼ teaspoon nutmeg
2 cups flour
2 teaspoons baking powder
¼ cup shortening
½ cup cold water

Cook apples in boiling water until soft. Add sugar, butter, cinnamon and nutmeg. Chill. Sift together flour, baking powder and salt. Cut in shortening with 2 knives. Add cold water gradually until flour is moist enough to roll into a ball. Roll dough thin and cut into 24 rounds (about the size of a saucer. Divide the mixture into and spoon into the middle of the rounds. Fold over the rounds and press the edges together with a fork. Fry in deep fat and drain on brown paper.

During the winter, Daddy would listen to the battery-powered radio for the weather reports as to when would be the best "hog killing" days. It had to be a certain temperature to start the processing of the meat.

Mama and us girls would cut up the meat that Daddy didn't hang or cure in the smoke house. We also canned sausage.

Daddy did not allow us to have an abundant amount of idle time so we were always busy. During the spring and summer months, Mama and we girls would garden, preserve, and can vegetables. We made jellies, jams and preserves. We made pickles, always an adornment to any meal and Mama's pickles were the best. Her sweet garlic dill pickles were always eaten first.

We had two apple orchards. We would gather the apples and take turns using a hand turning apple peeler. We would make jelly and preserves or dry out the apples and make those wonderful fried apple pies. She would slice the apples nearly paper thin and dry them in the sun or sometimes in the car so the insects would not get to them. She always seemed to know when the apples cured just right. It was a wonderful treat to come in from school or chores and have Fried Apple pies on the table waiting for us.

We also got out the cider mill and made cider. Cool apple cider was so good, but after a few days, Daddy and Mama stopped us from drinking the cider. You know, cider will ferment and has the ability to make you ever so slightly inebriated. Then, of course, after a while it turns to vinegar that you use for pickling. Daddy never did want us girls to eat the green apples but they were so good we would sneak and eat them before Daddy got home from work.

In the summer time when Daddy came in from delivering the mail, we ate lunch and there were always chores to be done.

We had a mill where we ground wheat and corn to feed the cows, pigs and horse. We also ground wheat for flour. It seemed like we were always preparing food for either the animals or ourselves.

Daddy owned the only threshing machine in our area. In late May or the first of June after school was out for the summer, we would go through the community cutting oats and wheat for the neighbors. We girls rode the machine tying up the bags as they filled. We really knew how important it was to tie the bags tightly and correctly. The farmers that we cut grain for would feed us dinner. We really enjoyed the meals, because their wives were good cooks.

Sometimes we would go with Mama and Daddy to "Corn Shuckins". Of course, the kids did more playing and eating than they did shucking. It was a wonderful way to socialize and really know your neighbors.

In the summer time, Ethelda and I would help some of them by working in tobacco. Daddy didn't raise tobacco but we could help our neighbors if we wanted to.

There were different foods to eat although I remember the bread pudding was the best.

Although we worked hard, there were fun times as well; we made and ate homemade ice cream. Our iceman's name was Slim. Daddy would let us buy a quarter's worth more ice just for the ice cream. We put the ice in the icebox on the back porch. We bought 200 pounds a week during the summer months and it would last just about a week. We would get out the old "White Mountain" ice cream machine and everybody got a chance to turn the crank. Whenever it was about ready we all took turns sitting on top of the machine to hold it down in the ice so it would freeze harder. Our machine usually made about 2 gallons.

> ## Bread Pudding
>
> 1 egg
> 3 cups milk
> 1 tablespoon vanilla flavoring
> ½ cup raisins
> ⅔ cup sugar
> 3 biscuits (crumbled)
> Dash of nutmeg
> Dash of cinnamon
>
> Beat egg in a 1 quart baking dish; add remaining ingredients. Mix well and bake until light brown at 350°. Yield 4 servings.

Mama and Daddy loved to go to the movies and so did we. We had no television so Daddy and Mama would take us into Siler City to the "Elder Theater" We would go to the movies and have drinks, candy and popcorn. We used our allowance money to pay our way.

When we grew out our chickens and sold them it was our money to keep and we had to make sure it lasted till we sold again. We also used that money for personal things that we wanted to buy from the "Sears and Roebuck Catalog". The Wish Book was a favorite past time for all of us.

On Sunday afternoons, we would meet up with the neighborhood children and play "cow pasture ball".

We never knew when relatives or company was coming because there was no phone. Sometimes relatives would show up and stay the night. Mama would cook a lot of food for those meals and our company never went away hungry. In the summertime our Uncle Ray (Mama's brother) from Forsyth County and his family would frequently come for an over night visit. He had eight children.

As I mentioned, there were eight of us children, so as expected, all five of the girls grew up doing house chores and cooking.

Mama and Daddy always liked to read after supper so that left us girls to clean the dishes. We got into big trouble if we made too much noise because that was 'quite time,' used to read and do home work.

The boys did not help at all in the kitchen. They did no cooking and they sure did not wash any dishes. Well, to my knowledge they never even learned to boil water.

Cousin Gene Phillips, my sister Sue, my sister Ethelda, Me, and my cousin Dottie Phillips. We played together when young. You can tell the difference between the country girls and the city girls by the wearing of shoes.

As I have reminisced over the years I've often wondered why my brothers were exempt from the cooking and kitchen duties. It seems strange now, since Daddy was such a good cook.

We girls were more accomplished at cooking sweets than an actual meal with vegetables and meat. We made cakes and lots of candy. Candy was our specialty because every member of the family had a sweet tooth. These sweets did not last long at our house.

Every year around Christmas time, we would take a trip to Siler City. Beane's Grocery Store was the place. We would buy all the ingredients for our fruitcakes and candy. We would all join in and crack the nuts in the evening and Mama would make the fruitcakes the next day. She would make some of the cakes in loaf pans and always one or two of the cakes were made in round tube pans. The cakes were soaked in grape juice until we ate them at Christmas.

We made lots of different kinds of candy for Christmas. We really enjoyed the candy made with brown sugar and black walnuts called "penuche". It didn't matter that the candy didn't have a long shelf life because we ate it before it went bad.

When we were growing up we girls enjoyed making this "Penuche" candy, especially at Christmas. We would sit and pick out black walnuts. The walnuts gave the candy a distinct flavor. This was one of our favorite Christmas candies.

Life then and now has changed tremendously but an exception to change is curiosity. My siblings and I were not exempt. My sisters and I were never mischievous, just inquisitive. There is an incident that has always remained vivid to me.

Ethelda was 14 years old at the time; I was 12 and Sue Ann was 10. We were out on a very cold winter's day. There was a large creek nearby and we decided to see if the water had frozen over hard enough to play on. Of course, we did not obtain permission to play on or near the ice. We were all on the ice and not as close to the bank as we should have been and I ventured further out than Ethelda and Sue Ann. The ice started to crack and down I went into the frigid icy cold water. Ethelda got on her knees and tried to reach me and the ice broke with her as well. With the cold water and the ice up to our armpits, we were struggling to escape. Every time we thought the ice would be strong enough to hold us so we could get out, it would break again. Sue Ann, the smallest, was able to walk off the ice but Ethelda and I had to walk in the icy water and break the ice as we headed toward the bank to get out. When we finally reached the bank and escaped the icy water, we rushed home hoping not to be found out. Mama and Daddy didn't see us as we snuck up the stairs and changed clothes. The hot meal that Mama prepared that night was more than welcomed to our cold bodies.

Penuche

2 cups brown sugar
1 cup white sugar
1 cup cream
2 tablespoons light corn syrup
¼ teaspoon salt
2 tablespoons butter
1 teaspoon vanilla
1 cup chopped black walnuts

Combine sugars, cream, corn syrup and salt in saucepan. Stir over heat to dissolve sugar. Cook to 238°; stir occasionally. Remove from heat, add butter and let stand without stirring until bottom of pan is lukewarm or 120°. Add vanilla and beat until creamy, mix in nuts. Pour in greased 9 inch greased pan. Cut into squares.

Hot Chocolate Recipe

½ cup sugar
¼ cup cocoa (we used Hershey's)
Dash of salt
⅓ cup hot water
4 cups milk
1 teaspoon vanilla extract

Mix sugar, cocoa and salt in sauce pan. Stir in water and cook over medium heat until mixture boils. Stir for 2 minutes. Add milk and reheat. Do not boil after milk is added. Remove from heat and add vanilla and serve.

That particular secret we kept between ourselves for years. I will forever be grateful to Ethelda for helping me. The three of us have realized that guardian angels are evident in our lives and are watching over us.

Daddy was a man of strong work ethics and determination. He wanted things easier for Mama. He built the washhouse and it still stands today.

He wanted all his children to grow up knowing the value of a dollar, and how to make a dollar. He was determined that his children would not grow up lazy or dependent on anyone.

Daddy worked hard for his family, not only at his public job, but also the work he did with the farm and securing the development of his family.

As my siblings and I grew up and left the family to start our own families, we all left with high school diplomas where we graduated from Bonlee School. Some left after they completed courses in college.

My sisters, Ethelda and Sue, were registered nurses. Allene was an LPN, Jane, a Laboratory Technologist, and me a Licensed Cosmetologist. My brother Russell was in construction, my brother Bill Joe followed in Daddy's footsteps and took over his mail route and continued to farm; my brother Gary took over the family farm and continues to raise chickens and cows. As we all went our separate ways, I followed my own path in life.

I value the independence that Daddy instilled in me by the heritage that he provided. There were times growing up that I didn't understand the sternness or the drive that was my Daddy. I realize now that our lives are molded by not only the love that we received, but also the love in correction and discipline that we have received.

Daddy passed away in 1976.

This family picture was taken in 1974, at Mama and Daddy's
Fiftieth Wedding Anniversary. From left to right; Jane,
Russell, Ethelda, Allene, Mama, Daddy, me, Gary, Sue Anne
and Billy Joe.

Hoyt's Family: The Scotts

Hoyt Scott was born in Chatham County to Lonnie and Nellie Dixon Scott. Lonnie's first wife, Nellie Porter, had died and left him with five small children.

Nellie Dixon had a son from a previous marriage. In 1925 Mr. Scott and Nellie Dixon married.

Over the years Lonnie fathered fourteen children and with Nellie Dixon's son, they raised a total of fifteen children. Mr. Scott and the boys farmed and raised chickens.

In 1949 some of the older children had already left the home in pursuit of their own ambitions.

One day as the family was visiting a local neighbor, they noticed a big black cloud of smoke getting higher and higher in the sky. This billowing cloud of smoke appeared to be located over their home. With urgency they headed in the direction of their farm. When they reached their home, it had been burned to the ground. There was nothing left. The family had lost their home and the entire contents. There were no telephones at this time or they might have been able to respond faster.

Lonnie and Nellie Dixon Scott

Mr. Scott was a Deacon at his church and very well respected by the community. The Church, the neighbors, and the community rallied and worked together. Those wonderful people raised money, cut logs, and rebuilt the home. Within two weeks the Scott family was moved into a new house. Of course the inside was not completed, but it was comfortable to live in as they finished the interior.

Mr. Scott passed away a year and a half after Hoyt and I were wed. Mrs. Scott passed away several years later.

I met Hoyt Scott while I was in High School. The first encounter was brief but memorable. At fifteen years old I was invited to go out with a group on a Sunday afternoon; there were six of us. There was a young man in the group who was not my date, and whom I guess you could say, was "flirting" with me.

We all decided to go to see the construction of a new bridge. Once we were at the bridge this young man picked me up, held me over the side of the bridge, and pretended to drop me. Naturally I hung around his neck tightly and wouldn't let go.

That young man was Hoyt "Teet" Scott. I never really saw Hoyt again after that incident until about a year later when the opportunity presented itself again.

I just wish I had been given a heads-up!

I played guard position on the high school basketball team. I played in a lot of basketball games. A girl friend of mine who went to ball games with me a lot asked if I would go with her and her boyfriend to a ball game. She also said they had a friend who wanted to meet me. I told her that would be fine and the date was set.

That particular evening I was running behind on my chores and it seemed the fellow who was picking me up was running ahead of schedule.

Of course he had to wait on the porch for me to get ready. At that time I didn't know who I was going with to the ball game.

I came down the stairs and opened the door and my mouth at the same time saying, "What did you come so early for?" I looked up into the face of Hoyt Scott. Hoyt never missed another ballgame in which I played.

I've always thought that Hoyt had found a treasure in me; but he has allowed, over the years that he should have dropped me over that bridge.

Hoyt and I continued to date through my junior year in high school and decided to get married at the end of that year. Hoyt was a painter then and his income was not the highest.

14

Berta and Hoyt Marry and Start A Family

Running off to South Carolina was the thing to do in those days, so we ran off to Chesterfield, South Carolina.

Before we left Hoyt gave me money for clothes. At that time I was between sales on my chickens. I thought the gesture was extremely sweet. I didn't know that by spending this money, all of it of course, we started our beginning as husband and wife in a slight bind financially.

We lived with his parents for a short while after the wedding. I still remained in school at Bonlee. I walked to the school bus stop every day. After a few weeks we decided to look around and find somewhere else to live.

My friend Sara had married Hoyt's cousin Lester. They were living in a house on his father's farm. This house was just around the corner from Hoyt's family. Sara and Lester were only using a small portion of the back of the house. They told us that we could live in the front of the house if we wanted to.

I had sold a house of chickens and decided to go furniture shopping while Hoyt was fishing. By the time he got in that weekend, I had moved.

It was a move of convenience for me, because of the school bus stop. I walked to the bus stop, which was located where the Fruitcake Factory stands today. While waiting for the bus it never crossed my mind that we would ever own a Fruitcake business at that location.

The bond that Sara, Lester, Hoyt and I had developed continues to grow. Sara later became a vital part of the Fruitcake business as Head Cake wrapper. Hoyt and I will always be grateful to Sara and Lester for our first home. We developed a special bond and it is irrevocable.

I graduated High School in the spring and later that year our first child was born. She was so beautiful and we named her Belinda Ellen. Sara had her first child Mike, 2 weeks before our first-born. Together we would rock our babies on the front porch.

Hoyt built us a small house on his Daddy's land and we left the home of our friends. But, we were still just around the corner. The year following we had our first son, Ricky.

I felt the need to contribute to the family so I went to work at the Kellwood Hosiery Mill in Siler City. My school friend Elmo consented to baby-sit for me. Elmo later came to work with us and headed our Fruitcake Kitchen. Soon, Sandra Lou, our third child, made her appearance in our lives. I did not return to Kellwood.

I was taught from an early age to be independent. I had a personal need to help with the household expenses. With three babies, I decided to go to Cosmetologist School. I enrolled as a student at

Ricky, Belinda, Randy and Sandra in Grandma's flower garden.

Troutman's Beauty Academy in Greensboro. I had hoped that in this profession I could possibly manage or run a beauty salon and still be able to be with my children and contribute. After completing my course, Hoyt built me a small beauty shop. Within a couple of years of having the shop open and building my business, Randy, our fourth child was born.

My clientele grew and grew. I was very busy trying to work, manage a business and raise the children. I was always concerned that my family was missing a few meals. Even though it seemed I was constantly working, our family always went to church every Sunday at Tyson Creek. Hoyt had followed in his father's footsteps, and he is a Deacon at the Church. We would come home from church and have a big Sunday dinner. Going to church has always been an important part of our lives.

In 1970 we decided to build a larger home with more space for the children. Our home was completed and we moved in the fall of 1972. We were just around the corner yet another time. After Hoyt built our new home, the gas market skyrocketed, and that was an increase that we did not factor into our budget. Our heating bill was more than our new house payment. Our new home was larger than we had been accustomed, so Hoyt starting thinking of alternative heating methods.

Teet came up with an idea to design a fireplace insert with an electric blower. Later he and a partner designed a freestanding wood heater. They started a factory and the business took off.

They opened a store in Asheboro and stayed in operation for ten years. At that time they had two hardware stores, a manufacturing facility and a warehouse. It took all these facilities for the supply-in-demand for their freestanding woodstoves as well as the

Hoyt working on his wood stoves.

fireplace inserts. *After ten years, gas and heating prices fell and the demand for the wood heaters dropped. The business closed and we were again looking for another business to take its place.*

During the building of our new home and the wood heater venture, our children started to get on with their personal lives. Now I was in the midst of dealing with an "empty nest". I decided to go to Sandhills Community College and took business and computer courses. I attended off and on for about three years.

With a little more time to devote to myself, I realized that times had changed. Our

Cutting Hugh, my son-in-law's hair.

children had led far different lives than their parents. We had no animals to water, feed, or milk. Therefore, their chores were at a minimum. My sons have expressed over the years how they had to learn to cook and clean because their Mama was a busy hairdresser.

"Teet" is a nickname I use for Hoyt. Teet had two hobbies or vices- hunting and fishing. He put every possible minute he could spare into his hobbies, and with great passion I might add. He was such a master at attending to these hobbies that our sons followed in his footsteps.

Deer hunting.

The boys joined their Daddy fishing and hunting as soon as they were big enough to carry a fishing pole or a gun and the grandsons that later came into our lives also mimicked the master. All the males in our family are true gamesmen; they not only get what they go after but they can clean and cook it as well.

Proud of his catch!

Venison Country Style Steak

Using fresh venison cured approximately 5 days in cooler and using Ham steaks.
4 pounds Venison Ham steaks cut
¾ inch thick
Salt
Pepper
Corn Oil
Flour

Heat oil to 325°°; Sprinkle steaks with salt and pepper. Roll in flour and cook until brown both sides. Remove from pan. If gravy is desired, using drippings in pan from steaks add approximately 2 tablespoons flour to thicken and 2 or more cups milk until medium thick. Serve gravy and venison together or separately.Serve with vegetables of your choice.

Randy, Hoyt, and Ricky on their annual Outer Banks fishing trip.

Fish Fry At Hoyt's

Type of fish to Fry:
Brim. Crappie. Flounder. Trout. Catfish.
Prepare fish-scale and dress.
Place in container for soaking.
Add:
1 gallon water
3 tablespoons salt
3 tablespoons baking soda

Place in refrigerator for 2-3 days

When ready to cook-roll in corn meal, salt and pepper. Pan-fry in corn oil or peanut oil on both sides; brown on one side before turning. Serve with Cole slaw, french-fried potatoes, onions sliced in vinegar, fried corn-bread.

Our children have always been a major part of our lives, as they grew and went their separate ways there is still, "no place like home".

Belinda, our first born, was the first to leave the nest. She married a local boy, Wayne Jordan. She completed college with a degree in X-Ray and Mammography.

Ricky, our first son, married his "High School sweetheart", Gail Binkley. Ricky followed in his Daddy's footsteps as a painter. As the wood heater business grew, Ricky managed one of the hardware stores and Gail was Teet's secretary.

A year after we moved in to our new home, Sandra, our second daughter, married Hugh Brown. She is a registered nurse.

Randy, our youngest son, married Lisa Wilson, who happened to be my dear friend Sue Wilson's youngest daughter.

Our lives are constantly changing, but family and good friends are always a blessing.

I continued working as a hairdresser. The loyalty and friendships that developed will always be a special part of my life. Little did I know as we visited each week that their support would later become a valued asset to another phase of my life.

The Beginning of a Vision

*A*lways at Christmas time I wanted to do a little extra something for my customers and their loyalty. Some of my most loyal customers were Elmo, Sara, Evelyn, Faye, my sister Ethelda, and a special friend indeed, Sue Wilson. Every year a few weeks before the holidays I would start cooking and baking. I would make cookies, candy and fruitcakes for all my ladies and freeze what I needed till the time was ready for gift giving.

Hoyt and I were in search of another way to supplement our income. I kept thinking about the reviews I had received about the Christmas Fruitcakes that I gave as gifts. I became obsessed with the idea of marketing this cake. It seemed as though I could not get the idea out of my thoughts. The fear factor kicked in, but I could not turn loose of the idea. I prayed to the Lord to help in directing me in this venture. It seemed that the more I prayed the more it was in my thoughts.

I approached the one person who would never tell me "no" my daughter Belinda; I told her of my idea and, as usual, her reply was "anything you want to do, Mama".

Hoyt and I discussed this vision with the rest of the family. We told the family that it would be a part-time seasonal job. The pay for their help would be little or nothing. We wanted to put any profits back into the business for expansion if it turned out to be lucrative.

Gail, our son Ricky's wife agreed as well as our son Randy's wife, Lisa.

I decided to ask my loyal and dear friends their opinions. Their thoughts were encouraging. They gave me the push to try to market my idea. When I discussed my idea with my long time friend Sue Wilson, she supported the idea. She overwhelmed me with her enthusiasm to seek this dream and encouraged me to get started.

I went to Belinda once again to see if her garage would be available to convert into a kitchen because my garage had my beauty shop in it. Of course "anything you want to do, Mama", was her reply. We started closing in the garage. We bought a used pizza oven, mixer, and bakers rack. Actually we bought only the bare necessities. I kept getting closer and closer to seeing this venture open its doors.

Every one of us had full time jobs, which meant we were going to need more help. I thought of my sister Ethelda and the cooking that we had done together over the years. There was no doubt in my mind that together we could manufacture a product that would maintain the perfection of our cake as well as keep it consistent.

Obviously, I could not commit full time due to the beauty shop business, as it was my steady income. My hours ran late into the evenings. Ethelda agreed to come in after her work in the evenings. At that time she was Head Nurse for the Emergency Room at Chatham Hospital.

So the preliminary stages needed to be set and acted upon. This was where the details of manufacturing, packaging, rules and regulations came into play. There were so many factors to be considered and dealt with and every aspect created more challenges. The more obstacles that came and went the easier it all seemed to come together. We discussed the things that could hurt the Fruitcake business as far as competition and location and other factors that might be needed to assess the situation toward a "yes" or a "no."

The fruitcake business was contingent not only on the cost of this cake but the taste. Competitors had the quality, the packaging, the looks and the market. But this market had not been introduced to my cake.

I ordered cakes from all over and planned a testing party. We tasted the cakes and judged the looks, texture, glaze, quality, packaging and the convenience of getting this cake to consumers. We also took into consideration what the best strategies were for the overall concept contingent on a market that was small. I was convinced that my cake had the taste and the looks. .

The first thing I did was to perfect this recipe. I worked on the glaze for a year before I got it exactly like I wanted it. We ran tests to check the shelf life of the cake.

At the same time we started looking into the packaging. Packaging and presentation of any product is one of the most vital parts of success. I knew that the product tasted good and looked good; but it also needed to have an eye-catching appeal and slogan that caught the consumers' eye.

The box for the Fruitcake, the name, and every aspect of this endeavor was time consuming. There was so much 'leg work' to be done before we could actually introduce our product to the consumers. I began working with a box company that led me to Mr. Foster Shaw. I went back and forth from vendor to vendor until I was pleased with the design and the box itself. I found a manufacturer for the box and now I needed a name for my cake.

I got the children together. Over the breakfast table we struggled to find the perfect name. A product name speaks volumes. We chose "Southern Supreme." Southern Supreme to me means old southern tradition and goodness, and I knew my cake was good.

I also knew that a more personal touch was needed. It was decided to put a small letter into each box about us, and our appreciation to whomever made the purchase. We also had a brochure printed up to distribute so customers could locate us and order more cakes if they wanted to.

I never dreamed those classes that I took at Sandhills would give me the help I needed to start this business.

We contacted the Health Department to make sure we did everything by the book. Learning and applying what was necessary to get this endeavor off the ground took lots of preparation and hard work.

Rome wasn't built in a day and neither was our fruitcake business. Hoyt was available and with construction to the garage almost completed we started gathering up our possible part-time help. Every family member knew that there would be no income or profit margin for us. They knew that if there was any money made it would go back into the business to use to expand if we were lucky. We were also going to need more help.

I knew who I wanted and I knew they would not turn me down. I went to school with Elmo Phillips; and Sue Wilson was a friend and customer of mine for years. They are the ones that encouraged me to pursue this dream. Elmo Phillips, her mother Miss Nina and Sue Wilson were our first paid employees. I had known these women most of my life. I could count on them and trust them to help with the production of my product.

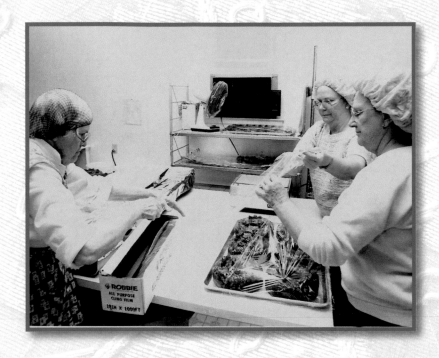

It was time to start purchasing the ingredients to make our cake.

We had limited knowledge on wholesalers and most of our purchases were made at grocery stores, especially the fruit. Most of the nuts were purchased from local neighbors, which meant that they were still in the shell. At the time, I thought to save on production costs that we should crack the nuts ourselves. It didn't take me long to realize that was a terrible idea.

Baking our Cake for Marketing

Bake day was upon us. Our three employees and some of the family gathered in the garage and preheated the pizza converted to "Fruitcake" oven. Everything was done by hand. We took our time, produced our first hand weighed, packed down, and molded "Southern Supreme" Fruitcake. At that time we were only equipped to produce nine pounds at a time.

My daughter Belinda and Daughter-in-law Gail working in Belinda's garage.

Berta holding our first boxed fruitcake!

The cakes were then taken into Belinda's kitchen and glazed and from there to her dining room table to be wrapped and boxed. Every cake that we made was made individually. These cakes were made on faith.

While we were building an inventory of approximately 1,000 cakes, we were also scoping out our marketing possibilities. What was I to do with all this fruitcake?

I had heard of a Christmas Show in Raleigh at the Civic Center called a "Carolina Christmas". I contacted the promoter Frances Dell and reserved a space. All of us were so excited. We all racked our brains trying to decide how to present our cake to the public. We had the dimensions of the booth and knew we needed to design an appealing backdrop for our product.

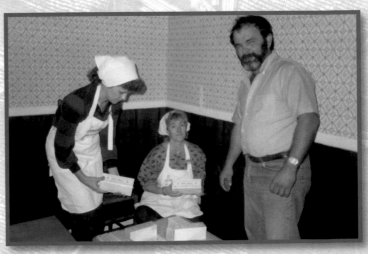

Gail, Belinda and Wayne on Wayne and Belinda's dining room floor boxing cakes.

Hoyt and our son Randy came up with an idea. They decided to build a stage with a fence and a log cabin front. The big day arrived. Behind the fence was a front porch to a log cabin. This log cabin had steps, windows with curtains. Displayed on the front porch were the cakes. We thought it was beautiful. Everyone showed up; Randy and Lisa even brought our two-week old granddaughter Rae. Grandmother Sue Wilson stayed behind the door to the cabin rocking our mutual granddaughter.

When the show doors opened, we were ready. We started out by offering samples of my fruitcake and a brochure. We got the usual comments "I don't like fruitcake"; "has it got that green stuff in it"; and of course "no thank you".

It was difficult work just to get people to even sample my cake. After a while there were a few adventurous brave souls who took the chance and took a bite. You could see the surprise on their faces as they realized it was indeed good. About an hour after giving out samples of the cake, people started purchasing our cake.

By the end of the day we were sold out. With two more show days to go we knew that production of our cake had taken another turn. We went home to bake more cakes for the remainder of the show.

During the next couple of days there were people returning to the show just to get another or a larger cake.

It certainly looked like we were in the Fruitcake Business for sure.

The Carolina Christmas show has always been special to us; our business got its birth in that first Christmas show. We grew from that show immediately. The brochure that we had given out in Raleigh was generating business. There were calls and orders, which meant we had returning customers. We sold cakes off my dining room table. I was still working in the beauty shop and would take the calls and orders from there. By the end of the year we had sold 2000 pounds of fruitcake. At this point in the game, we were very pleased.

Hoyt and I decided to take the profit from the sales and build a small building behind our house. The building would consist of two rooms and a walk-in cooler. This building would be used to glaze, wrap and box the cakes. Hoyt and a couple of carpenters got together and started on the building. Soon the building was completed and we were comfortable with our workspace. Our plans were to continue selling the cakes from my dining room table.

Also that spring we had decided we needed to find another source to purchase our fruits and shelled nuts. We needed the convenience of delivery. Fruitcake is really a seasonal item so we knew our best profit margin would be from October of each year until after Christmas around New Years.

Always researching for marketing strategies to increase our sales, we talked to numerous vendors. It seemed the Christmas show to be associated with was the "Southern Living Christmas Show". This show takes place in Charlotte every year at the Merchandise Mart. At that time it was called "The Twelve Days of Christmas", meaning the length of this show was twelve days.

Dawn Stumpt, Evelyn Cheek, Fay Oldham, Amy Goodman and Ray Cheek working the Charlotte Christmas Show. This Group has helped make Southern Supreme a success in Charlotte.

It seemed every vendor we spoke with had a success story about the show. We contacted the show coordinator and we were accepted as a new vendor.

The booth rental for this particular show was more expensive than the Raleigh Show. We decided we could make do with a single booth and to our knowledge there was no other "Fruitcake" vendor.

On Faith and high hopes we started planning for the seasonal events that we had signed up for. The inventory

needed for this show was questionable. We had no way of knowing how the cake would sell. With the Raleigh show and the Charlotte show coming up we guessed at the projected sales and went to work. At that time, one batch of fruitcake was only 18 pounds. We got our help together and went to the garage to work. Keep in mind that we all had full time jobs, so we worked at night and on our days off.

The show date for Charlotte was upon us. Teet and I were the only ones available to do this show. At that time we were not generating enough income to justify staying in a hotel. It was 120 miles to the

Evelyn Cheek, Faye Olham, and Harriet Burk working the show!

show and 120 miles back home. This took approximately 2 ½ to 3 hours one-way. The show hours for this particular show were very long, nine and twelve hour days.

We faced opening day with a lot of anticipation. Our booth was set up and open for business. Cake samples in hand, we were ready. The crowd soon made their way toward our booth. It did not take long to realize that no matter where you are, people still have the same remarks when approached to try our cake.

"I don't like fruitcake" or "Has it got that citrine stuff in it?"

We spent a lot of time in our booth explaining the contents. We would tell the inquirers that our fruitcake contains a lot of nuts. We explained that our recipe calls for no citrine and none of the green stuff. After a while, a select few would brave the old "fruitcake" myths and mysteries. As they tasted the cake you could see the surprise over take their facial expressions. Each day at the Charlotte show drew a different crowd. We went through the same routine and responses concerning our fruitcake.

Teet set the groundwork for this type of selling venture. His persistence set a precedent for every show that we've done or are yet to do. All the people who have worked for us still hear the same comments and are asked the same questions that we heard at our first show.

Reminiscing with Teet one day, I asked, "Just what did you think at that first Charlotte Show?" There was no hesitation in his reply, "This old country boy felt out of place." Teet elaborated on the vendors that we made friends with and remain friends today. He mentioned Mr. and Mrs. Hanes. They were in a booth beside us in the Charlotte show for years. They have a Moravian Cookie business. The relationship that developed by their encouraging words and experience at shows has been very valuable. We continue to stay in touch and visit occasionally.

Duplin Winery was on the other side of us in Charlotte and we visit their establishment as well.

The trial and error phases that we went through told us success does not always come easily and we have really worked hard at this business.

Teet reminded me how I was so tired that I was ready to pack up and go home. It was our faith and persistence that pushed us, that and the fact that we knew our cake was good.

Thinking back to nameless faces that I have observed over the years, I could tell their mind was set for the terrible flavors that were about to attack their palate. I have almost laughed as pure astonishment and a great deal of relief washed over their once composed faces. Some of the people would take a piece of cake and look at it, then smell of it; some would even lick it first. Then tasted it because they did not want to be rude. It still amazes me to watch the skeptical faces.

I must say Teet's persistence and patience out weighed mine by the time the week ended.

The Twelve Days of Christmas at the Southern Living Show in Charlotte proved to be a building block that year. When the show ended we returned home tired and apprehensive about our debut. It wasn't long before the phone was ringing and we were sending cakes to people who had bought one or they wanted us to send one to someone for them. The exposure that this show gave our fruitcake solidified the marketing technique, proof we needed for increasing our sales.

Soon we were in our fifth season and our production of fruitcake had grown from 2000 lbs our first year to about 20,000 pounds. Let me stress that in our marketing strategy we gave a lot of fruitcake away as samples. Our show schedule had grown. We were booking and attending at least

10 shows a season. During those five years my sister Sue came to do seasonal work for us. Sue was retired from Rex Hospital where she was head nurse over thirteen operating rooms. We had invited her to work in the house taking phone orders and handling the "dining room" sales.

As the demand for our cake grew we would hire more ladies to help in the garage kitchen with the cooking. We would hire different ladies from the community.

One day a couple, Ray and Evelyn Cheek, walked into our dining room to buy our Fruitcake. When I was young and going with my Daddy to cut grain for the public, Ray's family was one of many we helped. I also worked in tobacco for his family. They had moved back to his home place. Evelyn became one of my clients in the beauty shop. Ray was a retired truck driver. As our sales grew we hired Ray to go for the ingredients for our cakes because by that time we were buying in bulk. He would also haul cakes and supplies that were needed to set up our shows as well as assisting with the set up.

Ray Cheek giving out samples at the Charlotte show.

As our business grew both Ray and Evelyn took over doing a lot of shows for us. Evelyn would run the cash register and Ray would give out samples and keep the show inventory stocked.

By 1990 Hoyt decided it was time our fruitcake needed a home. He thought that a kitchen and showroom combined would work out on a piece

Evelyn Cheek in our showroom.

of property across the road from our house. This parcel of land, the future home of our fruitcake, was the cow pasture. This was also the place I waited for the bus to school when Teet and I first married. I was concerned about being so far out in the country. Would anybody really drive out here to get a fruitcake? Would they even be able to find us?

Hoyt, our son Randy, and Belinda's husband Wayne, got together and decided that we needed a 2400-square foot building. At that time we were still in the garage and, on a good day producing no more than 500 pounds of cake. That was quite a lot, but being able to produce the supply in demand was becoming overwhelming. This was when we called on our good friends at First Bank in Bennett. With everything in order we started the construction of our new building.

In 1990 we had the Ribbon-Cutting and dedication of our new building. Reverend Bob Wachs said

Ethelda, Gail, Kyle & Rae cutting ribbon for first open house.

the prayer and gave a dedication speech. It was indeed a momentous occasion for the entire family and the employees to move into the new facility.

When the building, the move and the dedication ceremony were completed, we were so proud to have a new facility and a "show room" to go with it. We could not only display our fruitcake but we could also display a few retail gifts.

We started carrying a few coffees and teas to compliment our cake. Our showroom was dressed up with curtains and a welcoming atmosphere and soon our customers began to show up. There was a glass window in our showroom so the customers could stand for hours to watch our kitchen in action. We had a small office area with a computer and, of course, my sister Sue was there to take the phone orders.

Daughter-in-law Lisa makes designer baskets for our showroom.

My sister Sue Ann Farlow took phone orders and processed them for us for several years.

A small break area was designated for our employees and we had a small warehouse. But the area that was built to manufacture our fruitcake was so spacious we knew that we could produce as much cake as we could sell.

We soon started coming in the evenings and on Saturdays to get ready for the season. Elmo and Sue enjoyed the room and the convenience of our new kitchen. Elmo's mother Nina Goins joined us and continued to work every season until her health interfered. Joyce Hussey started working with us and continues today. Other seasonal employees were added as the production and sales grew.

Ethelda and I gathered family recipes that we had uised when we were growing up, and began testing these recipes for the purpose of bringing them to the market. From this testing we launched our "Maple Crispy Peanuts," "Hot pepper Peanuts," "Cinnamon Pecans" and later we added our "Southern Pecan Pralines."

Each year Ethelda and I concentrated on something new to produce and introduce to our customers.

1990... A milestone 28,000 lbs.

Randy, Belinda and Zac.

With all the abundance of fresh fruits grown locally, we took the opportunity to perfect some recipes, so in 1999 we introduced our garden fresh jams and jellies.

The next couple of years we continued to grow and we started adding more "gourmet" foods to our showroom.

Within three years, our new building was in need of more space and plans for an additional kitchen for the nuts was in the making.

Somewhere during this time, Judy Presler came to work for us. Judy has become a valuable employee.

She runs our nut kitchen, which not only makes our nuts but the brittles and our crunches. She continues to be an asset to our staff. To this day all products that are made in the nut kitchen, which includes the jellies and jams, are made in small batches; just like we did at home when I was young.

Judy and co-workers making Spiced Pineapple Pickles.

Wayne Jordan and Judy Preslar in the kitchens.

Our showroom was crowded with our expanded food products. The Christmas shows that we had originally started out doing were generating more business.

We had also started doing more shows in different locations as well. Therefore, our warehouse space seemed to get smaller and smaller. The warehouse was used not only for the finished product but also for housing the boxes, jars, ingredients and anything else needed for the finished products that we were now making.

The packaging of all our products was a very important part of our business. We had ribbon, labels, boxes, and tins stacked everywhere. We have always realized the more attractive your product is, the more attention it gets. We decided to broaden our scheme of product displays and design gift baskets to show off our products.

Daughters-in-law Lisa and Gail working at one of the first shows.

Rita Garner packages our 'cheese florets'.

Our packaging department in peak season.

The amount of people that were coming to our showroom to buy our products and observe our fruitcake making skills seemed to grow as well. Our showroom began to burst at the seams. Teet decided he could give up some more of his cow pasture so we went forward with our plans. This time our original show room turned into a chocolate kitchen.

Our cake wrapping department during peak season.

Everybody gets to take a break. Elmo (in the center) has been with us since the garage days.

Deborah Stephenson and My Daughter Belinda are treated to sausage gravy and biscuits by coming in early. The kitchen staff makes breakfast during the peak season while the cakes are baking because they are at work so early.

Our shipping basket department is always busy making baskets to be shipped all over the world.

Barbara Dowd has worked in the showroom basket department for several years; she is masterful at making bows.

We built a bigger showroom and our old showroom converted into a "Sample Area".

By then we had started doing small tours through our facility. Our employment numbers grew from season to season.

Teet and Randy designed a "Tour Walk" so that the people who came to visit could see our kitchens in full production. This walk started out in the warehouse, came through the kitchens and ended with sampling our products and shopping in our showroom.

Our Chocolate Kitchen stays busy.

Joanne hard at work.

My sister Ethelda and Joanne Jones our head Candy Makers.

Our son Randy helps out in the kitchen.

We have reached peak production with a hydraulic "cake molding" machine, which Teet and Randy designed and had built.

We also bought a bigger oven and a new mixer. Our mixer was bought in Patterson, New Jersey. The family, along with enough ingredients to fill the mixer, made the trip.

We tried out the display model of the mixer in the showroom. We had to be sure that this mixer that held a 250-pound batch of fruitcake would not break or crush our nuts. We left the showroom with that mixer and we left the sales man with 250-pounds of cake that needed baking.

Our last addition included a warehouse built large enough to hold all our raw ingredients, boxes, and jars. We also needed space for inventory for the showroom, the shows, and the shipping department.

Hoyt and I stock the shelves.

Ruth Oldham and Nellie Brewer ready to serve guests at our Sample Bar.

We added more office space to accommodate all employees' needs for the telephone orders.

We also added a bigger shipping area, which needed two more shipping computers and easier access for UPS to pick up.

We added a "sun room" that is a holding area for our group tours. This area keeps them out of inclement weather. In addition, this induction area acquaints them with our tour guides.

Of course, members of the Scott family are our tour guides. The family members that are constantly on "tour duty" are Hoyt, Belinda and Randy. Occasionally, when needed we have employees that can stand in for this duty. Judy Councilman is one of our great tour guides. She has been with us for several years.

Son-in-law Wayne and Randy and Lisa's son Zachary trying out the mixer in a showroom in Patterson, New Jersey.

Grandson Kyle (Ricky and Gail's son) in our production warehouse.

Pam Cameron in our new shipping department.

When the tour is completed, every one gets to sample our cake with coffee and try a bit of our other products at our sample bar. We look forward to seeing all our visitors. Some come back year after year.

When our season is over in January, we immediately start planning for the next year. Our decorating, our show schedules, the themes, the inventory needed and the upcoming season trend is also taken into consideration.

Through the years, we have been very fortunate to receive recognition from all types of "Media" concerning our Company. "Our State" magazine was the first to report our story and introduce our products to the public that we might not otherwise reach at the time. Being the only fruitcake factory in the area, we seem to be the "ideal" Christmas feature in magazine and newspaper articles. Local television stations have and continue to feature us during the holiday season.

Mary Margret Holt in the shipping department.

Brenda Williamson takes orders in the showroom shipping department.

Employees Hazel McMath and Elizabeth Rea wait in Sun Room for Open House Visitors.

While working in the kitchen son-in-law Wayne and Alan "Ziggy" Zimmerman can't wait for January, the end of the rush and the motorcycle rally at Myrtle Beach!

Randy stays busy between the tours, but I can always find him when I need him.

Judy Councilman a long time, part-time employee.

Josh Holt and Keith Josey our stockmen are relieved that the season is at a close, it has been a busy year.

I think the most exciting media coverage that we have yet to experience was when Kate Snow, co-anchor of the weekend edition of "Good Morning America," 'googled' us. We came up under "Good Fruitcake." She and her camera crew flew in from New York and spent a whole day with us. She put on an apron and a hair net and went to the kitchen to help make fruitcake. She also toured and interviewed every department.

What a milestone, my vision was being viewed on National television.

Kate Snow places an order
with me to be shipped.

We love to decorate for the Christmas Season
and we look for the newest trends.

Where We Are Today

As Southern Supreme continues to grow, we are still making quality products and introducing new ones.

We have added more shows to our list over the years and we continue to do the original shows from 21-years ago. The Charlotte show has grown from a single booth to a store in 'The Village'. Where two people could comfortably work previously, we now have six to eight people working the show. We start setting up and decorating three days before the doors open to the public.

This past year we received the 'First Place' award for decorating and the best-looking store. Our Charlotte show has been very good for us. Ray and Evelyn Cheek have been the main employees at that venue and they retired this past year. Their dedication to Southern Supreme for 16-years has contributed to our success.

Today I am still coming in to work and handling details of this business with the help of my family. As I delegate to my assistant what I want to convey in this part of my book I know that now is the time for you to 'meet' my children and their families, and to know their involvement and responsibilities and to realize how they have contributed to the business as we have evolved.

Never, when standing at the bus stop many years ago had I dreamed of such a business or such attention. I am very thankful for the maturity of this dream that started in such a meek and small way.

Sometimes when the work is all done at the end of the day and everyone is gone home I take a walk through the building. Hoyt is with me sometimes and sometimes I am alone. I stroll through one end to the other and ask myself "How did I make this happen?" How did this all fall into place? I am amazed at the products, the packaging and the reality that my fruitcake is shipped all over the world. Over the past 25 years we have taken small steps and we have taken giant steps. None of this could have happened without the help of my husband Hoyt, my children and my sisters Ethelda and Sue Ann. They were all so wonderful. Maybe they didn't see my vision, but they had enough faith in me to follow my lead and give me the greatest experience I could ever know. What a warm and loving feeling when you follow God's plans that He has for our lives.

To start our business with 3 paid employees, we have grown to 125-150 during season's peak. We are truly blessed.

Children of Berta & Hoyt

Front row left to right: Sandy & Belinda
Back row left to right: Randy & Ricky

"Our Family is a circle of love and strength.
With every birth and every union the circle grows.
Every joy shared adds more love.
Every crisis faced together makes the circle stronger."

-- Author unknown

Me, and Mama.

Hoyt and me.

Hoyt, Berta, Ricky
(Top) Belinda, Sandy, Randy.

My sisters: Jane, Sue, Ethelda.
Me, Belinda.

Belinda and Wayne

Belinda was our first-born. She came into our young lives as the most beautiful baby we had ever seen. We were so excited about being parents. It is very true that you learn a lot about children when you are raising that first one. Belinda grew up to be a major help to me not only with the younger siblings but in the future business that would materialize in later years.

Belinda was the oldest, so I depended on her quite a lot. I had a very busy beauty shop, so I relied on her to help with her brothers and sister. She also did a lot of the cleaning and cooking for me. I can still see her carrying her baby brother Randy around on her hip when she herself was only ten years old.

When she was about thirteen years old, she decided she wanted to work in a hospital. I think being around my sisters who were nurses influenced her decision. But there was one thing for sure; she did not want to be a hairdresser.

At the age of fifteen my sister Jane hired her to develop x-rays at the local hospital. Her career was set in motion by that summer job.

During her high school years she met her future husband Wayne Jordan. Belinda and Wayne were married and settled across the street from her Mama and Daddy. They presented us with our first grandchild in 1969. Christopher Wayne was born three months premature and remained in the hospital for three months before finally coming home. He was a fighter and even though he was a preemie he was determined to survive. He was a beautiful baby. I tend to think he inherited his strong will from Hoyt. In 1971 they presented us with a second grandson, Jonathan Matthew. John was a full term baby weighing in at 6 lbs 7oz. Now we had two beautiful little boys.

In 1970 she pursued her dream and was accepted in the Radiology Technology program at Moore Regional Hospital. Belinda graduated from the program in 1972 and started her career at Chatham Hospital in Siler City, North Carolina where she remained for twenty-five years.

Through the years Wayne worked as a truck driver and was also working with heavy equipment doing some excavating. Wayne was a tremendous help with the boys as Belinda was on call with the hospital a lot of the time.

Belinda and Wayne never wavered when I asked to use their garage for a kitchen. They were both instrumental in every step and phase of our business. Never once did they tell me "No". Their answer was always "what ever you want to do, Mama". Not only did we use their garage but their kitchen and dinning room where we boxed and wrapped the fruitcakes.

Over the years they both continued to hold down full time jobs, taking vacation to help with the Christmas shows and working at nights and on the weekends to help the business get off its feet. They both realized that this was too much so in 1999, Belinda left her position at the hospital and came to Southern Supreme full-time, and Wayne came on board full-time in 2001. Of course the boys are all grown now with families of their own. Chris and Susie have twin girls, Abby and Annie, they are 3 years old, and they live in Hoffman, NC. John and Amy have two daughters Kayle who is 8 years old and Rebecca who is 6 years old. They live next to Belinda and Wayne or Meme and Poppy as the girls call them.

Wayne is currently managing the kitchens. He handles the ordering of ingredients and makes sure we do not run out of products. He works closely with the various department heads in each kitchen, making sure they have what they need to do their job. It can get very hectic around our busy season, but he handles very well. In the summer season he coordinates the buying of our fruits for our jams and jellies. He stays pretty busy all-year round.

Belinda and I work very close together taking care of the showroom where our products are for sale. We hire our employees during the early fall and start decorating for the season. Our employee staff can sometimes mount up to 15 to 20 employees. It keeps us very busy making sure shelves are stocked, customers are taken care of, and employees are happy. Belinda is responsible for booking all our Christmas shows. She takes care of the space sizes, ordering electricity and phones line, booking hotels and assisting in loading the trucks. She also hires the staff to work these shows.

Both Belinda and Wayne have sacrificed their time for this business. Never will they know the amount of gratitude that Hoyt and I have for them. Hoyt and I have very fortunate to have a daughter like Belinda; she has always been where we needed her and always been ready to help no matter what we ask.

Wayne and Belinda have always been a vital part of this business. I guess I could have found another place to make the fruitcake, but we have always appreciated the fact that Belinda and Wayne's door was open to us. This was truly the beginning.

Belinda and Wayne.

John helps Kayle on the ball field.

Chris and John
the younger years.

Annie and Abby
with their Mom Susie.

Belinda with her Dad Hoyt
during the "Season."

Having Twins can be hard work.
Proud Dad Chris has learned
to sleep when they sleep.

Wayne and Chris.

Rebecca and her friend.

Dress up time with
Meme #1 and Meme #2.

John and Amy with their daughters
Kayle and Rebecca.

Rebecca   Kayle

Abby and Annie
Chris and Susie's Twin Girls.

Abby and Annie.

Rebecca and Kayle.

Wayne and Belinda head
up the "Wild Hogs" of
The Fruit cake business.

Ricky and Gail

Ricky was our first son; he was born in 1952. Hoyt always wanted a son, he was the most handsome little man, and we were so proud. He was a good child and like all little boys he was very inquisitive.

I think Ricky came into the world hunting and fishing like his father. I must say he learned from the master and at an early age. I think one of his favorite pastimes was 'crabbing and fishing' at the beach. He was also involved in school sports as well.

As he grew older and before he got his driver's license, he was always on his little white Honda motorcycle. That bike went everywhere. During the summers, Ricky helped Hoyt as a painter. When Ricky got his license, he had a 1964 GTO. At that time, he also got a girlfriend. Gail Binkley was a student at Chatham Central where Ricky went to school. Gail was a middle child of a large family, although I did not know her as she was growing up. I was well aware of the match that she and Ricky made. They seemed to be ideal for each other. When they both had finished high school, they were soon married. Ricky and Gail were married on my parents' Fiftieth wedding anniversary May 30 1978.

Gail had already become a dear part of our family and now she was my daughter-in-law. Hoyt and I found Gail so easy to love and she immediately settled in as one of the family. When they first married, Ricky was working with Hoyt at his Hearthside Shop where Ricky managed one of the stores and Gail worked as Hoyt's Secretary.

During that time in 1980, Derrick their first son came into the world weighing a big 10lbs. I will never forget his first trip to visit us; they had him dressed in overalls. He was less than two weeks old and he looked adorable.

After the fall of the wood-heater business Ricky went back to the painting business. His roots in this profession had started by helping his father. Ricky started his own painting business. Gail went to work at Kayser Roth as the Human Resources Administrator.

In comes the Fruitcake business. Gail was so agreeable of helping to see my vision materialize. She has always been so generous with the giving of her time and help. She has been with us every step of the way. She would work her eight hours at her public job and then come to the garage and wrap cakes.

Ricky would watch Derrick at home and helped occasionally setting up and taking down the shows. When possible he would work at the shows. During this time Ricky and Gail gave us Kyle another precious grandson, he was born in 1987. Like their father and their grandfather, they two have acquired the passion of the outdoors, for they also are hunters and anglers.

Gail was always there when we needed her. The sacrifices that were made trying to work two jobs and school for the boys and let us not forget the fishing and the deer hunting.

Derrick and Kyle have always been sports minded. Derrick excelled in baseball and Kyle was proving himself in wrestling. He was the only student to play five sports his last two years of high school. Both have won awards for their athletic abilities. Ricky and Gail have always been supportive in all the boys did.

Gail has sacrificed a lot of time and effort through the years with the devotion to this business. I can truthfully say that her help has always been an asset and greatly appreciated. She is acclimated with all aspects of the business as well because she has been with us from the beginning. I am sure like me she felt that her family was at times put on the back burner. However, I know her contribution has been beneficial to where we are today.

Derrick has now graduated from Campbell College where he attended under a baseball scholarship. He is presently a Physical Education teacher in Harnett County. Kyle is currently in his second year of college majoring in Wildlife Management.

At the time the new building was completed everybody was still part-time. In 2000, Gail came to work with us full-time. Gail was already familiar with the ins and outs of the business. She had contributed to the growth and development in all areas of this business. Gail was traveling and doing shows almost every

Ricky, Gail, Derrick & Kyle.

weekend. Gail also took most of the responsibility of the shipping out of products. She would get the orders ready to mail or ship at night after she had worked her public job. Now that she is with us full time Gail still handles all aspects of the shipping. She is our Personnel Director and handles the human resource part of this business. Gail does the interviewing of all applicants and keeps up with our payroll system. Gail is a valuable asset to our company.

Ricky comes in during our heaviest part of the shipping season and helps Gail while he still maintains his painting business. I hope that one day Ricky will want to join us full-time.

Our Favorite Family Meal:

Venison Swiss steak

Hand Mashed Potatoes

Green Beans

Biscuits

Rick and Gail's family shares this meal together quite often. Rick is the head chef in charge of preparing the Swiss steak, which is delicious. This meal is one that they cook as often as they can and no one ever complains.

The boys' favorite dessert is their Mom's famous brownies.

Gail's Brownies

1½ cup shortening
2 squares unsweetened chocolate
2 eggs
1 cup sugar
1 teaspoon vanilla flavoring
¾ cup sifted all-purpose flour
¾ teaspoon salt
½ teaspoon baking powder
1 cup coarsely chopped walnuts

Melt shortening and chocolate in a two-quart saucepan on low heat. Cool slightly; place cooled chocolate mixture, eggs, sugar and vanilla flavoring in mixing bowl. Beat vigorously until well mixed and smooth. Sift together flour, baking powder and salt. Add nuts to chocolate mixture. Beat until thoroughly blended. Pour into greased pan. Bake at 350° for 25-30 minutes. Let cool in pan, cut into squares.

Rick's Venison Swiss Steak

2-3 lbs Venison cubed steak
2 Large Cans Diced Tomatoes
2 Medium Onions (sliced
1 Sliced Green Bell Pepper
Enough flour to coat steak
Salt and Pepper to taste

Dredge meat in flour, cook in frying pan with hot oil until brown. Add salt and pepper to taste. When steak has browned, add tomatoes, onions and green peppers. Cover and simmer until onions and peppers are tender. They love a big spoonful of the tomato gravy on their potatoes.

Ricky and Gail.

Derrick gets a turkey.

Kyle and Derrick with "Mimi."

Derrick always wanted to play baseball and we knew he would be a great player.

Derrick pitching for Campbell University.

Kyle poses in his football jersey.

Jessica Cockman and Kyle leaving for the prom. Jessica also works for Southern Supreme.

Ricky always proud of his sons.

Grandpa proud of Kyle getting a deer.

Derrick Scott
Male Athlete of the Year.

Zachary and Kyle at the prom.

Grandpa and Kyle "crow hunting."

Gail on Hoyt's tractor.

Sandy & Hugh

*I*n 1955, we had our third child, a girl, we named Sandra Lou. What a happy child. She was just a bundle of love. Our Sandy came into the world with a kind, warm and tender heart. She is the most beautiful person you could ever meet. Her kindness just spreads like sunshine. Sandy, as we call her today, has kept this persona, all through her childhood and continues to this day.

She married Hugh Brown, a high school sweet heart; they have two sons, Jason and Scott. Jason made Sandy and Hugh grandparents in 2005. Scott is in the 10th grade and enjoys baseball and hunting. When Sandy had settled into married life and Motherhood, she decided she wanted to be a nurse. So off to nursing school she went. After she received her RN, she worked at the local Hospital in Siler City for many years. She mostly did Operating Room nursing, but over the years she has performed in almost all aspects of nursing. Her patients loved her and she loved her patients.

Sandra helped me in the fruitcake business as much as she could. In the early years she was raising her sons and it was hard for her to give me as much time as she wanted. She did manage to help at shows; she also helped many years on weekends in the showroom, at the sample bar or the cash register. Whatever time she could give us was well needed, wanted and greatly appreciated.

Sandy & Company busy with the "Sweet Garlic Dills".

When the kids got older and she had more time on her hands; the entrepreneur bug bit her. She has always loved Mama's pickles. Being from the south she knew there was a market for a good pickle, so she went to work and developed and perfected recipes for sweet garlic dill pickles and a Cinnamon Spiced Pickle. She made a couple of batches and passed them out to the family to taste and we all loved them. Her next step was to find her a jar and design a label. She names her company "Sandy and Co." Just like her Mother she started in a garage making her pickles. We carry her pickles in our showroom at "Southern Supreme" and our customers just love them. They have been a great success.

All of Sandy's pickles are outstanding in taste, whether eaten alone or as a condiment, so here is a recipe that highlights her Sweet Garlic Dills.

Sandy's Potato Salad

6 cups potatoes (cubed)
¾ cups celery (chopped)
1 medium purple onion (finely chopped)
2 tablespoon pimento (drained and chopped)
1 eight ounce jar Sandy & Co. Sweet Garlic Dills (drained and chopped)
¾ cup Mayonnaise
1 tablespoon of yellow mustard
Salt & pepper to taste
1 to 2 chopped boiled eggs (optional)

Peel and chop potatoes. Place in sauce pan and cover with water, add ½ teaspoon of salt. Cook over high heat to a rapid boil, boil for 2 minutes, turn heat off and cover. Let potatoes sit for 10 minutes.

In large mixing bowl combine celery, onions, pickles, pimentos and mustard. At this time add chopped boiled eggs if desired. Mix well. Drain potatoes and add to mixture. Lightly toss. Add mayonnaise and stir gently, until all ingredients are combined. ENJOY

Hugh and Sandy.

Sandy and Mom.

Jason, Sandy, and Scott.

Scott gets a deer.

Scott and Jason.

Jason, Liesel, and their daughter Kaitlyn.

Hugh and Sandy.

Ricky and Gail's son Derrick and Jason.

Mom, Dad & Sandy.

Sandy and Belinda, sisters and friends.

53

Randy and Lisa

Randy my youngest son was born in 1959. He came to us in what we call a more mature time in our life.

He grew up doing the things all little boys do. He loved Little League in the summer time and football in the fall. He enjoyed woodworking, even when he was a little boy he had to have a hammer in his hand. When he grew older he ventured into bull riding. That was a scary time for us, but he eventually came to his senses and gave it up. My husband Hoyt made sure he knew how to hunt and fish.

Between the hunting, fishing and bull riding he discovered a neighborhood girl, Lisa. I had known Lisa all her life. Her mother, Sue, brought her to the beauty shop every week for her regular hair appointment. Lisa had lost her father at a young age, but she had her Mother, her brothers Jerry and Jimmy and her sister Cindy. Even though they had lost a big part of their family, their love and devotion to each other carried them though a difficult time. Randy and Lisa knew each other as children in the beauty shop. As the years went by they met again in High School, they both were attending Chatham Central in Bear Creek. Lisa was playing basketball when Randy discovered her again. In their sophomore and junior year they started dating steady. They dated until graduation.

Randy left for Catawba Valley in Hickory, North Carolina to study furniture production and design, Lisa went to Chapel Hill to attend the University of North Carolina enrolling in the Dental Assistant School. She was already endeared to us; we considered her part of the family. After they graduated they came home and married. The love that we have for Lisa continues to grow and now she is a part of our family. They were married on June 6, 1981.

In 1984 when we began the Fruitcake business both Randy and Lisa were there to help. Their first born, Katherine Rae Scott was born on October 8, 1985. Rae was only 2 weeks old when we did the first show in Raleigh. Randy and Lisa brought Rae with them; she sat very quietly in the back of the booth. All the family took turns helping take care of her. Rae, as we call her, was our first granddaughter. As it seems, she has turned out to be our only granddaughter.

While working full time and raising Rae, they both worked in the garage helping with the fruitcakes. There was late night packaging, shipping, and sometimes cooking to do after they had already worked a full day at their regular jobs. The weekends brought Christmas shows to load, samples to hand out, and the showroom to staff. Randy was instrumental in the designing and construction of our first real building. We moved in the building in the fall of 1990 and Randy and Lisa blessed us with a grandson. Zachary Bruce came into our lives December 18, 1990.

In 1991, the business needed a full time person. Lisa was content to leave her job and came in Southern Supreme as a full time office employee. Lisa was able to be at the business as I continued to work part-time in my Beauty Shop. Lisa was able to get our business ready for the season with staffing and booking shows. She helped with product display and general decorations of the showroom. Lisa also helped with the designing of the baskets and helped selecting the types of baskets that we would display in our catalog and showroom. Lisa was helpful in all aspects of the business. At this point in time Lisa still continues to be a part of all aspects of the business. Her major role that is so important to any business is the financial and office portion of this business.

Randy would still come in the evenings and on weekends. That was when the majority of our work was done because all the rest of us had other jobs to attend. It was not many years before Randy would take a three-month leave to help us full time during the busy season. We credit Randy for being the best Brittle maker in the family. Randy helped with our tours. He felt it was important for one of the Family members to meet and greet the customers and give them first hand information. Randy generally did anything that needed to be done except make a bow! Randy helped with the designing of the hydraulic machines to mold our cakes so that we could reach full-production. In 2005 Randy joined us full time. He is now the President of our company.

Their children have grown up in the business. Rae has graduated high school and college and is employed as a Radiological Technologist specializing in mammography. She attended the same high school as her parents. Today she continues to help us in our basket department, and with our Christmas shows. Rae's fiancé Justin Fields also helps with our shows. They will be married September 13th, her Daddy's birthday and I will be making a fruitcake for the wedding. Hopefully, even with their busy lives they will continue helping during the season.

Zachary is attending high school also where the rest of the family did and excels in baseball. He is also like his father and grandfather by being a devout hunter and fisherman.

Lisa and Randy

Randy, Lisa, Rae and Zac.

Rae loves to help in the kitchen.

Rae can also play ball as well as the boys.

Randy can make the best brittle.

Zac hits another homerun.

Rae and Zach with Missy and Remington.

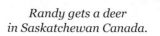

Randy gets a deer in Saskatchewan Canada.

Randy congratulates Zac on his deer.

Hoyt restored this tractor
for Randy.

Zac enjoys
duck hunting as well.

Lisa with her sister Cindy
and their Mother.

Zac and Rae with Granny.

Rae and Justin relax
after a big meal at Christmas.

Justin and Rae's
engagement picture.

Rae and Zac will always remain close.

One of their all time favorite family meals is Sunday lunch. With all their busy schedules Sunday is usually their family time. They enjoy baked ham, macaroni and cheese, creamed potatoes, English sweet peas dumplings and pear salad.

English Pea Dumplings

(Rae's favorite)

2 cans Sweet Peas
1 stick margarine
1 can Biscuits
1 cup water

Place peas in sauce pan, add water and margarine and bring to boil. When you have a full boil, drop small pieces of biscuit dough into boiling mixture. Peas will thicken. Salt and pepper to taste. I use to make this for Rae when she was a little girl. Now she is all grown up and makes it for herself.

Baked Ham

One semi-boneless ham, score top about 1 inch apart and ¼ inch deep. Spread one jar of Southern Supreme Hot Pepper Jelly on top of ham. Wrap in foil and cook at 350° until done.

Pear Salad

6 large leaves iceberg lettuce
1 large can sliced pear halves
¼ cup mayonnaise
1 ½ cup shredded sharp cheddar cheese
6 to 8 maraschino cherries

Line serving platter with lettuce leaves. Place pear halves on top of lettuce. On each pear half drop a dollop of mayonnaise, then sprinkle with cheese and top with a cherry.

Ethelda

When one is growing up, there is always that person that you look up to, follow around, and inspires one to be like. To me that person was my sister, Ethelda. We were only two years apart in age; so we were close. Raised on a farm we both had chores to do every day, there were chores to do before school and chores to do after school. We always helped Mama with the meals and the cleaning of the kitchen. We were always a team when we worked and when we played. When we grew up, Ethelda left home to go to nursing school, and I felt left behind. She eventually graduated from school and moved to Virginia to work at a hospital and there she met her husband Merle Stumpf.

Ethelda

Ethelda has four children, three daughters and one son. Dawn, her oldest, is the Director of the Board of Elections for Chatham County. Douglas Merle, her second child, is a welder and makes custom knives. Bonnie, the third child, is married to Wayne Reynolds and they have 2 children, Holly and Chad. Bonnie works in the business office at Moore Regional Hospital in Pinehurst. Jamie, the fourth child, is married to Rodney Brady and they have 2 children, Jordan and Aaron. Jamie is a Cytotechnogist at Moses Cone Hospital in Greensboro.

All the children have worked in some category at Southern Supreme. They all have helped with Christmas Shows, shipping and all aspects of the business.

Forever Wedding Cake

1 rounded cup of true love
1 heaping cup of perfect trust and confidence
A pinch of unselfishness
A very large sprinkle of interest in all that your partner and family do

Mix all ingredients with a pint of sympathy and flavor with a bear hug and loving kiss.

Bake well for all of your life.

ALL MEMBERS OF THE
STUMPF FAMILY

The People Who Stood Behind Us

*I could never express in words what I feel in my heart
for these special people.*

Sue Wilson

Sue Wilson was not only a very good friend, but a weekly customer in my beauty shop for many years. My youngest son Randy married Sue's youngest daughter Lisa. Sue had lost her husband when Lisa was small.

When my idea of marketing my fruitcake came to me, I was still working in the beauty shop. Sue was a great influence and encouraged me to grasp the concept to a reality. I knew I could count on her help. Indeed Help is the key word. From the very beginning, Sue helped in all aspects of our fruitcake venture. During fruitcake season, she helped with any thing we needed. She also helped us with the Jams and Relishes in the summer time. Her life experience with cooking and food enhanced everything she did, we learned from her experiences, and it made us better.

Sue loved to help us give samples of fruitcake at the shows we attended. Seeing and meeting the people was a true enjoyment for her.

A special time for Sue and us was our annual Open House. Sue loved greeting the customers who came each year and toured our kitchens and tasted our products.

The most important things in Sue's life was God, her Church and her family. In 2003, Sue became ill and passed away at the age of 85. She was a wonderful woman with a beautiful soul and spirit. The void in our lives as well as her families is evident.

I will always be grateful to Sue for the encouragement and help that she gave me in the beginning of this journey.

Elmo Phillips

If there was one person I could trust to bake my fruitcakes it was Elmo. I have known Elmo since grade school. We both attended Bonlee School together. After finishing school we both married and started our families. I went to Beauty School and Elmo became a stay at home mom. She and her husband, Bobby raised five children, Joy, the oldest, Landis, Cary, Martha and Neal. When I decided to go to work, Elmo baby set my two oldest children. That was the first time I called on my friend.

Elmo was the hardest working woman I knew. She took care of her children and my two plus tending to a very large garden. She canned and froze garden vegetables all summer long. She was also one of the best cooks in the county. She has many great recipes I am sure you will enjoy in our recipe section. Elmo is one of these ladies in the community that you could always count on. She is constantly visiting the sick, taking care of an elderly friend or volunteering in her church.

When I decided to market my fruitcake the first person I thought of was my friend Elmo. When I approached her with my idea she said yes. Having raised their five children, she and her husband Bobby were empty nesters with time on their hands. This was the beginning of a twenty-two year commitment. Elmo was entrusted with the obligation of baking and supervising the fruitcake kitchen. She was given the task of ensuring that each cake met our strict criteria. She met and surpassed this duty many times over. No fruitcake was ready until Elmo said it was ready. She gained the support and respect of her fellow workers through the years.

I could never express all my gratitude to this wonderful woman. Her loyalty and hard work to Southern Supreme could never be re paid.

In 2008, Elmo retired. My family and I can hardly imagine baking the fruitcakes without her. She will surely be missed, so I say to my friend from the bottom of my heart "Thank You".

Nina Goins

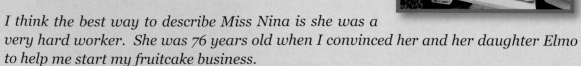

Miss Nina, that's what we always called her. Miss Nina was born in Chatham County in 1909. She came from a very large family and was raised just a few miles from where Southern Supreme is today.

I think the best way to describe Miss Nina is she was a very hard worker. She was 76 years old when I convinced her and her daughter Elmo to help me start my fruitcake business.

She could work circles around me and everyone in the kitchen. Miss Nina had always been a homemaker. She canned and froze vegetables from her garden every summer. She could cook those vegetables too; she was one of the best cooks in the county. She was famous for her 8 layer chocolate cake. You were a very lucky person if you got one of her chocolate cakes for your birthday.

What a gem she was to everyone she met.

Miss Nina worked when we were in my daughter's garage. The first season that we moved to our large kitchen Miss Nina informed us all that she thought she might get lost it was so big. Miss Nina worked with us until 1992. She passed away at the age of 87. I still remember the days when Miss Nina, Sue and Elmo made the most wonderful fruitcakes, they were so proud.

8 Layer Chocolate Cake

Nina Goins

1 box "Pillsbury Golden Butter Recipe"
1 box "Food Lion Butter Gold Cake" mix
1-teaspoon vanilla
3-heaping tablespoons cocoa

Follow directions on the boxes and add 1-teaspoon vanilla. Mix well and put in greased 9 inch cake pans. This will make 12 or 14 layers. Bake at 350° for 12 minutes. I freeze the left over layers for another time.

Chocolate Frosting

2 pounds confectioner sugar
1 stick margarine
2 blocks unsweetened chocolate
1 teaspoon vanilla
Small can evaporated milk

In the microwave, melt 2 blocks unsweetened chocolate with 1 stick margarine, takes about 2 minutes. Mix well. Make a well in confectioner and pour in chocolate. Add vanilla, and then add milk. Beat with hand or mixer; add milk as needed. I use this frosting on the 8 layer chocolate cake.

Kitchen Staff

Joyce Hussey

Joyce works in the fruitcake kitchen. She presses and molds the cake. Joyce has been with us since 1995.

I think the best thing about Joyce is her ability to make everyone laugh. She has this distinct laughter that you can't miss. If you walk through the fruitcake kitchen and hear everyone laughing you know Joyce is behind it. Joyce resides in Moore County with her husband Benny. During the off-season she enjoys riding with Benny on his motorcycle.

Sally Ryan

Miss Sally as we all call her came to us in 1996. Sally had retired from the management of the cafeteria at Bennett School and was bored sitting at home so we put her to work. Her first position was glazing the cakes, which she done very well. She also helped with the tours when she had time. Everyone always enjoyed Miss Sally's tours; she was so knowledgeable of the company, its products and family histories.

Standing: Sue Wilson, Me, Evelyn Cheek, and sitting is Ms. Sally.

In later year because of health problems she began the position of cracking the eggs for the fruitcakes. The customers who toured the fruitcake kitchen really enjoyed watching Sally crack eggs. They always ask her "How many eggs do you crack in a day"? She really got a kick out of that. Sally didn't work in the 2007 season and we really missed her, and many of the returning customers ask about her. She is a true friend to Southern Supreme and we wish her well.

Joyce Brown

Joyce has been working at Southern Supreme for 3 years. We appreciate the good job she does for us. Joyce presses the fruitcakes after they are weighed. It is very hard work and she does it very well. She lives in Robbins, NC.

Judy Ritter

Judy has been employed in the fruitcake kitchen for five years. She weighs the cake out of the oven. When we have tours coming through, Judy enjoys demonstrating to the crowd how she molds the cake. We feel very proud to have an employee as loyal as Judy.

Cliff Norris

Cliff has worked in the fruitcake kitchen for four years. His job is to assist in baking the fruitcakes. This is a very hard job and the heat from the ovens is terrible, but Cliff is great. He has a good attitude and enjoys his work.

Cliff is retired from Randolph Technical College where he taught Art. When he isn't making fruitcakes, he restores antique cars.

Marie Shamburger

Marie comes to us from Moore County. She works in the fruitcake kitchen. Marie's job is to weigh the fruitcake when it comes out of the oven. If we are making 1-pound fruitcakes, Marie weighs out 1 pound of cooked fruitcake and passes it on to be molded. She does a wonderful job for us, and we are proud to have her on the team. Marie has been with Southern Supreme for 3 years.

Alan (Ziggy) Zimmerman

Alan has worked with Southern Supreme for two years. He works in the fruitcake kitchen mixing the cake in the giant mixers. He also prepares the pans of fruitcake for the oven.

Alan also helps us with our Christmas shows around the east coast. He loves doing the shows, his bubbly personality just wins folks over and they will buy anything from him.

Alan is retired from the Highway Patrol after thirty years on the force. He spends his spare time between his wife Karen and his motorcycle. Alan and Karen are also members of Wayne and Belinda's "wild hog" group.

Wayne and Ziggy.

The All-Important Pastry Crust Flaky Pastry

Alan Zimmerman
Bear Creek, NC

2 ¼ cups sifted all-purpose flour
1 teaspoon salt
3 ¼ cup (2 tablespoons) shortening-'Crisco'
⅓ cup cold water
2 crust pie:

In bowl mix flour and salt. Cut in shortening until like coarse meal. Sprinkle water, 1 tablespoon at a time over different parts of mixture. Toss quickly with fork until particles stick together. When pressed gently and form dough clings to fork (use only enough water to make flour particles cling together). Dough should not be wet or slippery. Lightly form dough into smooth ball (on warm day, wrap in wax paper or aluminum foil and refrigerate up to ½ hour) Then divide in half to form 2 balls; makes enough for 8 inch or 9 inch pie. For baked pie shell, bake at 450° 12-15 minutes until bubbles appear, prick with fork. Unbaked pie in which filling is baked in the pie, fill and bake as specific recipe directs.

Linda Sheffield

Linda is one of our glazers. She makes the glaze for the fruitcake, along with spreading the glaze on the cake, plus decorating each cake with a cherry and pineapple. She has been with us for 3 years and does a great job. Linda lives in Moore County and has two children. She also works during the summer assisting with the jams and jellies.

Chewy Graham Brownies

Linda Sheffield
Carthage, NC
You will not believe these fudge-y brownies only have five ingredients. The thick batter is loaded with chocolate cookie crumbs.

1cup (6 ounces) semi-sweet chocolate morsels
½ cup creamy or chunky peanut butter
1 (14 ounce) can sweetened condensed milk
½ cup coarsely chopped pecans, toasted
2 cups chocolate graham cracker crumbs or chocolate wafer cookie crumbs

Combine first three ingredients in a saucepan. Cook over medium heat, stirring constantly until morsels and peanut butter melt. Remove from heat; stir in pecans and chocolate crumbs. (Batter will be very thick) Bake at 350 ° for 24 minutes; cool in pan. Cut into 2-inch squares. Yield 16 brownies.

Dixie Holt

Dixie is Hoyt's youngest sister. I found out early in life that Dixie didn't like to wash dishes, from the large dinners we had at Hoyt's Mothers house, but she can pack fruitcake.

Dixie came to work with us in 2003. She takes the cake after it is bagged and sealed then places it in the box and places a letter to our customer on top, lays the lid on and it is ready to go. She does a great job for us and we enjoy having her around.

Bean Salad

Dixie Holt
Bear Creek, NC

1 can yellow beans, drained
1 can green beans, drained
1 can dark red kidney beans, washed and drained
1 onion, thin sliced

Mix dressing:
¾ cup sugar
1 teaspoon salt
1 teaspoon celery seed
⅔ cup vinegar
⅓ cup oil
⅓ tablespoon pepper

Bobbie Phillips

Bobbie is a friend and neighbor who was retired but not ready to stop working altogether, so she helps us in the wrapping department during fruitcake season. Bobbie's job is to place the fruitcake in a bag and seal it. This is a very hard job and not everyone can do it, but she handles it great. My daughter Belinda and her daughter Debbie grew up together and are still best friends today.

Peach Fruit Smoothies

Bobbie Phillips
Bear Creek, NC
Smoothies are great for breakfast, dessert or a midday snack!

1 ¼ cup milk
1 cup (8 ounces) lemon yogurt
1 cup orange juice
3 teaspoons sugar
½ teaspoon vanilla extract
1 package (16 ounces) frozen or fresh unsweetened peach slices
(If peaches are fresh, add ice cubes)

In a blender or food processor, combine all the ingredients. Cover and process until blended and smooth; serve immediately. Yield: six servings

Sara Scott

Sara is one of my best friends. When Sara retired she approached me for a job and we found her something to do right away. She works in the wrapping department. She and Bobbie bag and seal all the fruitcakes. In the summer she helps with the production of the jams and jellies. We truly appreciate the loyalty and hard work that Sara gives to our company.

Easy French Onion Soup

Sara Scott
Bear Creek, NC

2 tablespoons butter or margarine
1 large onion, sliced
½ teaspoon sugar
1 (10 ½ ounce) can beef bouillon
1¼ cup water
2 tablespoons "French's Worcestershire Sauce"

Melt butter in medium size saucepan. Add onion and sugar, cook and stir 5-10 minutes until lightly browned. Add bouillon, water and Worcestershire sauce simmer 10-15 minutes. Ladle soup into a ram kin place a small slice of French bread on top of soup and sprinkle mozzarella cheese on top of the bread. Bake in oven until cheese has melted on bread.

Shelby Scott

Shelby is my sister-in-law. Her husband Bob and Hoyt are brothers. Shelby retired from a local manufacturing company and came to work in 2007. She helps in the wrapping department.

She places the fruitcake in the boxes and sends them down the line for letters and lids. Shelby stays busy in the summertime taking care of her four granddaughters.

Vegetable Chicken Wraps
Shelby Scott
Bear Creek, NC

4 flour tortillas (8 inches)
1 carton (8 ounces) spread-able garden vegetable cream cheese
2 cups shredded romaine
2 small tomatoes, thinly sliced
8 slices Provolone cheese
1 small red onion, thinly sliced
2 cups diced cooked chicken

Spread cream cheese evenly over each tortilla. Layer the romaine, tomato, cheese, onion, and chicken on the tortilla. Roll up tightly and cut in half to serve. Yield: 4 servings

Sara, Shelby, Dixie and Bobbie.

Nancy Williamson

Nancy is another local who came to work for us in 2004. I have known Nancy and her family for many years. We attend the same church. She also works in the wrapping department, placing cakes and customer letters in the boxes. We are proud to have Nancy in our employment.

Molly Woody and Linda Wicker

Molly and Linda are sisters who came to work for us in 2000.

They both do a great job working in the wrapping department. Molly seals the bag the cake is in and Linda packs the finished cake in a master box. They both live in Goldston, North Carolina.

68

Judy Preslar

Judy started work with Southern Supreme in September of 1996. She is the supervisor of one of our four kitchens. Judy brought an enormous amount of experience with her when she came, having managed the kitchen at a health care facility for thirteen years, as well as owning and operating a food business with husband Waylon.

Judy At "Open House."

She oversees all the day-to-day operation in the kitchen, which we call the nut kitchen. They cook all of our gourmet nuts; and no, it does not mean you are a nutty person if you work in this area. This kitchen is also responsible for producing the almond, pecan and cashew crunch as well as the brittle. We also use this particular kitchen to produce our jams, jellies, relish and mustards in the summer. Judy is really a people person and her ability to work with people as well as lead them speaks for itself. She is another one of our valuable employees which has contributed to the growth and success of Southern Supreme. Her commitment, flexibility and willingness to help, whether it is to cook nuts, bake fruitcake and cookies or to order supplies and ingredients for her kitchen or yes, even if we need help in the showroom waiting on customers we know we can depend on her. When Judy is not cooking, she enjoys watching her granddaughter play softball. She is also very active in her church where she plays the piano, not from a hymnal but by ear. She states that this is her God given talent. We think Judy has many talents and we thank her for sharing them with us through the years.

Crock Pot Macaroni & Cheese

Judy Preslar
Bennett, NC

8 oz. of macaroni (cooked)
1 ½ cup milk
2 eggs
1 tsp salt
3 cups sharp cheddar cheese
Pepper to taste
¼ cup melted butter

Oil Crock Pot, add and mix ingredients. Cook on low 3 to 4 hours.

Judy and Waylon reside in Bennett, North Carolina. They have 2 children, Rodney and wife Lisa, Ginger and husband Brian and 1 grandchild, Cori who is the apple of their eye.

One of Judy's favorite recipes can be made very easily.

Jane Maness & Thelma Purvis

Old Fashioned Peanut Butter Cookies

A Family Favorite from Jane Maness
Carthage, NC

1 cup butter or margarine softened
1 cup creamy peanut butter
1 cup sugar
1 cup firmly packed brown sugar
2 large eggs
2 ½ cups all-purpose flour
2 teaspoons baking soda
¼ teaspoon salt
1 teaspoon vanilla extract
Sugar

Beat butter and peanut butter
with an electric mixer until creamy. Gradually add sugars,
beating well. Add eggs, beating well. Combine flour, soda
and salt in a medium bowl; add to butter mixture, beating
well. Stir in vanilla, cover and chill 3 hours. Shape into 1 ¼
inch balls, place 3 inches apart on un-greased cookie sheet.
Dip a fork into additional sugar. Flatten cookies in a cross
design. Bake at 375° for 7-8 minutes. Remove to
wire rack to cool-yield 6 dozen.

Jane and Thelma have worked with Southern Supreme since 1999. As I was looking back at their history with us, I noticed something about these two ladies that I'm sure I knew but had forgotten through the years. Both of these ladies came and put their application in on the same day, they were interviewed the same day and both were hired to begin working on October 4, 1999. As you may have guessed they both work in the same kitchen. Our company has certainly benefited from these two loyal ladies. They are two of the most hard working, dependable folks that we employ. They have proven how valuable they are to us over and over through the years and we hope that they are here for many years to come.

Jane and husband Robert reside in High Falls, NC. They are the parents of five children, Rita (who works with us), Roger, Benita, Audrey and Christine. They also have ten grandchildren, eight great grandchildren and 3 great great grandchildren. Jane loves to go to the beach and she also enjoys playing the piano.

Thelma is married to Robert and they live in Robbins, NC. They have two daughters, Sheila and Brenda, four grandchildren and one great grandchild. Thelma is very involved in her church and supports different ministries there. She and her husband really enjoy traveling when time permits.

Cheese Sauce For Vegetables

Thelma Purvis
High Falls, NC

2 tablespoons butter
2 tablespoons flour
¼ teaspoon salt
⅛ teaspoon pepper
¼ teaspoon dry mustard
1 cup milk
½ cup shredded cheddar cheese

Heat over low heat, stir constantly until cheese melts and sauce is smooth. Cook for about one minute.

Rita Garner

Rita joined our company in 1999. I interviewed Rita myself and I knew right away that I wanted her to be in charge of our packaging department. It was a decision that I have never had to question.

Rita has proven herself many times over as she supervises our packaging department. Some may think the packaging would not be as stressful as working in the hot kitchens, but I am sure Rita would beg to differ. In the packaging department they probably have ninety to one hundred different items that they package, bear in mind that all of this is done by hand. Rita knows where every bag, band, label, tag, container, doilies, ribbon or anything that is used in packaging. She also sees that each product is packed and tagged correctly. During a single day they may have to package fifteen to twenty different products. Rita keeps up with what was packaged, sizes and how many. She also supervises our wrapping department. In this area they wrap and box all the fruitcakes. On most days in season we will bake 2500 to 3000 pounds of fruitcake, which again is wrapped and boxed by hand. Needless to say that she has a big responsibility and she uses her pleasing but firm manner as she works with her staff to do the job. She will never ask of them more than she will do herself. I am very fortunate and happy to have Rita as a part of our staff at Southern Supreme. Rita and husband Buddy reside in High Falls, NC They have three children, Gary, Justin and Whitney and are the proud grandparents of Jayden. Rita and family love to go to the beach when they can and they also enjoy camping.

Salsa With Black Bean & Corn

Rita Garner
Carthage, NC
This is a yield for a big party-
If it's more than you need cut it in half.

1½ teaspoon cumin seeds-toasted 1-2 minutes until brown & fragrant, stirring often
2 (15 ounce) cans black beans, rinsed and drained
1 (15 ½ ounce) can whole kernel corn, drained
1 red pepper, minced
1 small purple onion, minced (1 cup)
½ cup chopped fresh cilantro
½ cup chopped fresh parsley
⅓ cup lime juice
¼ cup olive oil
3 cloves garlic, crushed
½ teaspoon salt
1 teaspoon dried crushed red pepper
½ teaspoon freshly ground black pepper

Combine cumin seeds, black beans, and remaining ingredients; toss well. Cover and store in refrigerator.

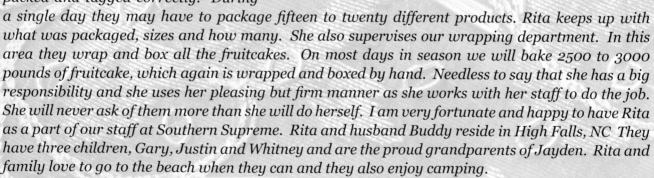

Hazel McMath

Hazel's position is in the Packaging Department. Hazel is a fiery little thing, she never slows down. She can package products and seal bags faster than any one. She knows where every, bag, box, tin, label and bow is in the warehouse and put her finger on it in an instant. She is definitely Rita's right hand woman. Hazel works in Jams and Jellies in the summertime, she washes and labels all the jars by hand. Employees like Hazel are hard to come by and we truly appreciate her. Hazel has been with us for 5 years and lives in Goldston, NC.

JoAnn Jones

JoAnn is a neighbor who joined us in 1998. She assists Ethleda in the candy kitchen. JoAnn is responsible for many of the great chocolate recipes that are produced in the candy kitchen. Her and Ethelda work hard all summer to come up with new chocolates and other delicious items. One of many successes was their Creamy Pralines. It took many months to perfect this wonderful delight. Her enthusiasm is seen throughout her department in the candy she produces and in her staff.

JoAnn hard at work in the candy kitchen.

JoAnn was born in Alamance County and moved to the Bennett area in 1948. There she met her husband Ralph. They raised two daughters Jenny Lynn and Donna Sue. JoAnn has four grandchildren.

I truly appreciate the hard work and loyalty that JoAnn has given to me and my family and proud to have her at Southern Supreme.

Cream Cheese Oreo Balls

Hazel McMath
Goldston, NC

1 package 'Oreo Cookies'
1 (8 ounces) cream cheese
White chocolate

Use blender or food processor to blend the cookies until fine. In mixing bowl, add cream cheese and cookies together. Roll in balls and chill in refrigerator on wax paper until mixture hardens. Dip in white chocolate. Put back in refrigerator until chocolate hardens.

Banana Bread

Joann Jones
Bennett, NC

⅓ cup oil
1 cup sugar
3 eggs
3 cups mashed dead ripe bananas
2 ⅓ cups "Bisquick"
½ teaspoon vanilla
Nuts

Mix by hand. Pour in 2 loaf pans. Bake 55-60 minutes in 350° oven.

Karen King

Karen works in our Cookie Kitchen. She is responsible for all the great cookies from that kitchen. She also makes our wonderful cheese florets. When Karen first came to work she was in the chocolate kitchen, but our cookies were such a success we needed someone full time to take over. Karen has been with us since 1999. She lives in Sanford with her small daughter.

Fluffy Pumpkin Cheesecake Pie

Karen King
Sanford, NC

12 ounces cream cheese, softened
½ cup sugar
1 ½ teaspoons pumpkin pie spice
2 eggs
1 cup canned pumpkin
1 Graham cracker crust

1. In large mixing bowl beat the cream cheese until fluffy on medium speed of electric mixer. Add sugar and spice. Beat until combined.

2. Add eggs, one at a time, mixing until just combined after each addition. Stir in pumpkin.

3. Pour into crust. Bake at 350° for 30-35 minutes or until center is almost set. Cool for 1 hour on wire rack. Refrigerate at least 3 hours.

4. Garnish as desired. Keep refrigerated.
Yield: 8 servings

Rosetta Oldham

Rosetta came to work in 1999. She first worked in the fruitcake kitchen glazing. After a couple years she decided she wanted to work in the cookie kitchen, so she has been Karen's assistant since that time. Rosetta loves to make fruitcake cookies. We appreciate the years that she has given to us.

Office Staff

Kristy Cheek

Kristy is another one of our valuable employees. She has been with us since 2002. She works in our customer service department. Kristy is capable of answering and making decisions pertaining to customer concerns.

Kristy has a strong computer background that has been a big asset to our business. Her help in developing our website as well as maintaining our site has been a bonus for us.

Kristy's knowledge of all aspects of our business has made her very versatile to us. Her quiet and mild manner has made her a pleasure to work with. Kristy resides with her husband Kevin in Robbins NC, they have one daughter Kaci. They all enjoy outdoors, especially hunting and fishing together. Southern Supreme feels very fortunate to have Kristy as a part of our company and we appreciate her dedication and loyalty.

Baked Beans

Kristy Cheek
Robbins, NC

1 large can pork & beans
1 chopped onion
½ cup ketchup
1 tablespoon mustard
4 teaspoons brown sugar

Mix all ingredients well. Place strips of bacon on top of beans and cook covered 1 hour at 350°.

Kim Cheek

Kim has been with Southern Supreme since 1998. Her first position was in the kitchen that produces our gourmet nuts; from there she went to assisting with the jelly making. Kim, today, is employed in the shipping department.

Kim lives in Bonlee, NC with her husband Darien and their 11 year old daughter Autumn. She enjoys mountain hiking and going to her daughter's baseball games.

Kim is one of those employees that will work any where you ask her to! Multitasking is one of her best virtues. Her co-workers really enjoy her happy-go lucky attitude.

Spaghetti is Autumn's favorite meal. She is a picky eater so Kim makes her spaghetti special and easy.

Autumn's Spaghetti

Kim Cheek
Bonlee, NC

1 pound Hamburger
1 can Hunt's Plain Spaghetti Sauce
1 box Spaghetti Noodles

Brown hamburger and drain. Add sauce to hamburger. Boil noodles until tender. Pour sauce over noodles and sprinkle with Parmesan cheese.

74

Dottie Josey

Dottie began her career at Southern Supreme in 1993. She started in the packaging department wrapping fruitcakes by hand. After two seasons we started our basket department and Dottie began designing baskets for the showroom and the catalog. She joined the showroom staff in 1995. During these early years while working for Southern Supreme Dottie was also attending college for degree in computers. She brought Southern Supreme out of the dark ages and into the world of computers. Her expertise has slim lined our operation, made it more productive and more computer savvy. Her knowledge of computers has greatly enhanced the growth and future growth of Southern Supreme.

Dottie advanced in 1996 to Office Manager and Customer Service where she remains today. One of her responsibilities, among many, includes the development of our mail order catalog. She spends many hours placing photos and writing text. The success of our website and its design can be contributed to her knowledge and hard work.

Lasagna
Dottie Josey
Bear Creek, NC

Cook 1 lb Lasagna noodles according to directions. Add ¼ cup of cooking oil. Drain noodles and lay out flat if possible.

Mix:
1 ½ pounds ricotta cheese
2 eggs beaten
⅓ grated Parmesan cheese
⅓ cup chopped parsley
1 ½ teaspoon salt
¼ teaspoon pepper
2 cans Hunts Meat Sauce (you can add more or less to taste)
1 large bag Mozzarella cheese

Place a layer of noodles in bottom of baking dish and follow with a layer of ricotta cheese (can use cottage cheese). Sprinkle with a layer pf spaghetti meat sauce, a layer of shredded mozzarella cheese, and a layer of grated Parmesan cheese. Repeat for 5 to 6 layers. Top with Lasagna noodles, meat sauce and grated Parmesan cheese.

Bake at 350° for 15 minutes and turn off oven and leave for 5 minutes. Remove from oven and let stand for 15 minutes before serving.

During the busy season, we rely on her to keep Customer Service running smooth. She is also responsible for Accounts Receivable. Dottie has been a pioneering force in the development and growth of Southern Supreme; we could never repay her for all the work and dedication she has given to this company.

Dottie lives in Bear Creek with her husband Roger Sr. and her four children, Jennifer, Roger Jr., Keith and Brandy. Dottie also has two grandchildren Tyler and Haley.

She would like to share her favorite recipes.

And to go with the Lasagna

Pepperoni Bread

Dottie Josey
Bear Creek, NC

2 ¼ cup warm water (110-115°)
2 packages Yeast
1 tablespoon salt
1 tablespoon margarine
6 ½ cups All Purpose Flour
1 tablespoon sugar
1 ½ cup pepperoni (chopped)
1 egg beaten

Pour warm water in large bowl, sprinkle in yeast, and stir. Add sugar, salt, margarine and 3 cups of flour. Beat until smooth. Stir in remaining flour to make soft dough. Knead 8 to 10 minutes. Place in greased bowl, cover and let rise for 1 hour. Punch dough down and divide into 3 pieces. Roll each ball to a 12 x 8. Place pepperoni slices or chopped pieces on each. Roll and seal. Grease baking sheets and cover to rise for 1 hour. Splash tops with egg wash and bake a 400° for 20 -25 minutes.

Sandra Cook

Sandra is one of our most valued employees. Her position is Customer Service Representative. She has been with Southern Supreme since September 2000. Sandra and her husband Elton live in Siler City, NC and have two grown children, her son Chris and her daughter Beverly. When Sandra is not at work she enjoys, reading, church activities and spending time with her family.

I always enjoy coming in and seeing her smiling face. Sandra is filled with knowledge of our products, which makes her great at her job. It always gets crazy at the Christmas season, but she handles it great.

Crock Pot Pork Chops

Sandra Cook
Siler city, NC

4-6 Pork Chops (bone-in)
1 can Cream of chicken Soup
12 ounces water
½ cup Self Rising Flour
⅓ cup flour
2 tablespoons shortening

Lightly flour pork chops. Heat shortening, then brown pork chops (both sides) in skillet. Place pork chops in crock-pot. Add soup and water to pork chops and cook on low setting 6-8 hours. Served over rice or mashed potatoes makes a great meal.

Sandra and her husband Elton work our Myrtle Beach Show.

Sandra and her family also help with our Christmas Show schedule. Sandra and Elton and their family do the Charles Dickens Christmas Show in Myrtle Beach. She also assists with Holly Fair Christmas show in Fayetteville. Sandra's dedication and loyalty to Southern Supreme makes her an asset to our company.

Stuffed French Toast

Judy Councilman
Siler City, NC

1 stick butter (½ cup)
1 cup brown sugar
¼ cup maple syrup
Sliced bread (preferably French bread or cinnamon raisin)
Cream cheese (enough to spread liberally over bread slices)
Fruit of your choice (such as berries, apricots, peaches or thinly sliced apples)
Walnuts or pecans (amount to suit your taste)
6 eggs
1 ½ cups milk (adjust amount to density of bread)
1 teaspoon vanilla extract

Start with a 9X12 inch pan. Place butter, brown sugar and maple syrup in a dish that can go into the microwave and in the oven. Microwave until the butter melts. Stir to dissolve sugar and mix the ingredients well. Sprinkle nuts over this mixture. Spread cream cheese on half of the bread slices. Place berries, fruit or apple slices on top with the plain bread to make a "sandwich". Cut in half diagonally and place in a baking pan with the butter, sugar and syrup mixture. Do not overlap the slices. Mix eggs, vanilla and milk. Pour over the bread. Cover and refrigerate overnight. Bake at 350° for about 45 minutes, uncovered. Flip over to serve, so that the syrup side is up. Top with powdered sugar and additional fruit or syrup if desired.

Judy Councilman

Judy Councilman came to us in 1994. She started out in the office helping answer the phone and invoiced our orders for shipping. Judy is an asset at whatever she does. Although she is still a part of the office functions she has other responsibilities. Judy's knowledge of our company allowed her the opportunity of helping us with our daily tours. Judy is married to Harold. They live in Bear Creek NC. They have 2 sons Lee and Brian and are proud grandparents of 4 grandchildren.

Caramel Popcorn

Elizabeth Rea
Robbins, NC

8 quarts popcorn, popped
In saucepan put:
2 sticks butter
2 cups light brown sugar
½ cup Karol light syrup
Bring to boil; boil 5 minutes. Remove from heat and add:
½ teaspoon soda
Pinch of cream of tartar
Dash of salt

Pour over popcorn. Put into roaster pan. Bake 200 °
for 1 hour. Put on waxed paper and separate grains.

Elizabeth Rea

Elizabeth joined our staff in 2006. She is responsible for ordering ingredients and supplies for our company. Elizabeth is our liaison between all departments and truly keeps us on our toes. She is good at finding things that I have lost.

She deals with our vendors and handles most correspondence with them. Responsible for Accounts Payable, she pays all the bills.

Elizabeth is a single mom and is devoted to her 19 year old son Zachery. She loves antiques and does a lot of shopping for deals. She retired from Moore Regional Hospital in Pinehurst, NC after 28 years as a division secretary. Even though Elizabeth hates to cook, her Mother has contributed many delicious recipes to my book. I really enjoy Elizabeth and hope to have her here at Southern Supreme for many years to come.

Shipping Staff

Pam Cameron

Pam works in our shipping department and has been employed with us since October 1999. She usually works from September through December each year. Pam has lived in many places during her life as she comes from a military family. She claims California as her home state. Pam had postal experience as she worked as a mail clerk in the Air Force. After relocating to North Carolina she was looking for part-time work and that is how she came to us. Pam handles all the day to day operations of our shipping department during our peak season where probably 85 – 95 percent of our shipping is done. She trains all our new personnel each year. Packages are normally shipped by UPS or the Postal Service and she has the responsibility to see that they are shipped timely and accurately with a minimum of errors. We certainly appreciate her service and dedication to Southern Supreme by her willingness and flexibility in the mail order part of our business.

In her spare time Pam is an avid shopper who knows how to find a bargain. She also makes beautiful beaded artwork for all occasions which she sells at local craft shows.

Showroom Staff

Deborah Stephenson

Deborah has been with us for three years. Her talent lies with decorating and basket making. She manages our showroom basket department, making sure our showroom is stocked with beautiful gift baskets and gift boxes. Since her relationship with Southern Supreme, she has been responsible for decorating our showroom. Her expertise for color and her talent to put it altogether is truly admirable. Anyone who has visited our showroom during the season can honestly appreciate her efforts.

Deborah also assists us in buying gift items for sale in our showroom. She has also been very instrumental in helping me write this book, and, I appreciate the one on one time she gave me. Talented employees like Deborah are hard to come by and we are grateful to have her.

Deborah lives in Carthage, North Carolina with her husband Hal and his two sons. Her two sons, Aaron and Zachary, are married and live near her. She has four grandsons and a granddaughter. She feels God has truly blessed her.

Black Forest Christmas Cookies

Deborah Pickard Stephenson
Carthage, NC
Showroom Employee

1 (8 ounce) package cream cheese
1 cup butter
1½ cup sugar
1 egg
1 teaspoon vanilla
2½ cup flour
⅓ cup cocoa
1 teaspoon baking powder
½ cup chopped pecans
½ cup chopped maraschino cherries, drained

Preheat oven to 375°. Cream cheese, butter, and sugar. Stir in egg and vanilla. Mix together flour, cocoa, and baking powder and stir into creamed mixture. Stir in nuts and cherries. Drop by teaspoons onto greased cookie sheets. Bake for 12-15 minutes. Makes 5 dozen.

Kathryn Brennan

Kathryn came to work with us in 2006. She is responsible for the Showroom registers, and assisting any customer who may need help. Kathryn is a loyal and dedicated employee and we depend on

"The General", Kathryn Brennan checking the inventory before tours arrive.

Grandma Brennan's Coconut Pie

Mary K. Brennan
Makes 2 regular 9 inch pie crusts

2 cups sugar
2 tablespoons flour
2 cups coconut
8 eggs (separate 6 eggs from yolk saving whites for meringue later)
1 can evaporated milk plus 1 can of water
1 teaspoon vanilla flavor

Mix in a double boiler in this order: sugar, flour, eggs, milk, and water. Put coconut in when mixture starts to boil. Cook until thick; keep in mind mixture will thicken more when cool. Add flavor after removing from heat. Pour into cooked pie crust. Top with meringue. Cook at 350° until meringue browns.

Meringue: Be sure egg whites are room temperature. Beat at high speed until stiff. Add 1 tablespoon of sugar per egg white; add ½ teaspoon of flavoring.

My daughter would request these pies every year for her birthday. The same recipe can also make a banana pudding. Just leave out the coconut and do not cook as thick.

Yellow Squash Patties

Mary K. Brennan

Fresh yellow summer squash
1 egg
Chopped onion
Salt and pepper
Flour

Mix egg, onion, salt and pepper together. Add flour until you have a dry batter. Thinly slice squash and add to batter. Add a little water if batter is too dry. Mix squash well into batter. Spoon batter into frying pan of hot oil. Fry until golden brown. Drain onto paper towel. Can also add green peppers if desired.

her enormously. Kathryn retired from the State Bureau of Investigation in Raleigh. Sometimes that stern attitude comes out, so we have nicknamed her "The General", but actually she is just a pussycat.

Kathryn relaxes by quilting, reading, gardening and going to the beach with her quilting club. She lives in Sanford with her daughter Annette and son-in-law Brad.

Kathryn Frazier

Kathryn began her employment with Southern Supreme in September 2003. She is a showroom coordinator along with customer service. Kathryn assists customers as they shop and answers any questions that they may have. She keeps inventory flowing and makes sure all shelves are full. Her smiling face and fun attitude calms all flustered shoppers down. In 2005 Southern Supreme expended their market to a kiosk at South Point Mall in Durham, North Carolina.

Kathryn was instrumental in the success of that venture, sometimes working 11 to 14 hours a day. In 2006, Kathryn's husband Bill was suddenly stricken ill. Kathryn remained by his side until his death in May 2007. We truly missed her that season. In August of 2007 she came back to us. Kathryn confided to me that coming back to work was her saving grace. The truth was we needed her as much as she needed us. Her warm personality is felt by everyone she comes in contact with. Kathryn still resides in her home in Liberty, NC that she shared with Bill. She has two daughters, Annalisa who lives in Arizona and California, and Leigh Anna who lives in Greensboro. Kathryn loves to visit and spend time with them. Kathryn enjoys collecting teapots, attending her Eastern Star activities and taking care of her four dogs. Our showroom shines a little brighter at Christmas time because of her presence, she welcomes all that enter our doors.

Winter Vegetable Soup
Kathryn Frazier
Liberty, NC

2 medium onions-chopped
3 large carrots-chopped
3 stalks celery-chopped
2 large potatoes-diced
⅓ cup flour
3 tablespoons butter
2 (12 ounce) cans "V-8" vegetable juice
2 cups water
Salt and pepper-to taste

Combine all ingredients in crock-pot. Cook on low 6-8 hours.

Lorrie Moore & Denise Holt

Lorrie is our weekend basket designer. She is also my & Hoyt's niece. Lorrie can design the most beautiful baskets. Her expertise is large baskets. We call her large baskets, "The Lorrie Baskets". Hoyt can walk through the showroom and if there is an empty spot on the floor, he goes right to Lorrie and tells her "Lorrie I need a basket". She has earned a couple nicknames over the years, but the best is The Basket Queen. Lorrie lives in Bonlee with her husband Ronald. They have three children, Chance, Brooke and Lauren.

Creamy Herb Dip
Lorrie Moore
Bonlee, NC

¾ cup sour cream
¾ cup mayonnaise
1 tablespoon minced parsley
1 tablespoon minced chives
1 teaspoon minced dill
1 teaspoon lemon zest
1 tablespoon lemon juice

Stir together all ingredients. Cover and refrigerate until ready to serve. Serve with raw vegetables, or crackers. Makes 1 ½ cups.

Denise is also my and Hoyt's niece. She works in the basket department on the weekends. Denise's specialty is bow making. She makes the most beautiful bows; they really make our baskets pop. She is so good with our customers, she really makes us proud. I only wish I had two more just like her. Denise lives just down the road from

Denise & Lorrie.

Southern Supreme. She is married to our nephew Phil, and they have three great kids, April, Mary Margaret and Tyler.

Raisin Walnut Waldorf Salad

Denise Holt
Bear Creek, NC

½ cup raisin
1 cup boiling water
4 cups chopped unpeeled red apples
2 celery ribs, thinly sliced
2 tablespoons lemon juice
1 cup (8 ounce) plain yogurt
2 tablespoons instant vanilla pudding mix
2 tablespoons sugar
½ cup chopped walnuts

In a bowl combine raisings and boiling water. Let stand for 5 minutes, drain. Combine raisins, apples, and celery and lemon juice; toss together. Combine yogurt, sugar and pudding mix. Pour over apple mixture, toss to coat. Cover and refrigerate for 1 hour. Stir in walnuts before serving.

Peggie Gaines and Terry Liles

Peggie and Terry are our weekend "Bar Maids." They do a great job of keeping fruitcake and other items for customers to sample on the bar. Terry is always encouraging customers to try this and try that and they usually do! They love talking to the customers and answering all the questions that they may ask. We appreciate the great job that they do.

Peggie is from Goldston, NC and is a Teachers Assistant at Bonlee School in Bonlee, NC. Terry is from Siler City, NC and is the Ultra-Sound Technologist at Chatham Hospital in Siler City.

Terry & Peggie.

Giant Spice Cookie

Peggy Gaines
Goldston, NC

1 package (18 ¼ ounces) spice cake mix
½ teaspoon ground ginger
¼ teaspoon baking soda
¼ cup water
¼ cup molasses
6 teaspoons vanilla

Combine cake mix, ginger and baking soda. Stir in water, molasses and vanilla. Mix well with flour or hand scoop out into balls 3 inches apart on greased baking sheets; flatten slightly. Bake 350° for 12-15 minutes until top cracks and cookies are firm. Remove from pan after 5 minutes.

Chocolate Peanut Squares

Terry Liles
Siler City NC

2 cups confectioners' sugar
¾ cup creamy peanut butter
⅔ cup graham cracker crumbs
½ cup butter melted
TOPPING:
⅔ cup semi-sweet chocolate chips
4 ½ teaspoon creamy peanut butter
½ teaspoon butter

Line a 9 inch square pan with foil and butter the foil-set aside. In a large bowl, combine confectioner's sugar, peanut butter, graham cracker crumbs and butter. Spread into prepared pan.

Combine topping ingredients in a microwave safe bowl; heat until melted. Spread over peanut butter layer. Refrigerate until cool; using foil, lift out of pan. Cut into 1" squares. Store in airtight containers in the refrigerate, Yield about 1 ½ pounds.

Brenda Williamson & Kara Joyce

Brenda and Kara are our Showroom Shipping Clerks. They assist customers who come into the showroom and want to ship items to friends or family. These girls are very knowledgeable of our products and shipping regulations, so they are a big help to our customers. They both have such a great personality and are so helpful it makes it easy for the customers to ship their orders.

Brenda works during the week and lives in Goldston, NC. She has been with us for three years.

Kara lives in Bonlee, NC and covers the weekend position; Kara has been with Southern Supreme for eight years.

Brenda Williamson

Faye Oldham

Faye has been with us for over 12 years. She is a local friend who lives down the road in Robbins, NC. Faye helps in most of our out-of-town shows. She can decorate the booth and set up the displays like a pro. She can also lift heavy fruit cake master boxes like they are feathers. She and Harriet and Nettie are a geat team. Faye also works in the showroom on weekends during the summer. We feel very blessed to have such an employee who is as dependable, trustworthy and loyal as Faye.

Faye Oldham, Harriet Burks and Nettie Sue.

White Chip Cookies

Faye Oldham
Robbins, NC

1 package (9 ounces) devils food cake mix
2 tablespoons baking cocoa
1 egg
2 tablespoons cream cheese (softened)
1 tablespoon milk
¾ cup vanilla or white chips

Combine the cake mix, cocoa, egg, cream cheese and milk; mix well. (Batter will be thick) Stir in chips. Drop by scoop spoon 2-inches a part onto greased baking sheet. Bake 350° for 14-16 minutes. Cool before removing from pan. Optional: may add 1 cup macadamia nuts.

Harriet Burks & Nettie Sue

Harriet has been doing Christmas shows for Southern Supreme for about 10 years. She enjoys the Charlotte show the best. That's the twelve day show called "The Southern Christmas Show." Harriet's husband Ray also joins her at the Holiday Fair in Greenville, S.C. A couple of years ago she persuaded her sister-in-law Nettie to join in. Nettie has proven to be a great asset. We feel very lucky to have people like Harriet, Ray and Nettie representing us at these most important events.

Nellie Brewer & Ruth Oldham

Nellie and Ruth are as we call them our "Bar Maids". Their job is to keep the bar full with fruitcake, nuts, candy, jams and jellies, along with coffee and hot cider for all of our customers to enjoy. It can get hectic during the height of the touring season, with sometimes more than 50 people at one time passing by for samples, but, they handle it just fine. Sometimes people just stop and talk, and they enjoy that. They have met many interesting people from all over the world who just stop and chat. Nettie and Ruth are both from Bennett, NC. We are proud to have them on our staff.

Nellie Brewer   *Ruth Oldham*

Employee Appreciation

As I come to the end of my story there have been many people along this journey that I want to recognize who have helped us bring our company to where it is today. Some of these have come and gone, others are still with us. I will name a few, hoping not to leave anyone out.

Amy Bryant	Dawn Kidd
Mike Burns	Caroline Liles
Beth H. Caviness	Katie Liles
Kim Caviness	Pat Lowe
Lauren Caviness	Amber Martindale
Rachel Cheek	Edith Martindale
Jessica Cockman	Julie Martindale
Leslie Cockman	Anne Millette
Martha Cox	Brooke Moore
Megan Frye	Lauren Moore
Stephanie Hackney	Janice Oldham
Maxine Hill	Bea Phillips
Nancy Hogan	Dean Phillips
April Holt	Melva Phillips
Mary Holt	Shirley Phillips
Clara Hunsucker	Robin Reavis
Clara Hussey	April Roberts
Jabo Hussey	Jennifer Russell
Brandy Josey	Andrew Scott
Keith Josey	Jennifer Simpson
Grace Kaiding	Rachel Sutton

There is another group of people that played a vital role in the growth of our company.

In the early years of our business when we first started to do craft shows to help build our business, it was hard work (and still is) and hard to find enough people to do them. You had to find people who could get off work, did not mind traveling, heavy lifting, five-minute breaks and long days. I will often refer to these people as our Show People.

Below we have listed folks who did that for us many times and I would like to applaud them for their service to us in the past and for their service to come.

Keisha D Allred	Megan Frye
Jamie Brady	Amie Goodman
Linda Brady	Nettie Sue Helfrich
Tina Brady	Chris Jordan
Jason Brown	John Jordan
Scott Brown	Pat & Carl McClelland
Ray & Harriett Burk	Sharon Munden
Debbie Cheek	Carla Norris
Ray & Evelyn Cheek	Faye Oldham
Lori Cockman	Carol Lee Phillips
Sandra & Elton Cook	Rebekah Phillips
Judy Councilman	Derrick Scott
Cindy& Keith Dixon	Kyle Scott
Meredith Dixon	Rae Scott
Cindy Ellis	Ricky Scott
Sue & Frank Farlow	Zac Scott
Beverly C. Fields	Deborah & Hal Stephenson
Justin Fields	Patrick Stephenson
Mitchell Fields	Carlene & Jimmy Stevens
Kathryn Frazier	Bub Stumpf
Alan Zimmerman	Amy Sugg

To each of you listed above I want to say thank you! All of you contributed to the success of Southern Supreme through the years with your hard work and jobs well done.

Appetizers

Finger Jell-O

Elmo Phillips
Bear Creek, NC

4 packages "Knox" unflavored gelatin
(there are 4 to a box)
3 boxes (3 ounce size jell-o any flavor)
4 cups boiling water

Mix jell-o and gelatin together. Add
boiling water-mix well. Pour into 9x13
pan. Chill until firm, 1-2 hours. Cut
into squares and remove from pan. It
will become tough if not removed from
original pan.

Salmon Roll

Marilyn Sehen
Sanford, NC

1 can (16 ounces) pink salmon
½ cup chopped pecans
1 (8 ounce) package cream cheese,
softened
3 tablespoons chopped fresh parsley
2 drops liquid smoke or "Worcestershire
Sauce"
Crackers

Combine salmon, cream cheese and
liquid smoke or "Worcestershire Sauce".
Mix well. Shape into a ball or log. Roll in
mixture of pecans and parsley. Roll up in
plastic wrap or wax paper. Chill to blend
flavors. Serve with crackers.

Helpful Hint

Fresh lemon juice will remove
onion scent from hands.

Spinach Balls

Carolyn Savina
Sanford, NC

1 ½ sticks butter or margarine

6 large eggs

2 (10 ounce) packages frozen chopped spinach defrosted

1 (6 ounce) chicken flavored stuffing mix

1 cup grated parmesan cheese

¼ teaspoon black pepper

Melt butter, place defrosted spinach in a colander and squeeze out most of water. Break eggs into a large mixing bowl and whisk until foamy. Add butter, spinach, stuffing, cheese, and pepper. Stir ingredients until well combined. Roll into 1 ½ inch balls or use a cookie dough scoop. Place on a cookie sheet and bake at 350° 8-10 minutes. Remove from oven and use a spatula to transfer to a serving platter. Cool and serve. Makes about 60 balls. Can freeze balls, put into zip-lock bag and store in freezer. Frozen balls-bake time changes to 12-15 minutes. Delicious!

B-L-T Bites

Elmo Phillips
Employee
Bear Creek, NC

16 to 20 cherry tomatoes

1 pound bacon, cooked and crumbled

½ cup mayonnaise or salad dressing

⅓ cup chopped green onions

3 tablespoons grated Parmesan cheese

2 tablespoons snipped fresh parsley

Cut a thin slice off each tomato top. Scoop out and discard pulp. Invert the tomatoes on a paper towel to drain. In a small bowl, combine the remaining ingredients; mix well. Spoon this mixture in the tomatoes. Refrigerate for several hours. Yield: 16-20 servings.

Mushroom Logs

Mary Lois Thomas
(Moosie)
Sanford, NC

2 packages of canned Pillsbury Crescent rolls

1 package of cream cheese (8 ounce)

1 jar of sliced mushrooms (6 ounce)

1 teaspoon of seasoned salt

Mix softened cream cheese, drained mushroom and seasoning salt. Spoon onto crescent rolls and roll up. Brush with beaten egg and bake according to package directions. This is a family favorite.

Shrimp Hors d'Oeuvres

In memory of my sister Allene Watts
Berta Scott
Bear Creek, NC

1 (8 ounce) package cream cheese (softened)
8 ounces cooked shrimp (chopped)
Spread the soften cream cheese about ¼ to ½ inch thick in a Pyrex pie plate. Spread the chopped shrimp on top of the cream cheese. Add Cocktail Sauce. Serve with party crackers.

Cocktail Sauce
¾ cup catsup
2 tablespoons finely chopped celery
1 teaspoon of cream style horseradish
1 teaspoon "Worcestershire Sauce"
1 teaspoon lemon juice
½ teaspoon onion salt
¼ teaspoon salt

Mix ingredients well. Spread over shrimp and cream cheese.

Sausage Balls

Jamie Brady
Daughter of Co-owner
Bennett, NC

1 pound "Neese's" hot sausage (cooked & drained)
1 (10 ounce) package sharp Cheddar Cheese grated
3 cups "Bisquick"

Mix all ingredients thoroughly. Shape into 1 inch balls. Bake in 350° oven for about 18-20 minutes until lightly browned.

Chipped Beef Ball

Marilyn Sehen
Sanford, NC

3 (8 ounce) packages cream cheese
3 (4 ounce) packages dried chipped beef
1 medium onion, chopped fine.
1 tablespoon "Accent"
1 tablespoon "Worcestershire" sauce

Mix softened cream cheese with 2 packages of chopped chipped beef, onion, and seasonings. Shape into a ball. Roll in chipped beef. Serve with crackers.

The Ultimate Grilled Cheese

Holly Reynolds
Granddaughter of Ethelda
Carthage, NC

1 package (3 ounces) cream cheese, softened
¾ cup mayonnaise
1 cup (4 ounces) shredded cheddar cheese
1 cup (4 ounces) shredded mozzarella cheese
½ teaspoon garlic powder
⅛ teaspoon seasoned salt
10 slices Italian bread (½-inch thick)
2 tablespoons butter or margarine, softened

In a mixing bowl, beat cream cheese and mayonnaise until smooth. Stir in cheeses, garlic powder and seasoned salt. Spread five slices of bread with the cheese mixture, about ⅓ cup on each. Top with remaining bread. Butter the outsides of sandwiches; cook in a large skillet over medium heat until golden brown on both sides. Yield: 5 servings

Orange Toast Fingers

Elmo Phillips
Employee
Bear Creek, NC

½ cup unsalted butter, softened
½ cup granulated sugar
3 tablespoons freshly grated orange rind
12 slices very thin white bread

Cream together thoroughly the butter and sugar. Add orange rind and mix well. Cut crusts from bread. Spread each slice thickly with orange mixture. Cut in thirds. Place on baking sheet (two vertical rows and two horizontal rows, fix a 10x15 inch jelly roll pan perfectly) and toast in a preheated 300° for 30 minutes. (Toast will not be brown. Do not worry; they are not supposed to be.) Cool before serving or storing in airtight container. Yields: 36

Shrimp Topped Cucumber Rounds

Elmo Phillips
Employee
Bear Creek, NC

¼ cup plain low fat yogurt
¼ teaspoon curry powder
⅛ teaspoon garlic powder
1 small cucumber cut in 12 slices
12 cooked and shelled small shrimp

In small bowl, mix yogurt, curry powder and garlic. Spoon 1 teaspoon yogurt mixtures on each cucumber slice; top each with shrimp. Makes 4 servings of 3 appetizers each.

Crispy Homemade Tortilla Chips

Lorrie Moore
Bonlee, NC

Make your own tortilla chips. Get 4 large flour tortillas; spray both sides with cooking spray and cut each into 8 wedges. Using one of the variations for season, arrange in single layers on two baking sheets; about 10 or 15 minutes at 350°; store in air-tight container.

Hot ranch:
Sprinkle tortillas evenly with 1 tablespoon powdered ranch salad dressing. Mix with ¼ teaspoon cayenne pepper.

Sesame-Curry:
Sprinkle evenly with 1 ½ teaspoons each curry powder and sesame seeds with ⅛ teaspoon cayenne pepper.

Barbeque:
Sprinkle evenly with 2 teaspoons chili powder, 1 teaspoon ground cumin and ¼ teaspoon salt.

Pizza:
Sprinkle evenly with 1 teaspoon Italian seasoning, 1 teaspoon paprika, 1 teaspoon garlic powder and ¼ teaspoon salt.

Glazed Fruit And Franks

Jamie Brady
Daughter of Ethelda Co-owner
Bennett, NC

1 cup Apricot preserves

⅓ cup Real lemon juice from concentrate

1 tablespoon cornstarch

½ teaspoon ground cinnamon

1 (8 ounce) package cocktail frankfurters
or ½ pound frankfurters cut into 1-inch
pieces

1 (8 ounce) can pineapple chunks,
drained

1 large red apple, cored and cut into
chunks

1 (11 ounce) can mandarin orange
segments, drained

In medium saucepan, combine preserves,
real lemon, cornstarch and cinnamon.
Cook and stir until well blended and
slightly thickened. Stir in frankfurters
and pineapple, heat thoroughly. Just
before serving, stir in apple and oranges-
serve warm. Refrigerate leftovers. Makes
3 ½ cups

Meatballs

Lisa Scott
Bear Creek, NC
Co-owner

2 pounds ground beef

1 pound hot sausage

2 eggs, beaten

1 onion, finely chopped

2 tablespoons cornstarch

½ teaspoon salt

2 (12 ounce) bottles chili sauce

1 (16 ounce) jar grape jelly

Mix beef, sausage, eggs, onion,
cornstarch and salt together. Shape
into small balls. Place meatballs into
frying pan and brown on all sides. Place
meatballs into crock-pot and cover with
chili sauce and grape jelly. Simmer for 45
minutes or until ready to serve.

Hot Sausage Balls

Keith Dixon
Bear Creek, NC
Brother-in-law of Lisa Scott

1 (8 ounce) jar 'Cheese Whiz'

1 pound hot sausage

3 cups 'Bisquick' mix

½ cup milk

Mix "Cheese Whiz", sausage, 'Bisquick'
mix and milk. Shape into 1-inch balls.
Place on ungreased cookie sheet. Bake at
400˚ for 15 to 20 minutes.

Shrimp, Crab Spread

Randy Scott Co-owner
Son of Hoyt and Berta Scott
Bear Creek, NC

1 (8 ounce) package cream cheese
1 (6 ounce) can crab meat, drained
1 (12 ounce) bottle cocktail sauce
1 (4 ½ ounce) can shrimp drained
Fresh shrimp/crab meat-can be used

Mix cream cheese and crab. Mix well. Spread mixture on serving plate. Spread cocktail sauce over mixture. Cover with shrimp and serve with crackers. Great appetizer!

Oyster Cracker Snack

Cindy Dixon
Bear Creek, NC
Sister of Lisa Scott

⅔ cup vegetable oil
1 teaspoon dill-weed
1 teaspoon garlic salt
1 package ranch dressing mix
1 (12 ounce) package oyster crackers

Combine oil, dill weed, garlic salt and dressing mix. Mix until well blended. Pour over crackers. Put in bowl with sealable lid, cover. Shake lightly to coat. Let set 2 hours turning bowl every 30 minutes.

Cheese Ball

Mary Lois Thomas
Sanford, NC
(Moosie)

2 packages of cream cheese (room temperature)
1 small can crushed pineapple (drained)
¼ diced onion (optional)
⅓ diced sweet green pepper
1 cup chopped pecans divided
1 ½ teaspoon seasoned salt

Mix cream cheese, pineapple, onion, pepper and seasoned salt together.

Add ½ of the pecans and mix well. Sit the bowl with the mixed ingredients in the refrigerator for two hours or more. Put cooking oil on your hand and shape into a ball. Roll in the remaining pecans. Serve with crackers.

Goat Cheese Spread

Mary John Resch
Siler City, NC

1 (8 ounce) package cream cheese
1 (3 ounce) package goat cheese
1 tablespoon fresh basil, chopped
1 tablespoon fresh chives, chopped
1 tablespoon fresh dill, chopped
1 tablespoon fresh parsley, chopped
1 teaspoon fresh garlic, chopped
1 teaspoon fresh shallots, chopped
1 dash salt

Blend the cream cheese and goat cheese. Add all the herbs and the chopped garlic and shallots, then the salt. Taste and adjust seasonings. Serve with assorted crackers or thin slices of French bread.

Dips

On The Go Dip

Donna W. Maness
Greensboro, NC

1 pound of country sausage (your choice,
mild, hot or low fat)
1 (8 ounce) block of cream cheese (can be
low fat)
1 (16 ounce) jar of Chunky salsa

Fry your sausage and crumble. Pour off
the grease. Add the cream cheese and stir
into the crumbled sausage until it melts
over low to medium heat. When melted,
add salsa.

You can transfer to a crock-pot for
keeping heated during a gathering or it
can be frozen and reheated.

This recipe is easy to carry to parties.
It is quick and easy to make. Make
ahead of time and can be frozen and
then reheated. Substitute with low fat
ingredients and it is still a winner. It is
high protein and low carbohydrates.

Fruit Dip

Carl Horst
Niagara Falls, NY

1 (8 ounce) package cream cheese
brought to room temperature
1 small jar of marshmallow cream
3 or 4 teaspoons of maraschino cherry
juice

Combine all ingredients, mixing well.
Serve with your choice of fresh fruit.

Vegetable Dip

Jamie Brady
Daughter of Ethelda Co-owner
Bennett, NC

8 ounces sour cream
8 ounces cream cheese
"Good Season Zesty Italian" dry mix
salad dressing

Mix well. Serve with chips.

Avocado Dip

Peggy Gaines
Goldston, NC

2 ripe avocados
¼ cup mayonnaise
2 tablespoons lemon juice
1 garlic clove, mashed
Ground black pepper

Peel avocados and mash pulp. Add other ingredients, cover and let stand at least 1 hour. Chill and serve with corn chips.

Spaghetti Sour Cream Dip

Amy Jordan
Bear Creek, NC

1 ½ envelope of spaghetti sauce
2 cups sour cream
½ cup finely chopped green pepper

Combine all ingredients blend well. Chill overnight to blend flavors. Serve with crackers. Yields: 2 cups

Fresh Fruit Dip

Amy Bryant
Siler City, NC
Employee

½ cup mayonnaise or salad dressing
½ cup sour cream
⅓ cup orange marmalade
1 tablespoon milk
½ pound green grapes
½ pound strawberries

In small bowl, whisk the mayonnaise, sour cream, marmalade and milk. Refrigerate until serving. Serve with fruit. Yields 1⅓ cups

Honey Mustard Dip For Chicken Fingers

Bonnie Reynolds
Daughter of Ethelda Co-Owner
Carthage, NC

¾ cup Dijon mustard
½ cup mayonnaise
¼ cup Honey
¼ teaspoon ground red pepper
⅛ teaspoon garlic salt
2 pounds 'deli' fried chicken fingers

Stir together first 5 ingredients. Serve with fried chicken fingers. Makes 6-8 appetizer servings.

Barb's Onion Dip

Audrey Poe
Bear Creek, NC

4 cups Vidalia or other sweet onions
2 cups Hellman's mayonnaise
2 cups fresh grated parmesan cheese

Mix and put in greased casserole dish.
Bake 30 minutes at 300° or until
browned.

Cocktail Sauce

Douglas Stumpf
Son of Ethelda Co-owner
Bear Creek, NC

1 cup catsup
1 ½ tablespoons horseradish
1 teaspoon Worcestershire sauce
1 teaspoon minced onion
Dash of 'Tabasco sauce'
Dash of salt

Mix all ingredients together well. Serve
with shrimp or other seafood.

Sweet & Sour Sauce

Amy Jordan
Bear Creek, NC

Juice of 2 lemons
1 small green pepper, chopped fine
½ to ¾ cup water
¾ cup white or brown sugar
¾ tablespoon cornstarch
1 teaspoon vinegar

Combine ingredients and cook over
medium heat until sauce is thick and
green pepper is tender.

Caramel Dip

Dawn Kidd
Employee
Robbins, NC

8 ounces cream cheese
¾ cup brown sugar
¼ cup sugar
1 teaspoon vanilla
½ cup chopped pecans

Combine all ingredients and beat with
electric mixer until smooth. Refrigerate
for at least 2 hours before serving. Serve
with crisp apple slices.

Spinach Dip

Terry Liles
Siler City, NC

1 package (10 ounce) frozen spinach-
thawed and chopped
1 ½ cups dairy sour cream
1 cup real mayonnaise
1 package "Knorr" vegetable soup mix
3 green onions-finely chopped
1 can water
Chestnuts, chopped (optional)

Squeeze spinach dry in medium bowl. Stir together chopped spinach, sour cream, mayonnaise, soup mix, green onions and water chestnuts (if desired). Cover and refrigerate 2 hours. Serve with assorted crackers.

Veggie Dip

Amy Jordan
Bear Creek, NC

1 cup sour cream
1 cup mayonnaise
3 tablespoons onion minced
3 tablespoons parsley flakes
3 teaspoons dill-weed
1 teaspoon salt

Mix all ingredients and chill for several hours before serving. Note: Do not use salad dressing as it completely changes the taste.

Hot Clam Dip

Zac Scott
Bear Creek, NC
Son of Randy and Lisa Scott

3 large packages cream cheese
2 cans clams
1 can of clam juice

Melt cream cheese slowly in double boiler. Add clam juice slowly. Add clams. Stir and serve.

Caesar Dip With Parmesan

Amy Jordan
Bear Creek, NC

1 cup mayonnaise
½ cup sour cream
½ ounce grated parmesan (makes ½ cup)
1 tablespoon juice from 1 lemon
1 tablespoon minced fresh parsley leaves
2 medium garlic cloves, pressed with garlic press or minced (2 teaspoons)
⅛ teaspoon black pepper

Combine all ingredients in medium bowl until smooth and creamy. Transfer dip to serving bowl, cover with plastic wrap, and refrigerate at least 1 hour. Serve with vegetables. Makes 1 ½ cup.

Baked Vidalia Onion Dip

Elmo Phillips
Employee
Bear Creek, NC

2 cups chopped Vidalia or sweet onions
2 cups grated Swiss cheese
2 cups mayonnaise
2 cups slivered almonds
½ cup pimento peppers
¼ teaspoon cayenne pepper

Mix all ingredients together and place in 13x9x2 inch baking dish. Bake at 325° until completely melted, approximately 20 minutes. Serve with butter crackers. Yield: 20 servings

Tartar Sauce

Dawn Stumpf
Daughter of Ethelda Co-owner
Bear Creek, NC

1 cup mayonnaise
2 tablespoons chopped onions
2 tablespoons chopped pickle
1 tablespoons cider vinegar
2 tablespoons chopped parsley
½ teaspoon minced lemon zest
¼ teaspoon salt

In mixing bowl, mix all ingredients well. Chill until used.

Black Bean Dip

Dawn Stumpf
Daughter of Ethelda Co-Owner
Bear Creek, NC

2 medium ripe avocados, peeled and diced
2 tablespoons lime juice
1 can (15 ¼ ounces) whole kernel corn, drained
1 can (15 ounces) black beans, rinsed and drained
1 medium sweet red pepper, chopped
6 green onions, chopped
2 tablespoons minced fresh cilantro
3 garlic cloves, minced
2 tablespoons olive oil
1 teaspoon red wine vinegar
½ teaspoon salt
¼ teaspoon pepper
Tortilla chips

In a bowl, combine avocados and lime juice; let stand for 10 minutes. In a large bowl, combine the corn, beans, red pepper, onions, cilantro and garlic. In a small bowl, whisk the oil, vinegar, salt and pepper. Drizzle over corn mixture; toss to coat. Gently fold in the avocado mixture. Cover and refrigerate for at least 2 hours or until chilled. Serve with tortilla chips. Yield: 4 ½ cups.

Taco Dip

Deborah Pickard Stephenson
Showroom Employee
Carthage, NC

1 pound ground beef
1 medium onion, chopped
1 can (16 ounces) refried beans
1 can (8 ounces) tomato sauce
1 envelope taco seasoning
½ cup sour cream
½ cup shredded cheddar cheese
Tortilla chips

In a large skillet, cook beef and onion over medium heat until meat is no longer pink; drain. Stir in the beans, tomato sauce and taco seasoning. Spread into ungreased 9 inch pie plate. Top with sour cream and cheese. Bake at 350° for 5-10 minutes, uncovered, until cheese melts. Serve with chips. Yields 6 cups.

Hot Broccoli Cheese Dip

Keisha Allred
Bear Creek, NC
Niece of Lisa Scott

1 (8 ounce) cream cheese
1 (8 ounce) sour cream
1 tablespoon Italian seasoning
1 (10 ounce) package frozen chopped broccoli, thawed and drained
4 cups cheddar cheese, shredded, divided
Assorted vegetables, sliced
Assorted crackers

Mix cream cheese, sour cream and Italian seasoning. Add chopped broccoli and 2 cups cheese; spoon into 9 inch pie plate. Bake at 350° for 20 minutes. Sprinkle with remaining 2 cups of cheese. Bake 5 minutes more until cheese melts. Serve with sliced vegetables or crackers.

Peanut Butter Dip

Dawn Kidd
Employee
Robbins, NC

1 (8 ounce) cream cheese, softened
1 cup peanut butter
1 cup packed brown sugar
¼ cup milk
3 to 4 apples cut into wedges

In a mixing bowl, combine the first four ingredients; mix well. Serve with apples. Keep in the refrigerator. Yields 2 ⅔ cups.

102

Beverages

Wassail Punch

Historical Stagsville Plantation
Durham, NC
Jo Ellis
Durham, NC

1 gallon apple cider
1 large can (46 ounces) orange juice
1 large can (46 ounces) pineapple juice
1 cup lemon juice
1 cup sugar
1 tablespoon whole cloves
1 cinnamon stick

Tie spices in a cheesecloth bag. Mix all ingredients together in large pot. Simmer slowly for an hour or so. Remove spices and serve very warm. Refrigerate left over if any. Recipe makes 55, 4 ounce cups.

Creamy Hot Chocolate

Sandy Brown
Sandy & Co.
Daughter of Hoyt and Berta Scott
Bear Creek, NC

⅓ cup well-chilled heavy cream
1 tablespoon sugar
4 ounces fine-quality bittersweet chocolate (not un-sweetened)
2 cups whole milk

In a bowl with electric mixer beat cream with sugar until it just holds stiff peaks. Chop chocolate and reserve 2 teaspoons. In small saucepan heat milk with remaining chocolate over moderate heat stirring until it just comes to a simmer. Pour hot chocolate into two large mugs and top with whipped cream and sprinkle chocolate left from sauce over top. Serves 2.

Lemon Frappe'

Ethelda Stumpf
Bear Creek, NC
Co-ownerA frappe' is a slushy dessert beverage.

1 (6 ounce) can frozen lemonade or limeade concentrate-undiluted
½ cup cold water
1 pint lemon sherbet or vanilla ice cream
1 (12 ounce) can ginger ale

Process the first three ingredients in an electric blender until smooth. Pour into a pitcher; add ginger ale. Serve immediately. Yield: 4 cups.

Pink Cloud Float

Hoyt Scott
Co-owner
Bear Creek, NC

1 (10 ounce) package frozen strawberries
1 cup milk
2 cups strawberry ice cream

Add strawberries, milk and ice cream. Blend until smooth. Makes 4 shakes- Delicious!

Orange Freeze

Jordan Brady
Granddaughter of Ethelda, Co-owner
Bennett, NC

1 pint orange sherbet
2 cups orange juice
2 cups crushed ice

Combine all ingredients in blender. Blend until thick and frosty. Makes 6 servings

Creamy Chocolate Shake

Hoyt Scott
Co-owner
Bear Creek, N C

2 ½ cups cold milk

4 teaspoons instant coffee powder

½ cup chocolate syrup

1 quart chocolate ice cream

Put 1 cup of cold milk, coffee and syrup in blender; spoon in ice cream. Blend smooth, add rest of milk; blend. Makes six delicious milk shakes!

Pink Punch

Marilyn Sehen
Sanford, NC

2 quarts water

1 (6 ounce) package strawberry jell-o

¾ cup lemon juice

2 cups sugar

1 (2 liter bottle) ginger ale

Bring water to a boil. Add jell-o, lemon juice, and sugar. Mix well. Let cool. Pour into a gallon size, zip lock freezer bag. Freeze. When ready to serve add bottle of ginger ale.

Holiday Punch

Nellie Haith
Siler City, NC

1 quart cranberry juice cocktail

1 (6 ounce) can frozen orange juice concentrate

1 (6 ounce) can frozen lemonade concentrates

2 cups water

1 (16 ounce) ginger ale

Mix juices and water. Chill about 6 hours before adding ginger ale.

Cappuccino Icee

Dixie Holt
Package Department

⅔ cups chocolate syrup chilled

2 cups cold coffee

2 cups vanilla ice cream

1 tablespoon frozen whipped topping

Place syrup and coffee in blender. Cover and blend on high. Add ice cream, cover and blend until smooth. Serve over ice, top with whipped topping. Makes 6 (6 ounce) servings. Very delicious!

Sparkling Lemonade

Dottie Croker
Atlanta, GA

8 to 10 lemons
1 ½ cup sugar
Water
Ice cubes
Club soda

Grate lemons to make 1 tablespoon finely grated peel. Squeeze lemons to make 1 to 1 ½ cups of juice. Set juice aside. In a 1 quart jar with tight fitting lid put lemon peel, juice and sugar. Add 1 ½ cup very hot water. With lid fitting firmly shake jar until sugar dissolves; refrigerate. To serve, pour into pitcher with ice cubes and top with club soda or pour ¼ cup syrup over ice cubes in individual glasses, and stir in ¾ cup club soda.

Christmas Punch

Juanita McCormick
Greensboro, NC

1 quart pineapple juice
1 quart cranberry juice
½ cup sugar
1 teaspoon almond flavors
1 (28 ounce) bottled ginger ale

Chill, then add ginger ale before serving. Approximately 24 servings

Chocolate (Diet) Milk Shake

Jo Ellis
Durham, NC

1 cup skim milk
1 ½ tablespoons sugar free Jell-O chocolate instant pudding mix
2 packets sweet & low
12 small ice cubes
½ teaspoon vanilla

Put all ingredients in above order in the blender. Crush ice with "pulse" setting. Then use liquefy button until mixture is as smooth as you prefer. Approximately 70 calories and no fat.

Sparkling Apple Juice

Ethelda Stumpf
Co-owner
Bear Creek, NC

1 quart apple juice
1 quart ginger ale-chilled

Combine apple juice and ginger ale. Serve over ice. Yield 4-1 cup servings. Sparkling grape juice: Use grape juice instead of apple. Avoid diluting drinks served with ice by freezing a portion of the recipe or fruit juice included in recipe. Makes colorful ice cubes.

Johnnyseed

Chaplain Larry E Small
Asheville, NC

Vanilla ice cream
Apple cider

Put two scoops of vanilla ice cream into a 12 ounce frosted glass or I like using the "old fashioned" A&W mugs. Pour cold apple cider over the ice cream. Place a straw and long spoon in each drink, then sit back and enjoy!! Good served with warm ginger bread

Party Punch

Sandra Cook
Employee
Siler City, NC

1 quart pineapple juice chilled
1 quart orange juice chilled
1 quart apple juice chilled
2 quarts ginger ale chilled

Pour chilled juices into chilled punch bowl. Top with scoops of lime sherbet or your favorite sherbet.

Soups & Salads

Taco Soup

Nellie Haith
Siler City, NC

2 pounds ground chuck hamburger
2 cans (15 ounces) whole kernel corn
2 cans (15 ounces) chili beans
2 cans (15 ounces) diced tomatoes
1 envelope taco seasoning
1 can tomato soup

Open all cans and pour into large pot. Add taco seasoning. Brown hamburger in frying pan and drain well. Add to other ingredients. Simmer about 2 hours- stir often. Serve with tortilla chips or crackers. Add grated cheese on top of serving bowl.

Tomato Soup

Mildred Jones
Bennett, NC

1 peck tomatoes
6 medium onions
1 tablespoon salt
1 tablespoon pepper or less
2 sticks margarine

Cook above ingredients together until well done. Strain, put back in pot and bring to a boil.

Mix together, ¾ cup cold water, 1 cup sugar, and 1 cup flour together until thickened.

Put in jars. Cook in pressure canner 5 minutes on 5 pounds, or 10-20 minutes cold pack. Makes about 7 quarts.

Kick Up Your Heels Taco Soup

Donna W. Maness
Greensboro, NC

1 pound hamburger
1 medium chopped onion
2 packets of taco dry mix
1 small can chilies
1 (8 ounces) can Garbanzo beans
1 (8 ounces) can kidney beans
1 (8 ounces) can whole corn
1 (16 ounces) jar of chunky salsa
2 (8 ounces) cans of Mexican diced
tomatoes with chilies

Cook the hamburger and drain off the
grease. Add your chopped onion and
chilies. Add the two packets of taco
dry mix. Simmer. Add the rest of your
ingredients to crock-pot. Add your
hamburger mixture. Let simmer in crock-
pot for several hours.

This is great soup for the winter.
This recipe is easy to prepare, low in
carbohydrates, high in protein, very
filling. Can be prepared ahead of time
and frozen. You can also use low fat
substitutes.

Broccoli & Cheese Soup

Brenda Howell
Siler City, NC

½ cup butter
1 onion, chopped
1 (16 ounce) package frozen chopped
broccoli
4 (14.5 ounce) cans chicken broth
1 (1 pound) package "Velveeta" cheese
cubed
2 cups milk
1 tablespoon garlic powder
⅔ cup cornstarch
1 cup water

In a stockpot, melt butter over medium
heat. Cook onion in butter until softened.
Stir in broccoli, and cover with chicken
broth. Simmer until broccoli is tender,
10 to 15 minutes. Reduce heat, and stir
in cheese cubes until melted. Mix in milk
and garlic powder.

In a small bowl, stir cornstarch into
water until dissolved. Stir into soup; cook
stirring frequently, until thick. Makes: 12
servings

French Onion Soup

Berta Lou Scott
Founder and Co-owner
Bear Creek, NC

4-5 large yellow onions (about 1 ½ pounds)
3 tablespoons butter or margarine
¼ teaspoon coarsely ground black pepper
2 tablespoons all-purpose flour
3 cans (10 ¾ ounce size) beef broth, undiluted
3 cups water
1 bay leaf, optional

Topping:
3 tablespoons parmesan cheese
1 cup grated parmesan cheese
1 cup grated or sliced mozzarella cheese
6-8 slices French bread

Peel onions, slice the onions thinly, discard root ends, in a large 4-quart pot over med-high heat, melt the butter, add the onions, and coarsely ground black pepper to the butter. Sauté the onion mixture until onions are light and golden brown, sprinkle the flour over onions, stir until all flour disappears; cook 2 or more minutes stirring constantly. Turn heat down to slow.

Gradually add the beef broth and water stirring constantly, return to medium high until boils. Reduce to low and simmer uncovered about 3 minutes.

Toast the French bread in broiler pan or toaster. Pour the soup into individual broiler proof bowls. Place the bowls on cookie sheet. Place toast on top of each bowl and sprinkle parmesan cheese, and sliced thin or grated mozzarella cheese. Remove from oven and serve.

Low Fat Minestrone Soup

Dottie Croker
Atlanta, GA

3 (15 ounce) cans beef broth
½ cup chopped celery
½ cup chopped onions
2 (15 ounce) cans chop tomatoes
1 tablespoon olive oil
1 cup diced red potatoes
1 cup diced baby carrots
1 clove garlic, minced
1 teaspoon dried oregano
2 tablespoons snipped parsley
2 teaspoons crushed dried basil
1 bay leaf
¼ teaspoon pepper
¾ of (15 ounce) can red kidney beans, drained
1 ounce spaghetti, broken

In large saucepan, sauté onion, celery and garlic in oil until tender. Stir in broth, tomatoes, parsley, oregano, basil, bay leaf and pepper. Cover and simmer for 30 minutes. Add carrots and potatoes and simmer, covered 15 minutes or until vegetables are tender. Add beans and spaghetti and cook 15 minutes or until spaghetti is tender. Remove bay leaf before serving.

Your walk walks and your talk talks.

But your walk talks louder than your talk talks.

Easy Soups

Berta Lou Scott
Founder and Co-owner
Bear Creek, NC

Cheesy Broccoli Soup

Cook 1 large bunch chopped broccoli and 2 chopped carrots with 1 can (10 ¾ ounces) each chicken broth and water, until vegetables are tender. Let cool for 10 minutes. Pour into blender. Process until smooth and return to saucepan. Whisk in ½ cup milk and 1 cup "Cheese Whiz". Warm over low heat to melt cheese; do not allow the soup to boil.

Tip: For a more complete meal, add leftover cooked chicken or turkey to this recipe after blending the soup.

Cheesy Minestrone Soup

Prepare 1 can (10 ¾ ounce) condensed soup according to directions. Bring to boil and add ½ cup Minute White Rice; let stand 5 minutes. Add 1 can (19 ounce) drained kidney beans and 1 teaspoon Italian seasoning. Stir in 2 cups Italian-style shredded cheese. Serve immediately.

Hearty Onion Soup

Prepare 1 can (10 ounces) condensed onion soup according to directions; add 1 can (28 ounces) whole tomatoes with liquid. Stir in ¾ cup each of shredded Swiss and mozzarella cheese. Pour into bowl and top each with 1 slice toasted French bread. Sprinkle with grated Parmesan cheese and additional Swiss and mozzarella cheese.

Tex-Mex Corn Chowder

Prepare 1 can (10 ¾ ounces) condensed cream of mushroom soup; add 4 cut-up wieners, 1 can (12 ounces) kernel corn and 1 teaspoon chili powder. Stir in 2 cups Kraft Mexican Style Shredded Cheese. Serve with tortilla chips.

Cheeseburger Soup

Elmo Phillips
Employee

½ pound ground beef
¾ cup chopped onion
¾ cup shredded carrots
¾ cup diced celery
1 teaspoon dried basil
1 teaspoon dried parsley flakes
4 tablespoons butter or margarine, divided
3 cups chicken broth
4 cups diced peeled potatoes (1¾ lbs.)
¼ cup all-purpose flour
8 ounces process American cheese, cubed (2 cups)
1 ½ cups milk
¾ teaspoon salt
¼ – ½ teaspoon pepper
¼ cup sour cream

In a 3 quart saucepan, brown beef, drain and set aside. In the same saucepan, sauté onion, carrots, celery, basil and parsley in 1 tablespoon butter until vegetables are tender, about 10 minutes. Add broth, potatoes and beef; bring to boil. Reduce heat; cover and simmer for 10-12 minutes or until potatoes are tender. Meanwhile, in a small skillet melt remaining butter. Add flour; cook and stir for 3-5 minutes or until bubbly. Add to soup; bring to boil. Cook and stir for 2 minutes. Reduce heat to low. Add cheese, milk, salt and pepper; cook and stir until cheese melts. Remove from the heat; blend in sour cream. Yield: 8 servings

New England Bacon & Corn Chowder

Mildred Hester
Durham, NC

6 strips bacon, diced
1 (10 ½ ounce) can condense cream of
potato soup
1 (10 ½ ounce) can condense onion soup
2 cups milk
1 (12 ounce) can kernel corn, not drained

Fry bacon until crisp. Drain excess fat,
leaving 2 tablespoons in kettle. Add
soups, milk, and corn. Reheat stirring
occasionally, until soup bubbles. Serve
piping hot with buttered biscuits. Serves 6

Cream Cheese Potato Soup

Katherine Frazier
Liberty, NC
Showroom Employee

6 cups water
7 teaspoons chicken bouillon granules
16 ounces cream cheese-cubed
30 ounces frozen cubed hash brown
potatoes-thawed
1½ cups cubed fully cooked ham
½ cup chopped onion
1 teaspoon garlic powder
1 teaspoon dill weed

In a 'Dutch' oven, combine the water
and bouillon. Add the cream cheese;
cook and stir until cheese melts. Stir
in the remaining ingredients. Simmer,
uncovered, for 18-20 minutes or until
vegetables are tender. Yield: 12 servings
(about 3 quarts)

Helpful Hint

Instant potatoes are a good
stew thickener.

Mary Murphy's Clam Chowder

Kyle Scott
Rick & Gail's son

8 thin slices salt pork
¼ pound butter
3 cups diced onions
6 cups potatoes-peeled and cubed
½ cup flour
4 cups clam juice
3 cups chopped clams
1 pint light cream

In a large pot, gently sauté salt pork until rendered. Remove pork and add butter, still over low heat. When bubbly, add onions and continue sautéing until transparent.

Add cubed potatoes and cook about 5 minutes, stirring to keep moist. Add flour and cook an additional 3 minutes or so, stirring well. Add clam juice and cook until potatoes are tender. Add chopped clams and cream; heat through, taking care not to boil. When heated through, serve. Makes 1 gallon

Dressed Up Potato Soup

Katherine Frazier
Liberty, NC
Showroom Employee

2 tablespoons butter
1 onion-finely chopped
32 ounces frozen hash brown potatoes-thawed
3 cups milk
2 cups water
1 teaspoon salt
½ teaspoon black pepper
½ cup instant mashed potato flakes
2 cups shredded cheddar cheese

In a soup pot, melt butter over high heat. Sauté onions 6 to 8 minutes until golden in color. Add potatoes, milk, water, salt and pepper. Bring to a boil. Stir in potato flakes and cook 5 minutes or until thickened and heated through, stirring occasionally. Add cheese and stir until melted. Serve immediately.

Note: Top each bowl with a sprinkle of shredded cheddar and bacon bits.
Serves 6 to 8

Hearty Beef Soup

Kathryn Frazier
Liberty, NC
Showroom Employee

4 pounds boneless beef top sirloin steak,
cut into ½-inch cubes
4 cups chopped onions
¼ cup butter
4 quarts hot water
4 cups sliced carrots
4 cups cubed peeled potatoes
2 cups chopped cabbage
1 cup chopped celery
1 large green pepper, chopped
8 teaspoons beef bouillon granules
1 tablespoon seasoned salt
1 teaspoon dried basil
1 teaspoon pepper
4 bay leaves
6 cups tomato juice

In two 'Dutch' ovens or one large soup
kettle, brown beef and onions in butter in
batches; drain. Add the water, vegetables
and seasonings; bring to a boil. Reduce
heat; cover and simmer for 20 minutes.
Add tomato juice; cover and simmer
10 minutes longer or until the beef and
vegetables are tender. Discard bay
leaves. Yield: 32 servings (8 quarts)

Oyster Stew

Douglas Stumpf
Son of Ethelda Co-owner
Bear Creek, NC

2 pints oysters fresh or frozen
1 quart half and half cream
¼ cup butter or margarine
1 teaspoon salt
Dash pepper
Chopped parsley, optional

Cook oysters in oyster liquid for 3-5
minutes or until edges begin to curl. Add
remaining ingredients except parsley
and heat. Garnish with parsley if desired.
Serve with oyster crackers.

Vegetable Garden Soup

Bonnie Reynolds
Daughter of Ethelda Co-owner
Carthage, NC

2 (14 ½ ounce) cans chicken broth, undiluted
2 (12 ounce) cans tomato juice
1 ½ cups cooked chicken, chopped
1 (12 ounce) can whole kernel corn, drained
1 (10 ounce) package frozen lima beans, thawed
2 potatoes, peeled and chopped
1 onion, chopped
1 cup carrots, chopped
1 ½ tablespoons Worcestershire sauce
1 bay leaf, remove before serving
¾ teaspoon garlic salt
½ teaspoon pepper
Croutons, optional

Combine all ingredients except croutons in a large cast-iron Dutch oven. Bring to a boil; cover, reduce heat and simmer 1 hour stirring occasionally. Serve topped with croutons if desired.

Chili Soup

Holly Reynolds
Granddaughter of Ethelda Co-owner
Carthage, NC

2 onions, chopped
2 green peppers diced
1 tablespoon oil
2 pounds hamburger
2 tablespoons chili powder
1 large can tomato juice
1 small can herb tomato soup
1 regular size can kidney beans

Sauté onions and green peppers in oil; add hamburger and brown. Transfer all to a stockpot and add remaining ingredients. Add ½ cup water and cook 1 ½ to 2 hours on low heat.

Cheeseburger Chowder

Jamie Brady
Daughter of Ethelda
Bennett, NC

1 pound of ground beef
1 large onion chopped
1 cup celery chopped
1 cup shredded carrots
1 teaspoon parsley
1 teaspoon basil
2 cups chicken broth
3 cups chopped potatoes
1 cup milk
8 ounces Velveeta Cheese (I add a little more)
¼ cup sour cream

In Dutch oven, brown meat. Drain and set aside. Sauté onions, celery and carrots in Dutch oven in 2 tablespoons butter. Add parsley and basil. Cook for 10 minutes or until onions and celery is tender. Add 2 cups of chicken broth. Add potatoes and meat. Add salt and pepper to taste. Bring to boil. Reduce heat and simmer for 15 to 20 minutes or until potatoes are tender. Add 1 cup milk and Velveeta. Cook until cheese melts and remove from heat. Add sour cream.

Baked Potato Soup

Jamie Brady
Daughter of Ethelda Co-Owner
Bennett, NC

4 large baking potatoes
⅔ cup all-purpose flour
½ teaspoon pepper
⅔ cup butter or margarine
6 cups milk
¾ teaspoon salt
4 green onions (chopped and divided)
12 slices of bacon (cooked and crumbled and divided)
1 ¼ cups shredded cheddar cheese
8 ounces of sour cream

Wash potatoes and prick several times with a fork.

Bake at 400° for 1 hour or until done. Let cool and cut in half lengthwise. Scoop out pulp and set aside, discard skins. Melt butter in a heavy saucepan over low heat. Add flour stirring until smooth. Cook 1 minute stirring constantly. Gradually add milk. Cook over medium heat stirring constantly until mixture is thick and bubbly. Add potato pulp, salt, pepper, 2 tablespoons green onion, ½ cup bacon and stir in sour cream. Add extra milk, if necessary for desired consistency. Serve with remaining onion, bacon and cheddar cheese. Yield 10 cups.

Corn Chowder

Ethelda Stumpf
Co-owner
Bear Creek, NC

6 tablespoons butter
2 potatoes (½ pound peeled and diced)
2 celery stalks, minced
1 small green pepper, minced
1 small onion, minced
1 ½ teaspoon salt
2 tablespoons all-purpose flour
2 tablespoons paprika
1 ½ cups water
2 chicken flavored bouillon cubes
1 (16 to 20 ounce) package frozen
kernel corn
2 pints Half & Half

In 4 quart saucepan over medium heat in hot butter, cook next five ingredients until vegetables are tender, about 10 minutes, stirring frequently. Stir in the flour and paprika until blended. Cook 1 minute. Stir in water and bouillon over medium heat, cook, stirring constantly until mixture is smooth and thickened, about 5 minutes. Stir in corn and Half & Half. Cook, stirring frequently until corn is tender and mixture thoroughly heated, about 10 minutes.

Copper Penny

Wyanne L. Caviness
Bennett, NC
First Bank

2 lbs carrots (cut in rounds chunks)
1 medium bell pepper (cut in rings)
1 small onion (cut in rings)
1 can cream of tomato soup
¾ cup sugar
½ cup salad oil
¾ cup vinegar
1 teaspoon prepared mustard
1 teaspoon Worcestershire sauce

Cook carrots until tender. Drain water. Mix soup, sugar, oil, vinegar, mustard and Worcestershire sauce together. Blend well. Add carrots, bell peppers and onions. Refrigerate over night before serving.

Beatitudes for friends of the aged

*Blessed are they who understand
My faltering step and palsied
hand.
Blessed are they who know that
my ears too
Must strain to catch the things
they say.
Blessed are they who seem to
know that my eyes are dim and
my wits are slow.
Blessed are they who looked
away
When coffee spilled at table today.
Blessed are they with a cheery
smile
Who stop to chat for a little while.
Blessed are they who never say
"You've told that story twice
today.""
Blessed are they who know the
ways to bring back memories of
yesterdays.
Blessed are they who make it
known that I'm loved, respected
and not alone.
Blessed are they who know I'm at
a loss
To find the strength to carry the
Cross.
Blessed are those who ease the
days on my journey Home in
loving ways.*

--- Esther Mary Walker

Salads

Honey Chicken Salad

Jo Ellis
Durham, NC

4 cups chopped cooked chicken
1 ½ cup diced celery
1 cup sweetened dried cranberries
½ cup chopped fresh cranberries
1 ½ cup mayonnaise
⅓ cup orange blossom honey
¼ teaspoon salt
¼ teaspoon pepper

Garnish: chopped toasted pecan

Combine first 4 items. Whisk together the mayonnaise & next 3 ingredients. Add to chicken mixture, stirring gently until combined.

Vegetable Salad

Jo Ellis
Durham, NC

2 cans French style green beans
1 can bean sprouts
1 can water chestnuts, chopped
½ cup chopped celery
½ cup chopped bell pepper (yellow, and/or green and/or red for color)
Drain beans, sprouts & chestnuts.

Combine:
½ cup oil
½ cup sugar (or Splenda)
1 teaspoon salt
¼ teaspoon pepper
Dash of garlic

Stir until mixed well and sugar dissolved. Pour over drained vegetables and marinate several hours. Can be refrigerated several days.

Christmas Salad

Joanne Diggs
Gastonia, NC

1 large package strawberry jell-o
1 small can crush pineapple
2 mashed bananas
1 cup boiling water
½ cup chopped pecans
10 ounces frozen strawberries

Mix jell-o and water (save ¼ cup for topping) Mix in all other ingredients and jell.

Topping: 1 small cool whip, 1 small package cream cheese, 1 cup confectioner's sugar, ¼ cup jell-o mixture, ½ cup pecans chopped. Mix all together. Spread on jell-o.

Pea Salad

Marilyn Sehen
Sanford, NC

1 can French style green beans
1 can shoe peg corn
1 can green peas
1 cup finely chopped celery
1 cup finely chopped onion
1 green pepper chopped
½ cup vinegar
½ cup sugar
½ cup salad oil
1 teaspoon salt
½ teaspoon black pepper

Drain green beans, corn and peas. Mix all ingredients together and marinate overnight.

Fruit Salad

Martha Gilmore
Siler City, NC

1 can crushed pineapple, drained
1 can fruit cocktail, drained
1 can coconut
1 cup nuts
1 jar cherries, drained
Small marshmallows
One container sour cream

Mix all ingredients and let stand over night. This is a colorful salad to make at Christmas time.

Cucumber Salad

Elmo Phillips
Bear Creek, NC

7 cups cucumber (sliced)
1 cup onion (chopped)
1 medium green pepper (chopped)
1 tablespoon salt
1 tablespoon celery seed
2 cups sugar
1 cup white vinegar

Combine all ingredients. Cover and refrigerate.

Amaretto Fruit Dish

Dottie Croker
Atlanta Georgia

1 (15 ounce) can peach halves
1 (15 ounce) can pear halves
1 (15 ounce) can apricot halves
1 (12 ounce) can pineapple chunks
1 (15 ounce) can black sweet cherries
3 bananas
12 coconut macaroons
½ cup amaretto
½ cup sliced almonds
2 tablespoons lemon juice
½ stick butter

Slice and toss bananas in lemon juice. Lightly toast almonds. Combine pears, peaches, apricots, pineapple, cherries, and bananas. Place half the mixture into 2 quart casserole dish. Top with ½ the macaroons and ½ the almonds. Dot with ½ the butter. Repeat with the rest of the ingredients. Pour amaretto over the top. Heat in 325° oven, uncovered, 30-35 minutes or until heated through and top is golden.

Apple Salad

Marilyn Sehen
Sanford, NC

1 can (20 ounce) crushed pineapple, un-drained
⅔ cup sugar
1 (3 ounce) pkg. lemon gelatin
1 (8 ounce) pkg. softened cream cheese
1 cup diced red delicious apples unpeeled
1 cup chopped celery
1 cup cool whip
1 cup chopped toasted pecans

Combine pineapple and sugar in pot. Bring to a boil. Boil for 5 minutes. Add gelatin-stir until dissolved. Add cream cheese-stir until well blended. Cool.

Fold in apples, celery, cool whip, and nuts. Refrigerate

Frozen Fruit Salad

Eleanor Stumpf
Big Run, PA

8 ounces cream cheese softened

¾ cup sugar

3 bananas sliced

1 large carton frozen strawberries

1 container Cool Whip

1 large can crushed pineapple drained

½ to 1 cup pecans

Note: can add any frozen fruit as desired. Thaw fruit.

Mix cream cheese and sugar. Blend in Cool Whip; add pineapple, bananas, fruit and nuts. Makes 23-24 servings

Place about ¼-⅓ cup in aluminum foil cupcake papers and freeze. Thaw before serving.

Pasta Shell Salad

Lena Hollifield
Morganton, NC

1 (16 ounce) package shell macaroni

4 carrots, grated

2 green peppers, chopped

1 onion chopped

3 stalks celery, chopped

1 cup mayonnaise

½ cup sweetened condensed milk

½ cup sugar

½ cup vinegar

Salt and pepper to taste

Cook macaroni using package directions; rinse with cold water; drain. Combine macaroni with vegetables in a large bowl. Blend mayonnaise, condensed milk and remaining ingredients in a small bowl. Add to pasta mixture; toss to mix. Refrigerate overnight. Yield 20 servings.

Cherry Cool Whip Salad

Martha Gilmore
Siler City, NC

1 (9 ounce) Cool Whip
1 can Thank You cherries/ or other fruit
¼ cup lemon juice
2 cups small marshmallows
1 can Eagle brand milk
1 can crushed pineapple, drained

Mix together and freeze and sprinkle with nuts.

Low Calorie Salad

Deborah Pickard Stephenson
Carthage, NC
Showroom Employee

16 ounce cottage cheese
15 ounce can crushed pineapple
3 ½ box orange jell-o (dry)
8 ounce Cool Whip

Mix dry jell-o into cool whip, cottage cheese; drain juice from pineapple. Mix into other ingredients. Keep in refrigerator.

Special Fruit Salad

Martha Gilmore
Siler City, NC

3 medium apples
1 cup raisins
¾ cup shredded coconut
½ cup mayonnaise
2 bananas
1 cup chopped pecans
1 medium can fruit cocktail
⅓ cup sugar

Heat raisins in small amount of water until boiling; cool and drain chop unpeeled apples. Add the bananas sliced pecans and coconut. Then add the raisins and fruit cocktail, drained. (Save the juice) mix juice, mayo and sugar together; pour over the fruit mixture and stir until well blended.

Broccoli Salad

Berta L. Scott
Founder & Co-owner
Bear Creek, NC

4 cups broccoli florets
3 cups cauliflower (broken into small florets)
1 large red onion (chopped)
1 cup sour cream
1 cup salad dressing
3 tablespoons Worcestershire sauce
2 tablespoons lemon juice
2 tablespoons sugar
½ tablespoon salt

In a large bowl, combine broccoli, cauliflower, onions. In a small bowl mix the other ingredients. Pour over the vegetable mixture and stir well. Enjoy!

Marinated Vegetable Salad

Terry Liles
Bear Creek, NC

Dressing:
1 cup vinegar
1 cup sugar
½ cup water
2 tablespoons vegetable oil
2 teaspoons salt
1 teaspoon celery seed
1 teaspoon dill seed

Salad:
1 medium head cauliflower
1 lb carrots—sliced
2 medium cucumbers—sliced
1 medium green pepper—julienned
1 small onion—sliced into rings
1 jar whole mushrooms (4 ½ ounce)—drained
1 can sliced ripe olives (2 ¼ ounce)—drained

In a saucepan, bring dressing ingredients to a boil, stirring occasionally. Remove from the heat; cool to room temperature. Break cauliflower into florets and blanch. Place in a large bowl; add remaining salad ingredients. Add dressing; toss to coat. Cover and refrigerate for several hours or overnight, stirring occasionally. Serve with a slotted spoon.
Serving size: 16.

Wilted Lettuce Salad

Jane Phillips
Bear Creek, NC

1 quart torn Iceberg lettuce
1 quart torn Bibb lettuce
½ cup sliced radishes
⅓ cup sliced green onions
8 slices Armour Star Bacon (or more to taste)
¼ cup vinegar
½ teaspoon salt
Dash pepper

Combine lettuce, radishes and onions in a large salad bowl, toss lightly. Cook bacon until crispy, drain reserving drippings. Crumble bacon, sprinkle over salad. Add remaining ingredients to drippings; bring to a boil over medium heat, stirring constantly. Pour over salad; toss lightly and quickly until lettuce wilts.

Homemade Garlic Croutons

Rae Scott
Bear Creek, NC

Garlic Valley Farms Garlic Juice Spray
Loaf of French or Italian bread
Olive oil spray
Salt

Buy a nice loaf of French or Italian bread and cut it into cubes.

Spray the cubes of bread with olive spray and lots of Garlic Valley Farms garlic juice. Toss the cubes occasionally while spraying. Sprinkle with salt.

Bake at 350° until the croutons are as crisp as you like-usually for about 10 to 15 minutes, stir again and bake for an additional 10 minutes. Makes great croutons!

Broccoli Salad

Jamie Brady
Daughter of Co-owner
Bennett, NC

1 bunch of broccoli
1 cup raisins
1 cup toasted pecan pieces
1 cup shredded cheddar cheese
1 large tart apple cut into pieces

Dressing:
1 cup Miracle Whip
½ cup sugar
¼ cup vinegar

Mix dressing ingredients until smooth. Pour over salad and mix until thoroughly coated. (You can omit the apple and pecans and add 1 small onion and 1 pack of bacon cooked and crumbled instead)

Broccoli Salad

Elmo Phillips
Employee

1 large bunch broccoli florets cut into small pieces
½ cup raisins
½ cup chopped pecans
½ cup chopped green onions
1 jar Hormel bacon pieces (2 ounce)
½ cup shredded cheddar cheese

Dressing:
1 cup mayonnaise
½ cup sugar
2 tablespoon apple cider vinegar

Mix the night before and then pour over broccoli mixture right before serving.

Kraut Salad

Frankie Meuller
Siler City, NC

1 can kraut (2 ½ ounce)
1 cup sugar
1 large onion chopped
1 can pimento chopped
1 cup vinegar
1 cup chopped celery
1 large green bell pepper chopped

Drain and rinse the kraut, let drain well. Heat the sugar and vinegar until the sugar melts. Add kraut, celery, onion, pepper, and pimento. Put in a covered casserole dish and keep in the refrigerator.

Mousy Pear Salad

Elmo Phillips
Employee

2 cups shredded lettuce or lettuce leaves
1 can (15 ounce) pear halves, drained
24 raisins
Black shoestring licorice-cut into four 3-inch pieces and
Sixteen 1 inch pieces
1 red maraschino cherry, quartered
1 slice process American cheese

On four salad plates, place lettuce and a pear half, cut side down. Insert two raisins at narrow end of pear for eyes. Tuck four raisins under pear for feet. Insert one 3-inch licorice piece into wide end of each pear for a tail. Insert four 1-inch pieces into each face for whiskers. Place a cherry piece under whiskers for nose. For ears, cut small teardrop-shaped pieces from cheese; place just above the eyes. Yield: 4 servings

Grape Salad

Barbara Dowd
Employee

2 pounds seedless red grapes
2 pounds seedless green grapes
1 (8 ounce) soft cream cheese
1 (8 ounce) sour cream
¼ cup sugar
Brown sugar
1 small pack chopped walnuts

Mix cream cheese, sour cream and sugar together. Add grapes and toss well. Sprinkle brown sugar and walnuts on top. Keep refrigerated.

Roquefort Dressing

Peggy Fox
Asheboro, NC

1 (3 ounce) package cream cheese
½ cup light cream
¼ teaspoon salt
¼ teaspoon prepared mustard
½ cup mayonnaise
⅓ cup Roquefort or Blue Cheese
⅛ teaspoon garlic powder

Blend cheeses with seasonings, add mayonnaise alternately with cream. Whip until smooth. If too thick add a little sour cream. Makes 2 cups.

Garden Pea Salad

Sandy Brown
Bear Creek, NC

20 ounce frozen peas
2 cups cooked pasta (your choice)
Juice of ½ lemon
3 tablespoons chopped onion
½ cups grated cheese (your choice)
Grated fresh pepper
Pecan pieces
½ cup plain yogurt
½ cups light mayonnaise
Serve on lettuce. 6-8 servings.

Apple Salad With Grilled Chicken

Berta Scott
Co-owner
Bear Creek, NC

Grilled chicken or turkey can be used
Romaine lettuce
3 red chopped apples, your choice
1 cup raisins, golden
3 sticks of celery
1 cup of English walnuts, toasted and cut into pieces
Poppy seed dressing

Wash Romaine lettuce; lay into bottom of pretty salad dish. Place apples on top. Chop celery-next-sprinkle, raisins and walnuts. Place chicken on top. Serve with poppy seed dressing. My Favorite!

Thousand Island Dressing

Dawn Stumpf
Daughter of Co-owner
Bear Creek, NC

4 cups mayonnaise (Hellmann's)
½ cup relish
¼ cup vinegar (apple cider vinegar)
½ cup catsup

Place all the ingredients into blender and keep refrigerated.

132

Spinach Salad

Peggie Gaines
Goldston, NC

1 pound fresh raw spinach

3 hard cooked eggs

1 minced garlic

2 tablespoons lemon juice

1 grated onion

7 tablespoons olive oil or corn oil

Fresh tomatoes

Salt to taste

Wash and drain spinach thoroughly.
Cut into bite size pieces. Mix salt, garlic,
onion, lemon juice and oil well. Toss until
spinach is well coated, then garnish with
wedges of tomato and hard cooked eggs.
Serves 4-6

Citrus Avacoda Salad

Belinda Jordan
Bear Creek, NC

Citrus fruit pair well with this sweet
dressing!

12 cups torn salad greens

2 medium grapefruit, peeled and
sectioned

2 medium naval oranges, peeled and
sectioned

2 medium ripe avocados, peeled and
sliced

1 small red onion, thinly sliced and
separated into rings

Dressing:

½ cup vegetable oil

¼ cup sugar

 3 tablespoons lemon juice

1 ½ teaspoon poppy seeds

½ tsp salt

¼ tsp ground mustard

¼ tsp grated onion

In a large salad bowl, gently toss the
greens, grapefruit, oranges, avacados
and red onion. In a jar with tight fitting
lid combine the dressing ingredients.
Shake well. Drizzle over salad and toss to
coat. Yield: 12 servings.

Orange Delight

Peggie Gaines
Goldston, NC

1 large package orange jello
1 small can mandarin oranges
1 small can crushed pineapple
12-15 large marshmallows
3 ounce cream cheese
Small (8 ounce) cool whip

Drain oranges and pineapple. Add water to liquid to make 2 cups. Bring this to boil and add jello, marshmallows and cream cheese. Reduce heat, stir until dissolved. Cool slightly, add oranges and pineapple. Chill until syrupy. Fold in cool whip and chill.

Inez's Chicken Salad

Audrey Poe
Bear Creek, NC

1 cup chicken cubed
1 medium onion
½ cup small green pepper chopped
¾ teaspoon curry powder
½ cup chopped peanuts
½ cup mayo
1 tablespoon lemon juice

Mix in food processor on pulse until ingredients are mixed and the consistency desired. Spoon mixture into cream puffs or pastry shells.
Makes about 30 appetizers

Summer Time Fruit Dish

Deborah Pickard Stephenson
Carthage, NC

1 large can of drained pineapple chunks
Fresh strawberries (as many as you want) quartered
4 or 5 bananas diced
1 to 2 cups cooked rice chilled
1 large container of "Cool Whip"

Make sure rice is chilled and flaked. Mix in all the fruit stirring gently. Fold in the 'cool whip'. Chill and serve. Keep refrigerated.
I am not sure the amount that this makes. I only know that by using the rice you have a cool and refreshing dish that fills you. I have had this recipe for 30 years. I always enjoy on a hot day when it feels "too hot to eat" outside.

Delicious Cole Slaw

Sandy Brown
Sandy & Company
Bear Creek, NC

1 head cabbage, shredded
1 medium carrot, shredded
Mix dressing:
1 ½ cup salad dressing
1 teaspoon salt
1 teaspoon mustard
⅛ cup milk
2 teaspoons vinegar
⅓ cup sugar

Stir dressing good-pour over into the shredded cabbage; mix well.

Garden Slaw

Sandra Brown
Sandy & Company
Bear Creek, NC

8 cups shredded cabbage
2 shredded carrots
1 chopped green pepper
1 cup chopped onion
¼ cup cold water
1 or 2 teaspoons celery seed
1 ½ teaspoon pepper
1 envelope unflavored gelatin
⅔ cup vinegar
⅔ cup sugar, may be reduced
¼ cup cold water.

Mix sugar, vinegar, celery seed, salt, and pepper in sauce pan. Bring to a boil; stir in softened gelatin. Cool until thickens. Beat well; add salad oil, drain vegetables, pour dressing on top. Keeps well in refrigerator.

French Dressing

Dawn Stumpf
Daughter of Co-owner
Bear Creek, NC

1 cup sugar

2 cups salad dressing

⅓ cup vinegar

⅓ cup oil

⅓ cup catsup

1 teaspoon garlic salt

1 tsp salt

1 teaspoon mustard

½ tablespoon pepper

Dash paprika

Dash Worcestershire sauce

Place all the ingredients in blender
and mix well; medium speed. Place in
refrigerator.

Macaroni Salad

Denise Holt
Bear Creek, NC

½ pound macaroni

3 quarts water

1 tablespoon salt

1 cup celery chopped

½ cup green pepper

1 (5 ½ ounce) can shrimp

½ cup mayonnaise

½ cup sour cream

1 tablespoon lemon juice

1 ½ teaspoon salt

¼ teaspoon pepper

1 tablespoon parsley

Cook macaroni in boiling salted water
until done; drain, rinse in cold water.
Combine celery, green pepper, pimento
and shrimp. Stir in the mayonnaise, sour
cream, lemon juice, salt and pepper. Add
to the cooled macaroni and mix well.
Sprinkle with parsley. Chill several hours.
Makes 4-6 servings

7-Up Fruit Salad

Holly Reynolds
Granddaughter of Co-owner
Carthage, NC

2 packages lemon jell-o,(dissolved
in 2 cups hot water)
2 cups 7-up
1 (no 2) can pineapple, drained
2 cups miniature marshmallows
2 large bananas

When jell-o is partially set; add rest of
ingredients and pour into 9x12 inch pan.

Top Layer:
½ cup sugar
2 tablespoons flour
1 cup pineapple juice
1 egg, beaten
2 tablespoons butter
1 (8 ounce) Cool Whip

Combine sugar and flour; stir in juice
and egg. Cook, stirring constantly until
thickens. Add butter and cook. Fold in
whipped cream and spread over jell-o.
Delicious!

Crunchy Salad

Helen Wilson
Bear Creek, NC
Sister-in-law of Co-owner Lisa

3 bunches broccoli
1 head cauliflower
12 slices bacon, fried and crumbled
¼ to 1 cup raisins, to taste
½ cup onion, chopped
1 cup mayonnaise
½ cup sugar
2 tablespoons red wine vinegar

Wash broccoli and cauliflower. Divide
into pieces. Mix vegetables, with
bacon, raisins, and onions. Combine
mayonnaise, sugar and red wine vinegar.
Combine with vegetable mixture. Toss
until covered. Refrigerate.

Helpful Hint

Your fruit salads will look
perfect when you use an egg
slicer to make perfect slices
of strawberries, kiwis or
bananas.

Potato Salad

Jeanne Vaughn
Bear Creek, NC
Niece of Co-owner

8 medium potatoes
5 eggs, hard-boiled
½ medium onion, chopped
½ cup mayonnaise
½ cup sweet pickle cubes
Salt and pepper to taste

Cook potatoes in skins until done. Can peel potatoes or cube with skins on. Put potatoes in large mixing bowl. Cube eggs, and place in bowl with potatoes. Add onion, mayonnaise, sweet pickle cubes, salt and pepper to taste.

Strawberry Salad

Dawn Kidd
Employee
Robbins, NC

1 can crushed pineapple
1 package strawberry jello - can use lime or orange
Bring to a boil; cool.

Add:
1 carton cool whip
1 cup cottage cheese
Mix lightly and refrigerate

Orange Delight Salad

Jeanie Scott
Siler City, NC

1 large orange jell-o
2 cups hot water
1 ½ cold water
1 large can crushed pineapple (drain and save syrup)
2 bananas sliced
2 cups miniature marshmallows

Mix jell-o and hot water until dissolved; add cold water. Let cool then add pineapple, bananas and marshmallows. Refrigerate until congealed.

Topping

½ cup pineapple syrup
¾ cups sugar
2 tablespoons flour
1 egg
8 ounces of cream cheese
1 cup chopped pecans
1 small container of Cool Whip

Mix sugar, flour and egg. Cook on low heat until thick. Remove from heat and add cream cheese. Beat until well blended. Let cool. Fold in Cool Whip.

Spread on congealed salad, sprinkle with pecans and coconut.

Vegetable Salad

Mary Lois Thomas
Sanford, NC

1 can shoe-peg corn
1 can sweet peas
1 can French style green beans
½ cup onion (chopped fine)
½ cup green pepper chopped fine
1 cup light brown sugar
½ cup vinegar
½ cup oil

Drain all the cans of vegetables and mix with the onions and pepper. Boil sugar, vinegar, and oil and pour over the vegetables. Mix and refrigerate.

Fruit Bowl

Pat Brown

1 (11 ounce) can Mandarin oranges
1 medium size can pineapple tidbits
1 medium size can sliced peaches
2 small boxes instant vanilla pudding

Drain juices off all can fruits and save. Use two cups of the juice and mix with the pudding mix. Mix the fruits and pudding mix together. Add 1½ bananas (diced), 1 apple (diced), and some seedless grapes. Put in a bowl and top with Cool Whip and maraschino cherries.

Blueberry Salad

Wyanne L. Caviness
Bennett
First Bank

1 can blueberry pie filling
2 boxes (3 ounce) grape jello
1 (No. 2) can pineapple (crushed and un-drained)
Dissolve jello with 2 cups boiling water. Add pie filling and pineapple. Let congeal in refrigerator for 1 hour.

Topping
8 ounces softened cream cheese
½ pint sour cream
1 teaspoon vanilla flavoring
½ cup sugar
½ cup chopped roasted pecans

Mix first 4 ingredients well. Spread on salad. Top with pecans. Refrigerate

Vegetables

Pickled Carrots

Bonnie Reynolds
Carthage, NC
Daughter of Co-owner

Pack several jars of these pickled appetizers as gifts. They're wonderful served with a vegetable dinner.

1 ½ cups cider vinegar

1 ½ cups water

1 cup sugar

2 pounds carrots, scraped and cut into strips

2 tablespoons dill seeds

3-4 cloves garlic

Combine first 3 ingredients in a large saucepan. Bring to a boil, stirring until sugar dissolves. Add carrots, dill seed and garlic, bring to a boil over medium heat. Cover, reduce heat, and simmer 6-8 minutes. Remove from heat, cool. Cover and chill 8 hours. To serve, pour mixture through a large wire-mesh strainer discarding liquid. Discard garlic, if desired. Yield 16 appetizer servings

Dilled Cucumbers With Tomatoes

Lorrie Moore
Bonlee, NC

⅓ cup olive oil

3 tablespoons cider vinegar

1 tablespoon fresh dill weed, chopped
  Or ½ teaspoon dried dill weed

½ teaspoon salt

½ teaspoon sugar

1 dash pepper

1 cucumber, thinly sliced

3 large tomatoes, sliced

Combine oil, vinegar, dill, salt, sugar and pepper in bowl. Stir until well blended. Add cucumber slices and toss well. Best when chilled for a few hours. Arrange tomatoes on single plates, spoon cucumber mixture over tomatoes. Makes a delicious salad.

Vegetable Medley

Tina Brady
Bennett, NC

Drain:
1 can french –cut green beans
1 can green peas (LeSeur)
1 can Shoe Peg corn
Add:
4 ounces pimento
1 cup chopped onion
1 cup chopped celery
1 cup chopped green peppers
Mix:
¾ cup vinegar
½ cup oil
1 teaspoon black pepper
1 cup sugar

Pour over vegetables and stir.

Pickled Mushrooms

Lisa Scott
Bear Creek, NC
Co-owner

⅓ cup red wine vinegar
⅓ cup salad oil
1 small onion, thinly sliced, separated
1 teaspoon salt
2 teaspoons parsley flakes
1 teaspoon prepared mustard
1 tablespoon brown sugar
2 (6 ounce) cans mushroom crowns, drained

In a small saucepan, combine red wine vinegar, salad oil. sliced onion (separated in rings), salt, parsley flakes, mustard and brown sugar. Bring to a boil. Add mushrooms. Simmer for 5 to 6 minutes. Chill in a covered bowl several hours, stirring occasionally. Drain.

Cucmber&Onions In Sour Cream

Pearl Herndon
Coleridge, NC

½ cup sour cream
1 tablespoon. sugar
1 tablespoon. vinegar
½ teaspoon salt

2 medium cucumbers-sliced
2 small onions, sliced

Mix all together and toss gently. Cover and chill. Serves 4

Red Pepper Jelly Glazed Carrots

Frankie Meuller
Siler City, NC
Special Hairdresser friend to Berta

1 (2 pound package) baby carrots
1 (10 ½ ounce) can condensed chicken broth (undiluted)
2 tablespoons butter
1 (10 ounce) jar Southern Supreme Red Pepper jelly

Combine carrots and chicken broth in a skillet over medium heat. Bring to a boil and cook stirring often (6 to 8 minutes until carrots are crisp and tender), and broth is reduced to ¼ cup. Stir in butter and red pepper jelly. Cook, stirring constantly (5 minutes or until mixture is thickened and glazes carrots.)
This is a great way to boost the flavor to vegetables.

Feta Cheese Stuffed Tomatoes

Raymond and Amy Brewer
Bear Creek, NC

4 large tomatoes
4 ounces crumbled feta cheese
¼ cup fine dry breadcrumbs
2 tablespoons green onions (chopped)
2 tablespoons fresh parsley (chopped)
2 tablespoons olive oil
Italian parsley sprigs (optional)

Cut tomatoes in half horizontally. Scoop out pulp from each tomato half, leaving the shell intact. Discard seeds and chop pulp coarsely. Stir together pulp, feta cheese, breadcrumbs, green onions, fresh parsley, and olive oil in a medium bowl. Spoon mixture evenly into tomato shells and place in a 13x9 inch baking dish. Bake at 350° for 15 minutes. Garnish with parsley sprigs if desired. Yield eight servings.

Pimento Cheese

Wyanne L. Caviness
Bennett, NC
First Bank

1 ½ cups mayonnaise
1 4 ounce jar diced pimento (drained)
1 teaspoon Worcestershire sauce
1 teaspoon finely chopped onion
¼ teaspoon ground red pepper
1 (8 ounce) block extra sharp cheddar cheese (shredded and chopped)
1 (8 ounce) block sharp cheddar cheese (shredded and chopped)

Stir together first five ingredients. Add cheeses. Mix well. May use food blender. Refrigerate. Yields four cups.

Tomato Pie

Tina Brady
Bennett, NC

1 Deep dish pie shell, bake at 350° for 10 minutes.

Layer 2-3 sliced tomatoes in bottom of pie shell. On top of tomatoes place ½ jar of real bacon bits and 2 tablespoons of minced onions.

Mix 1 cup cheddar cheese (mild or sharp) with 1 cup Hellmann's mayonnaise and spread over top. Bake at 350° for 25 minutes or until brown.

Squash Casserole Squares

Tina Brady
Bennett, NC

3 cups yellow squash grated

½ cup oil

½ cup onion diced

3 eggs, beaten

1 cup Bisquick baking mix

1 cup grated cheese

Mix all ingredients. Pour into casserole dish. Bake at 400° for 20 minutes or until casserole is sufficiently brown. Cut into squares and serve.

Entrees

Venison Shoulder Roast

Hoyt Scott
Co-owner
Bear Creek, NC

Large oven bag. Add 2 tablespoons flour to oven bag as directed-shake well.
4-6 pound shoulder roast-rub with salt and pepper and garlic powder to taste.
Add 2 bay leaves to bag.
Also add: 2 cans beef broth
4 cups carrots-small
4 cups medium potatoes-cut ¼ pieces
2 cans mushroom
2 cups medium onions cut in ¼ pieces

After tying bags, cut slits in bag as directed. Place oven bag in large baking pan in oven. Bake 320° for approximately 2 ½ hours-serves 10. Enjoy!

Hot Dogs And Chili

Jeff Wilson
Bear Creek, NC
Nephew of Lisa Scott

1 pound extra lean hamburger
4 teaspoons chili powder
¼ teaspoon salt
¼ teaspoon pepper
½ cup ketchup
2 teaspoons paprika
1 cup water
2 (1 pound) packages beef franks

Brown beef and drain, chop finely. Combine chili powder, salt, pepper, ketchup, paprika and water. Stir into beef. Chop until mixture is very fine. Simmer for 30 minutes. Add franks to chili and simmer on stove or in crock-pot for 3 to 4 hours on low heat.

Garlic Rosemary Turkey

Shirley Gerken
Siler City, NC

1 Whole turkey (10 to 12 pounds)
6 to 8 garlic cloves cut into small slivers
2 Large lemons, halved
2 teaspoons. dried rosemary, crushed
1 teaspoon rubbed sage
Freshly ground or coarsely ground black pepper

Cut ten to twelve small slits in turkey skin. Insert garlic between skin and meat. Squeeze two lemon halves inside the turkey and leave them inside. Squeeze remaining lemon over outside of turkey. Spray the turkey with nonstick cooking spray; (I use olive oil spray to add flavor). Sprinkle with rosemary, sage and pepper. Place on a rack in a roasting pan. Bake, uncovered at 325° for 1 hour. Cover loosely with foil and bake 2 ½ to 3 ½ hours longer or until a meat thermometer reads 185°. Can also be cooked on the grill. Over the past two or three years, I have prepared it on the grill. This method provides a special taste. Leftovers are wonderful in sandwiches, salads or served with sautéed vegetables.

Michael James Turkey Recipe

Michael James

Start with an 18 lb frozen turkey. This will feed about 12 people. I like it frozen because they don't get bruised as easy during transport. It takes about 1 day for each 4 lbs in the refrigerator to thaw, or a quick method is immersing in cold water.

In an ice chest (big enough to fit the turkey) mix 128 ounces of vegetable broth (this is sold in 14 ounce cans in the grocery store for about 50 cents each) and 2 cups of Mortens Kosher salt. Add enough ice to bring the level of the brine/broth close to the top of the turkey. Mix it up every once in a while and let the turkey sit in the ice chest for 12 to 16 hours.

Remove the turkey and drain well. Stuff the turkey with fresh mint, oregano, sliced apples, etc. Never stuff with breaded stuffing. This will just dry out the bird. The apples and other fresh herbs are just for flavoring. Butter the turkey up and place in the oven at 325° uncovered and in a V type rack. In about forty minutes the breast should be browned. Cover the breast with a foil shield to protect from drying out. Let the bird cook until the interior temperature is 180°. Remove and let cool for about 15 minutes before carving.
THIS WILL GIVE YOU THE BEST COOKED TURKEY YOU HAVE EVER EATEN!

Quesadillas

Dawn Stumpf
Daughter of Ethelda Co-owner
Bear Creek, NC

Make these tasty Mexican sandwiches by filling tortillas with cheese, sour cream and guacamole.

8 to 6 inch flour tortillas
1 ripe medium avocado peeled and cut into chunks
½ small onion
1 tablespoon lemon juice
½ teaspoon salt
½ teaspoon garlic powder
½ cup Monterey jack cheese, shredded
¼ cup sour cream
1 cup shredded cheddar cheese
Hot or mild taco sauce

Steam tortillas as label directs until they become soft and hot-keep warm. In food processor, blend at medium speed the next five ingredients until smooth. In large bowl, take the avocado mixture, Monterey jack cheese, sour cream and ½ cup of cheddar cheese. Spread avocado mixture evenly on one side of four steamed tortillas, top with remaining tortillas pressing gently to seal. Preheat oven broiler-cut tortillas sandwich into eight wedges. Place on large cookie sheet, sprinkle with remaining cheddar. Broil 3-5 minutes until cheese is just melted-arrange on warm platter. Serve immediately, spoon taco sauce over quesadillas.

Awesome Pepperoni Pizza

Derrick Scott
Rick and Gail's Son
Bear Creek, NC

2 ½ cups all-purpose flour
½ teaspoon salt
1 package (¼ ounce) dry yeast
1 tablespoon plus 2 teaspoons olive oil
¾ cup pizza sauce
12 ounces mozzarella, sliced
1 ¾ ounces pepperoni slices (about 25 slices)
½ teaspoon dried oregano
⅛ teaspoon black pepper

Preheat oven to 400°. Lightly grease a 12x9 inch baking sheet. Sift the flour and salt into a large bowl. Stir in the yeast. Make a well in the center and add olive oil and 1 cup lukewarm water. Mix until a soft dough forms. Turn the dough out onto a lightly floured surface and knead gently for 5 minutes. Roll out dough and press into prepared baking sheet. Cover and wait for 10 minutes at room temperature, bake for 5-7 minutes. Remove the crust from the oven and spread pizza sauce on top, leaving a ¾ inch border. Arrange the mozzarella on top and then the pepperoni. Sprinkle with oregano and pepper. Drizzle with olive oil and bake until golden, 15-20 minutes. Using a pizza cutter or sharp knife, slice the pizza into six square slices. Serve hot.

Jerky

Ricky Scott
Son of Hoyt and Berta Scott

½ cup water
½ teaspoon onion powder
1 teaspoon old hickory smoked flavor (liquid)
¼ cup soy sauce
1 tablespoon Worcestershire sauce
¼ teaspoon lemon pepper
¼ teaspoon garlic powder
3 pounds venison, elk, antelope or any meat

Cut meat in long thin slices. Put all ingredients in a pan and leave overnight. Turn once, cook on a cake rack or a foil covered cookie sheet at 150°. Turn after 4 hours, it cooks in about 8 hours.

Meaty Baked Beans

Deborah Pickard Stephenson
Carthage, NC
Showroom Staff

2 large cans baked beans
1 small jar Grandma's Molasses
2 pounds of bacon (1 pound fried crisp and broken up)
2 large onion (diced)
2 cups brown sugar
2 pounds of hamburger

Cook hamburger until brown. Drain and add onions. Dump into a huge aluminum-baking pan. Add baked beans, molasses, brown sugar and crisp bacon. Mix and place the raw bacon on top. Bake at 325° for 30 minutes.

Brian's Pasta

Brian McDonald

1 (9 ounce) "Barilla" 3-cheese tortellini pasta
6 teaspoons olive oil
1 ½ teaspoons crushed red pepper
½ teaspoon salt
1 teaspoon crushed black pepper
3 tablespoons sun dried tomatoes
3 tablespoons chopped basil

Bring 2-3 quarts of water to a rolling boil: add tortellini, reduce heat to medium. Add 2 teaspoons olive oil and cook 9 minutes. Drain and return to pot. Add 4 teaspoons oil, 1 ½ teaspoons crushed red pepper, ½ teaspoon salt, 1 teaspoon crushed black pepper, 3 tablespoons sun dried tomatoes. Stir; serve with 3 tablespoons fresh chopped basil. Serves 2-3.

Seafood

Shrimp Fettuccine with Garlic Sauce

Kate Henry
Charleston, SC

1 pound shrimp
1 pound fettuccine
4 tablespoons olive oil
2 tablespoons minced garlic
2 tablespoons butter
¼ teaspoon salt

Peel and clean shrimp. Prepare fettuccine. Heat olive oil and garlic in skillet on medium heat until garlic begins to brown. Three minutes before fettuccine is fully cooked, add shrimp to skillet. When shrimp are pink on one side, turn and add salt and butter. Continue to cook shrimp until both sides are pink. Drain fettuccine and add to shrimp in skillet. Fold garlic, butter and olive oil mixture to coat fettuccine.

Herbed Crab Cakes

Ricky Scott
Bear Creek, NC

½ cup mayonnaise
½ cup chopped fresh chives
¼ cup chopped fresh parsley
2 tablespoons fresh lemon juice
1 teaspoon Old Bay seasoning or other seafood seasoning blend
¼ teaspoon cayenne pepper
1 ¾ pounds lump crabmeat, picked over
5 cups fresh bread crumbs made from crust-less French bread
3 tablespoons butter
3 tablespoons olive oil

Lemon wedges

Mix all above ingredients. Shape into desired size. Fry in skillet with vegetable oil on medium to high heat until brown. This is easy to prepare and delicious to eat!

Shrimp Scampi

Wayne Jordan
Bear Creek, NC

1 pound large shrimp, peeled and de-veined
¼ teaspoon salt
⅛ teaspoon white pepper
1 teaspoon paprika
½ teaspoon Worcestershire Sauce
3 tablespoons all-purpose flour
¼ cup butter
¼ cup chopped onion
½ cup (dry white wine) optional
or lemon wedges
Garlic butter (recipe below)
2-3 cups cooked brown rice

Season shrimp with mixture of salt, pepper, paprika and Worcestershire sauce; then coat well with flour. Melt butter in large skillet over moderate heat. Add onions and shrimp to butter and fry 3-4 minutes until brown, turning once. Stir in garlic butter and wine (if used) and simmer 3-4 minutes. Serve over hot rice. Garnish with lemon wedges. Serves 4

Garlic Butter:
¼ cup softened butter
3 teaspoon finely chopped parsley
3 small cloves, crushed
Mix Well

Crab Cakes

Sue Farlow
Sister to Berta and Ethelda
Raleigh, NC

3 cups crabmeat, cooked fresh or canned
1 ½ teaspoons salt
1 teaspoon dry mustard
½ teaspoon pepper
2 teaspoons Worcestershire sauce
1 egg yolk
1 tablespoon mayonnaise
2 teaspoons minced parsley
Butter for frying

Mix ingredients together. Press mixture firmly into eight small cakes. Chill well. When ready to cook dip the cakes in flour then in beaten egg combined with 2 tablespoons water and into buttered bread crumbs. Melt butter in skillet and fry cakes rapidly over high heat until golden brown. Serves 4

Crab Cakes For Two

Wendy Paschal
Siler City, NC

1 (8 ounce) container jumbo lump crabmeat, picked free of shell
⅔ cup panko (Japanese breadcrumbs), divided
2 tablespoons minced red bell pepper
1 tablespoon minced green onion
1 teaspoon Old Bay seasoning
2 large eggs, divided
1 tablespoon mayonnaise
1 tablespoon fresh lemon juice (about ½ lemon)
2 tablespoons butter
2 tablespoons olive oil

Creole Sauce (recipe follows)

In a medium bowl, combine crabmeat, ⅓ cup breadcrumbs, bell pepper, green onion, and Old Bay seasoning; set aside.

In a small bowl, lightly beat 1 egg. Whisk in mayonnaise and lemon juice. Add egg mixture to crab mixture, tossing to combine. Shape mixture into 4 patties.

In a small bowl, lightly beat remaining egg. Lightly brush each side of crab cake with egg, and dip in remaining ⅓ cup breadcrumbs.

In a large skillet, heat butter and olive oil over medium heat. Add crab cakes and cook 3-4 minutes, per side, or until golden. Serve with Creole Sauce.

Creole Sauce:
¼ cup sour cream
3 tablespoons mayonnaise
1 tablespoon minced green onion
1 tablespoon fresh lemon juice
2 teaspoons Old Bay seasoning
1 teaspoon creamy horseradish

In a small bowl, combine all ingredients; cover, and chill.

Sauteed Shrimp With Cheese Grits

Elmo Phillips
Employee

Grits
1 ¼ cups chicken broth
1 ½ cups milk
¾ cup quick grits
¼ teaspoon salt
1 cup shredded cheddar cheese

Shrimp
1 cup diced bacon
1 pound medium shrimp, peeled & de-veined
½ cup thinly sliced strips green bell pepper
⅓ cup thinly sliced strips red bell pepper
½ cup slivered onion
Sliced green onions and shredded cheddar cheese
For garnish
Tabasco sauce

To prepare grits, bring chicken broth and milk to a boil in large saucepan. Stir in grits and salt; return to boil. Cover and reduce heat to low. Cook 5 minutes until thickened, stirring occasionally. Stir in cheddar cheese. Keep warm.

To prepare shrimp dish, cook bacon in skillet until crisp. Remove from skillet and drain bacon on paper towels; set aside. Drain all but 2 tablespoons drippings from skillet. Add shrimp, peppers and onion; cook until vegetables are tender and shrimp turns pink, about 3-5 minutes. Season with Tabasco sauce; stir in bacon. Serve shrimp mixture over warm cheese grits. Garnish with chopped green onions and shredded Cheddar cheese. Yield: 6 servings

Sauces & Gravies

Low Fat Gravy

Shirley Gerken
Siler City, NC

½ Cup finely chopped onion
½ Cup finely chopped fresh mushrooms
2 tablespoons chopped fresh parsley
2 Cups reduced sodium fat free chicken broth, divided, or
2 Cups broth made from turkey drippings with fat removed
2 tablespoons cornstarch
Pepper to taste

In a saucepan, sauté onion, mushrooms and parsley in ¼ cup broth until vegetables are tender. Combine cornstarch, pepper and ½ cup of broth; stir until smooth. Add to pan with remaining broth. Bring to a boil, stirring occasionally; boil for 2 minutes.

Mabel's BBQ Sauce

Reba Gunter Thomas
Pittsboro, NC

1 gallon vinegar
1 tall can tomato juice
1 small bottle Worcestershire sauce
2 large bottles Heinz 57 sauce
1 pound box light brown sugar
3-4 tablespoons crushed red pepper
3 tablespoons black pepper
½ bottle Texas Pete
¼ cup salt

Mix together and bring to boil. Simmer for 2 hours. Great for Pig Picking

Champagne Sauce For Ham

"Razz" O'Keefe
Oswego, N.Y.

1 quart Ginger Ale
1 cup vinegar
1 pound dark brown sugar
Raisins if desired

Mix all ingredients together in a saucepan. Let it come to a boil and cook a couple of minutes. Thicken with cornstarch. Mix with sauce a little at a time as it boils. Don't let it got too thick or it will get lumpy.

James M. Hot Dog/Hamburger Sauce

Eleanor Stumpf
Big Run, PA

1 large diced onion
½ pound oleo
½ teaspoon ground cloves
½ teaspoon nutmeg
½ teaspoon allspice
1 quart water
1 pound hamburger
1 (24 ounce) bottle ketchup
½ teaspoon cinnamon
½ teaspoon red pepper-crushed or flakes
Salt and Pepper to taste

Cook onion in oleo and drain. Brown the hamburger. Add ketchup, water, and spices and cook for one hour.

Helpful Hint

A friend is someone who
steps in when others step out.

Beef

Macaroni & Hamburger

Belinda Jordan
Co-owner
Bear Creek, NC

1 pound hamburger
2 cans (8 ounce) tomato sauce
1 tablespoon sugar
Dash pepper & garlic salt
1 teaspoon salt
1 ½ cups macaroni
1 package (3 ounce) cream cheese
1 cup sour cream
½ cup grated cheddar cheese

Brown meat in pan, add tomato sauce, sugar, salt & pepper. Simmer 30 minutes. Cook macaroni, mix cream cheese and sour cream in bowl; when smooth and creamy add macaroni. In 2 quart casserole put layer of macaroni mixture then meat sauce; repeat twice. Sprinkle top with grated cheese. Bake 350° for 30 minutes.

Salisbury Steak

Marilyn Sehen
Sanford, NC

1 can mushroom soup
1 ½ pound ground beef
½ cup dry bread or cracker crumbs
½ teaspoon salt
⅛ teaspoon pepper
1 onion finely chopped
1 egg slightly beaten
⅓ cup water

Heat oven 350°. In medium bowl, combine ¼ of the mushroom soup with remaining ingredients except water. Mix well. Shape into 6 patties. Arrange in single layer in 13x9 inch baking dish.

Bake uncovered at 350° for 30 minutes.

Skim off fat. In a small bowl, combine remaining soup and water; spoon over patties. Return to oven and bake 10 minutes. Garnish with mushroom slices.

Old South Barbecue

Josephine Janowcki
Passed on from my husband's
Aunt Lucy Katzmorek

1 ½ pounds beef

1 pound pork

2 tablespoons white vinegar

1 tablespoon dry mustard

2 tablespoons pickling spice

1 Medium green pepper

1 Cup Catsup

½ Cup water

1 teaspoon salt

1 Yellow onion, egg size

Cut meat in small pieces, dice onion and green pepper (¼ inch). Place in a small enamel pan. Carefully measure out and add salt, mustard & vinegar. Add ½ Cup water, and catsup. Stir and bring to simmering point on stove, allow to simmer slowly for 2 ½ hours. Add pickling spices in cheesecloth bag during the last 10 minutes only, then remove from mixture. Serve hot on buns-about 12 buns. Also, the recipe freezes very well so I triple it and cook it in a slow cooker.

Great Burgers

Reba G. Thomas
Pittsboro, NC

5 pounds. ground chuck beef

1 cup crushed Ritz crackers

1 cup apple sauce

1 envelope Lipton onion soup mix

5 teaspoons Accent

5 teaspoons Worcestershire sauce

½ teaspoon garlic salt

Mix together and make into patties. I put wax paper or clear wrap between burgers and then seal with tin foil. Freeze until ready to use.

Beef Brisket

Evelyn Cheek
Asheboro, NC

1 beef (flat) brisket

1 package Lipton onion soup mix

Carrots and potatoes

Preheat oven to 325°. Put 1 package onion soup mix in pan, lay brisket flat side up on top of soup. Put carrots and potatoes around roast. Salt and pepper potatoes and carrots only. Put other soup mix on roast. Mix brown sugar and ketchup, place on potatoes and carrots. Bake covered for 2 ½ to 3 hours. Slice and enjoy!

Barbequed Hamburgers

Nancy Hogan
Siler City, NC

1 ½ pounds hamburger
1 can tomato soup
¼ cup sweet pickle relish
½ cup chopped onion
1 tablespoon brown sugar
1 tablespoon vinegar
1 tablespoon Worcestershire sauce

Make hamburger patties about 2-3 inches in diameter and not too thick. Brown patties and place in baking dish. Mix together soup, relish, onions. Brown sugar, vinegar, and Worcestershire sauce and pour over hamburger patties. Bake at 300° for 45-60 minutes.

Beef Stroganoff

Pauline Petcovic
Freedom, PA

3 pounds ground meat
2 medium onions (chopped)
2 cans mushroom soup
2 large cans mushrooms (drained)
4 tablespoons ketchup
2 teaspoons Worcestershire sauce
1 (16 ounce) carton sour cream
Garlic salt

Brown meat and onions; Drain fat. Sprinkle with garlic salt to taste. Add mushrooms, ketchup, and Worcestershire sauce. Stir well. Stir in mushroom soup and sour cream. Heat well. Serve over rinsed cooked noodles. Serves 6-8 people

Hamburger Pie

Kathy Gaines
Siler City, NC

1 pound lean ground beef
1 can biscuits
1can Hunts Italian tomato sauce
1 cup shredded mozzarella cheese
1 cup grated Parmesan cheese

Brown the beef and drain well. Add sauce. Spread ½ can of biscuits on the bottom of a 9 x 9 inch pan. Pour beef over biscuits. Add shredded cheese. Spread remaining biscuits over the top of meat. Sprinkle Parmesan cheese on top. Bake at 350° until brown.

No-Peek Beef

Chad Reynolds
Carthage, NC

2 pounds stew beef
1 cup water
1 package dry onion soup mix
1 can or jar mushrooms, drained
1 can mushroom soup

Mix well together in 3-quart casserole dish. Cover and bake at 300° for 3 hours. Do not peek. Serve over rice or noodles. Serves 6

Beef Stew

Gail Scott
Bear Creek, NC

3 pounds beef stew meat
4-5 carrots in chunks
1 small chopped onion
3 potatoes diced
1 cup wide celery slices
1 teaspoon salt
1 can cream of celery soup
1 can mushroom soup
1 cup ginger ale

Grease a large casserole and layer beef and vegetables in it. Sprinkle salt on top. Spoon undiluted soups over all and finish with ginger ale. Cover and cook 325° for 3 hrs, uncover last 30 minutes.

Rump Roast

Elmo Phillips
Employee
Bear Creek, NC

8 ½-9 pound rump roast
2 pounds whole mushrooms
4 large potatoes cut in half
8 whole carrots
1 cup chopped green onion with tops
½ cup fresh parsley
2 cups wine
1 cup water
Worcestershire sauce
Celery seeds

Place in a large roasting bag. Sprinkle bag with 2 tablespoons flour first. Place mushrooms around roast, then potatoes, & carrots. Put green onions and parsley on top of roast. Sprinkle with celery seeds. Mix wine, water and Worcestershire sauce together. Pour at front of roast. Seal with tie and punch a dozen holes in bag. Cook on 350°

Shish-Ka-Bob's

Elmo Phillips
Employee
Bear Creek, NC

Round steak, trimmed of all bone and fat.
Green bell peppers
White and yellow onions
Eggs, milk, flour, salt, pepper, oil, cracker crumbs
Round toothpicks

The amounts of ingredients vary due to size and weight, and amounts needed to serve. Cut round steak, bell peppers and onions into 1 inch square pieces. Thread onto round toothpicks in following order: steak, bell pepper, onion, steak, bell pepper, onion, and steak. Roll each in flour, dip into egg-milk mix, and then roll in cracker crumbs. Brown in oil; add salt and pepper to taste. Bake ½ hour at 350°.

159

Best Roast Beef

Elmo Phillips
Employee
Bear Creek, NC

Rub a 3 to 7 pound rolled or standing rib roast with salt and pepper; place in roasting pan. Place in preheated oven for one hour, front side up. Turn off heat and leave in oven no matter how long it is until dinner. DO NOT OPEN DOOR AT ALL. Turn oven to 375° for 30-40 minutes before serving time and you can open the door! (Size of roast does not alter these directions.) Use a shallow pan.

Swiss Steak

Jane Phillips
Bear Creek, NC
Sister to Berta and Ethelda

2 pounds boneless round or chuck ½-inch thick
½ teaspoon salt
⅛ teaspoon pepper
2 tablespoons fat or vegetable oil
½ pound mushrooms, sliced
1 large onion, chopped
1 green pepper, seeded and chopped
1 clove garlic, halved
1 can (8 ounce) tomato sauce
1 cup water
1 to 2 tablespoons all-purpose flour

Cut meat into serving size pieces. Sprinkle with salt and pepper. Heat fat in heavy skillet, add beef and brown on both sides. Remove meat and set aside. Add mushrooms to fat remaining in skillet. Cook, stirring occasionally until lightly browned. Return meat to skillet. Put remaining ingredients except flour into blender in order listed. Blend at high speed until smooth. Pour over meat and mushrooms in skillet. Cover, simmer 1 ½ hours or until meat is tender. Remove meat to heated platter. To thicken gravy, blend 1-2 tablespoon flour and a small amount of water to a smooth paste. Stir into gravy. Cook stirring constantly until desired thickness.

Sloppy Joes

Douglas Stumpf
Son of Ethelda Co-Owner
Bear Creek, NC

2 pounds ground beef

1 large onion chopped

1 ¼ cup ketchup

½ cup water

1 tablespoon brown sugar

1 tablespoon white vinegar

½ teaspoon salt

½ teaspoon ground mustard

½ teaspoon chili powder

¼ teaspoon ground allspice

8 buns-split

In a large skillet, cook beef and onion over medium heat until meat is no longer pink, drain. Add the ketchup, water, brown sugar, vinegar, salt, mustard, chili powder and all spice. Bring to a boil.

Reduce heat, simmer uncovered for 35-40 minutes or until heated through. Use about ½ cup for each bun-makes about 8 servings.

Deluxe Eye Of Round Roast

Douglas Stumpf
Son of Ethleda Co-owner
Bear Creek, NC

This roast is a one-meal dish. Vegetables, gravy and meat are together in oven bag.

1 large oven bag-turkey size

1 eye of round roast (4-5 pounds)

¾ cup Worcestershire sauce

⅔ cup soy sauce

3 cups water

4 medium size potatoes peeled and cut in ¼ size pieces

6 carrots peeled and cut in 1-inch pieces

2 onions peeled and halved

Prepare oven bag as directed with flour. Insert roast; add Worcestershire sauce and soy sauce with the water; tie bag closed. Place on large baking pan. Make small cuts in top of oven bag as directed. Cook 350° for 3-4 hours or until almost done (basting meat every hour) then open bag and add vegetables and more water if needed. Close bag and continue cooking vegetables until done. When done, remove roast from bag to serving platter waiting 10 minutes before slicing. Add vegetables around roast; reserving gravy to serve over slices of roast and vegetables.

Little Meat Loaves

Betty King
Siler City, NC

1 egg
¾ cup milk
1 cup shredded cheese
½ cup quick cooking oats
½ onion chopped
1 teaspoon salt
1 pound lean ground beef
⅔ cup catsup
½ cup brown sugar
1 ½ teaspoons mustard

Beat egg and milk together then add cheese, oats, onions and salt. Add meat and shape into 8 small loaves. Put into greased 9x13 baking dish. Mix catsup, brown sugar, and mustard together; spoon over loaves. Bake at 350° for 45 minutes.

Prime Rib

Jeff Wilson
Bear Creek, NC
Nephew of Lisa Scott

2 boxes rock salt
1 prime rib
Garlic powder to taste
Worcestershire sauce to taste
½ cup water

Pour one box of rock salt into baking pan. Lay prime rib fat side up in pan. Add seasoning of garlic powder and Worcestershire sauce, (heavily). Pour the second box of rock salt on prime rib, pat all over to cover. Pour the water over the prime rib. Bake in the oven at 500°, Reaching these meat temperatures; 12 minutes per pound for rare (140°), 14 minutes per pound for medium at (150°); or 14 minutes per pound for well-done (160-165°).

Saucy Meatballs With Pasta

Deborah Stephenson
Robbins, NC

Sauté in ¼ cup olive oil:

1 ½ cups yellow onion, diced

Stir in:

2 teaspoon garlic, minced

Add and simmer:

3 cans (14 ½ ounce each) whole plum tomatoes, crushed

½ cup reserved meatball pan drippings

½ cup minced fresh parsley

1 tablespoon sugar

1 teaspoon crushed red pepper flakes

Salt to taste

Add and simmer:

12 cooked meatballs

Stir in:

1 pound cooked pasta

Before serving, add:

¼ cup fresh basil cut in strips

Garnish with: Parmesan cheese, grated

Sauté onions in oil over medium-high heat in a large pan until translucent, about 4 minutes. Stir in garlic. Cook just until you smell it, about 30 seconds. Add tomatoes, pan drippings, parsley, sugar, pepper flakes, and salt. Simmer 15 minutes. Start boiling the water for pasta. Add cooked meatballs to the sauce and simmer, uncovered, for 10 minutes to heat through. Meanwhile, cook pasta according to package directions; drain. Stir in the cooked pasta and toss well to coat. Before serving, add the fresh basil strips. Garnish pasta and meatballs with grated Parmesan cheese.

Beef Stroganoff

Pauline Petcovic
Freedom, PA

3 pounds ground meat
2 medium onions (chopped)
2 cans mushroom soup
2 large cans mushrooms (drained)
4 tablespoons ketchup
2 teaspoons "Worcestershire Sauce"
1 (16 ounce) carton sour cream
Garlic salt

Brown meat and onions; Drain fat. Sprinkle with garlic salt to taste. Add mushrooms, ketchup, and Worcestershire sauce. Stir well. Stir in mushroom soup and sour cream. Heat well. Serve over rinsed cooked noodles. Serves 6-8 people

Beef Stroganoff

Mike Wilson
Bear Creek, NC
Nephew of Lisa Scott

1 ½ pounds sirloin steak
½ cup onion, chopped
3 small green onions, chopped
2 tablespoons butter
1 cup sliced mushrooms
1 (10 ¾ ounce) can cream of mushroom soup
1 (10 ¾ ounce) beefy mushroom soup
1 (10 ½ ounce) can beef consommé
Salt and pepper to taste
1 (8 ounce) sour cream
1 (8 ounce) package egg noodles, cooked, drained, buttered

Grill steak to medium rare doneness. Cut into bite size pieces, set aside. In large skillet cook onions in butter until tender, and then add mushrooms. Add soups and blend. Add meat to mixture. Add salt and pepper to taste. Cook for 15 minutes over medium heat. Add sour cream and egg noodles.

Sloppy Joes

Berta Scott
Co-owner
Bear Creek, NC

2 pounds ground round
1 cup chopped onions
2 tablespoons butter
1 teaspoon salt
½ teaspoon pepper
1 cup ketchup
1 tablespoon sugar
1 tablespoon vinegar
½ cup water
2 tablespoons prepared mustard
2 teaspoons Worcestershire sauce

Brown onions, beef and seasoning in butter. Stir in balance of ingredients. Simmer 20 to 25 minutes. Serve on warm buttered buns.

My children always enjoyed these at lunch.

Corned Beef Casserole

Olga Phillips
Bear Creek, NC

1 corned beef (no hash)
1 package frozen lima beans
1 small can of sauerkraut
1 can cream of mushroom soup
1 sliced onion

Cook lima beans. Add salt and sliced onions with 2 tablespoons of bacon fat. Drain when done.

Crumble corned beef, and then combine all ingredients in a greased casserole dish.

I prefer to top casserole with pastry or 'Butter Me Not' biscuits and bake for 20-minutes at 350°.

There is a destiny

That makes us brothers

None goes his way alone.

What you send into the life of others

Comes back into your own.

World Famous Meat Loaf

Douglas Stumpf
Son of Ethelda co-owner
Bear Creek, NC

2 pounds ground round steak
2 eggs
1 ½ cups bread crumbs
¾ cup ketchup
½ cup warm water
1 package onion soup mix
2 strips bacon (optional)
1 (8 ounce) can tomato sauce

Combine first seven ingredients and mix thoroughly. Put into loaf pan. Cover with strips of bacon if desired. Pour tomato sauce over loaf. Bake one hour at 350°. Serves 6.

Ruben Sandwiches

Berta Scott
Southern Supreme Co-owner
Bear Creek, NC

½ cup Thousand Island dressing
24 slices of Rye Bread
1 ½ cup chopped sour Kraut (well drained)
½ pound thinly sliced corned beef
¼ pound sliced Swiss cheese

Spread ½ teaspoon dressing on each slice of bread. Place 1 teaspoon Sour Kraut on each slice. Place a piece of corned beef and then Swiss cheese, cut to fit on each slice of bread. Place sandwiches on cookie sheet. Bake at 400° or until cheese melts.

One of my favorite sandwiches.

15 Minute Beef and Cream Gravy

Dawn Stumpf
Ethelda's daughter
Bear Creek, NC

Press or hammer stew beef cubes until tender. Sear in hot skillet. Cook one cup finely chopped onion in pan about 2 minutes.

Mix and add:
1 cup fat free Half & Half
2 tablespoons cornstarch
2 teaspoons bouillon granules
1 tablespoon Worcestershire sauce
½ cup fat free sour cream

Cook and stir until thickened into gravy. Add salt and pepper to taste. Add beef and simmer until done.

Rib Eye Steaks with Gorgonzola Horseradish Butter

Theresa O'Laughlin
Greensboro, NC

4 rib eye Steaks (20 to 22 ounces total)
1 tablespoon butter
½ cup chopped shallots
¼ cup dry white wine
1 cup heavy cream
1 cup Gorgonzola cheese (may substitute with blue cheese)
¼ cup prepared horseradish
1 tablespoon chopped parsley
Salt and pepper to taste

Season steaks with salt and pepper and set aside. In medium sauce pan, melt butter. Add shallots and sauté until soft and translucent. Add wine and reduce until almost dry. Add heavy cream, bring to simmer and reduce slightly. Whisk in cheese and cook until the cheese melts. Fold in the horseradish and season with salt and pepper. Remove from heat, add parsley, and keep warm. Grill steaks to desired doneness. Place on plates and spoon sauce on steaks.

Barbecue Meat Loaf

Clara Hunsucker
Bennett, NC

1 ½ pound ground beef

½ cup fresh bread crumbs

1 chopped onion

1 egg beaten

1 ½ teaspoons salt

¼ teaspoon pepper

½ can tomato sauce

Sauce:

1 ½ cans Tomato sauce

½ cup water

3 tablespoons vinegar

3 tablespoons brown sugar

3 tablespoons mustard

2 teaspoons Worcestershire sauce

Mix together for Meat Loaf: Beef, bread crumbs, onions, egg, salt, pepper and tomato sauce. Pour in loaf pan. Combine ingredients for sauce together and mix well. Pour over meat loaf and bake at 350° for 1 hour and 25 minutes.

Meat Loaf

Joe Vaughn
Bear Creek, NC
Lisa's niece's husband

2 pounds ground chuck

1 cup soft bread crumbs, loaf bread

1 cup ketchup

1 large onion, diced

1 egg, slightly beaten

1 teaspoon Worcestershire sauce

½ teaspoon salt

¼ teaspoon pepper

1 (8 ounce) can tomato sauce

Mix ground chuck, breadcrumbs, ketchup, onion, egg, Worcestershire sauce, salt, pepper, and tomato sauce. Press into greased baking dish. Bake at 300° for 1 hour.

Chicken Fried Steak With Cream Gravy

Sandra Cook
Siler City, NC
Office Employee

1 pound beef top round steak cut about ½ inch thick
All-purpose flour
3 tablespoons salad oil
½ cup water
1 cup milk
1 teaspoon salt
⅛ teaspoon pepper
3 cups hot mashed potatoes

On cutting board, coat top round steak with 3 tablespoons flour. With a meat mallet, pound both sides of meat well, cut into 4 pieces. In skillet over medium high heat and in hot salad oil, cook steaks 3-5 minutes each side, until well-browned and of desired doneness. Remove to platter-keep warm. In cup with fork, mix water with 2 tablespoons flour until smooth. Gradually stir flour into dripping in skillet stirring and scraping until brown bits are loose from bottom of pan. Stir in milk, salt and pepper and cook over medium heat, stirring constantly until gravy thickens and boils. Serve the chicken fried steak with mashed potatoes and serve the hot gravy in a gravy boat.

Chicken

Spinach With Walnuts Chicken

Theresa O'Laughlin
Greensboro, NC

½ cup mayonnaise
⅓ cup chopped walnuts
1 tablespoon plain bread crumbs
1 cup loosely packed, chopped fresh spinach
2 tablespoon grated Parmesan cheese
6 boneless/skinless chicken breast

Preheat oven to 425°. In medium bowl, combine mayonnaise, walnuts, bread crumbs, spinach and parmesan cheese. On baking sheet, arrange chicken. Evenly coat with the spinach mixture. Bake 20 minutes or until chicken is baked through.

Chicken Quick

Gen Murray
Bennett, NC

4 to 6 skinless chicken breast
1 teaspoon apricot preserves
1 (8 ounce) bottle Wishbone French dressing, plus
⅓ bottle of water

Place chicken in long baking dish. Spread apricot preserves on top of each piece. Shake French dressing and water to mix. Pour over chicken and bake one hour in 350° oven.

Helpful Hint

Egg whites need to be at room temperature for greater volume when whipped, especially when making meringues.

Chicken Dumplins

Ruby Brady
Bennett, NC

Boil chicken until tender. Remove chicken and cut into chunks. Set aside. Add 1 stick butter and a can of chicken broth.

Make dough as for biscuits. Bring broth to a boil. Pinch dough into chunks and add to boiling broth. Add chicken and cook until dough is done.

Crispy Chicken Strips

Elmo Phillips
Employee

4 boneless, skinless chicken breasts
¾ cup mashed potato flakes, dry
¾ cup seasoned bread crumbs
2 eggs
3 tablespoons vegetable oil

Flatten chicken to ½-inch thickness; cut into 1-inch strips. In a shallow bowl, combine potato flakes and bread crumbs. Dip chicken in beaten egg, then in potato mixture. Heat oil in skillet over medium heat. Cook chicken in oil 2-3 minutes on each side, or until golden. Yield: 4 servings

Chicken Puffs

Ruby Brady
Bennett, NC

4 boneless chicken breast, boiled and chopped
1 package cream cheese-8 oz. softened
Dash of sage
2 cans crescent rolls
½ bag Pepperidge Farm herb stuffing mix
3 to 4 tablespoons margarine (melted)

Mix chicken, cream cheese, and sage. Form into 16 balls about 1-inch wide. Place ball into crescent roll. Seal edges and roll in hand and slightly flatten ball. Roll ball in margarine, and then in stuffing mix. Bake 10 to 15 minutes in 350 degree oven.

Gravy for chicken puffs:
1 can cream of chicken soup
1 cup milk

Simmer until hot. Serve over individual puffs.

Chicken With Cheesy Mushroom Sauce

Carl Horst
Niagara Falls, NY

4 to 6 boneless skinless chicken breasts
1 small can of mushrooms-drained
1 can cream of mushroom soup
1 pint heavy cream
1 cup milk
1 teaspoon oregano
2 cloves of garlic finely chopped
2 tablespoons. grated parmesan cheese
1 pound of linguini
1 bag frozen broccoli florets 12 oz

Mix first 8 ingredients together in an oven safe dish. Bake at 350° for 1-½ hours. When chicken is almost done, cook linguini to desired doneness. Add broccoli to linguini during last 5 minutes of cooking.

Remove chicken from cheesy sauce. Pour sauce over linguini and broccoli and toss to coat. Serve with additional parmesan cheese. Serves 4 to 6

Poppy Seed Chicken

Lorrie Moore
Bonlee, NC
Showroom Staff

Jamie Brady
Bennett, NC
Ethelda's daughter

3 chicken breasts
1 can cream of mushroom soup
1 can cream of celery soup
1 (8 ounce) container sour cream
1 stack pack Ritz crackers, crushed
1 stick butter, melted
3 tablespoons poppy seeds

Remove skin and fat from chicken. Cook and remove bones. Cut into bite size pieces. In a large casserole dish, mix soups and sour cream. Add chicken pieces and mix well. Mix crushed crackers and poppy seeds. Spread on top of soup mixture. Drizzle melted butter over top. Bake 350° for 35 minutes.

This is a very popular recipe and was submitted by several people.

Cashew Chicken Bake

Rae Scott
Bear Creek, NC

1 cup sliced celery
1 medium onion, chopped
2 cans cream of mushroom soup
1 can mushrooms, or 1 package fresh mushrooms
½ cup (or more) cashews
2-3 cups shredded chicken
1 package chow mein noodles

Cook the celery and onion in a little butter until soft (if using fresh mushrooms, cook them with the onions and celery). Add the soups, cashews, canned mushrooms, and chicken. Mix well. Turn into a 2 quart casserole. Bake, uncovered, 350°, for about 30 minutes. Add ¾ of the bag of chow mein noodles. Mix well. Return to oven and bake about 10 more minutes. Top with the remaining noodles and bake 5 minutes more.

King Ranch Chicken

Deborah P. Stephenson
Carthage, NC
Showroom Staff

Cook 2 ½-3 lb chicken, remove bones and skin and cut into small pieces (or use two cans white meat chicken).

Cook ½ cup chopped green pepper and ½ cup chopped onion in butter or margarine until tender in large sauce pan. Stir in 1 can Cream of Chicken soup and 1 can Cream of Mushroom soup, 1 can Rotel Tomatoes with green chilies, ½ teaspoon chili powder and garlic salt or powder to taste and 1 cup grated cheddar cheese and chicken.

Spray 3 quart baking dish (13x9x2) with cooking spray and cover bottom with flour tortillas (they are in the dairy case with canned biscuits, etc) Cover with chicken, soup mixture. Cover with more tortillas (break them into approx 2 inch pieces to cover evenly, add more chicken, soup mixture). Top with ½ cup sharp grated cheddar cheese and sprinkle paprika over top.

Bake at 325° for 40 minutes or until hot and bubbly and cheese is browned.

Can be frozen before or after cooking.

Spicy Chicken Breasts

Elmo Phillips
Employee

Ingredients:
1 boneless chicken breast, halved
1 teaspoon sesame oil
2 teaspoons Dijon mustard
1 tablespoon low-fat sour cream
2 tablespoons chopped onion
½ tablespoon chopped garlic
½ teaspoon paprika
Fresh ground pepper to taste

1. Preheat the oven to 375°. Spray a small shallow baking dish with nonstick cooking spray and place the chicken in the baking dish.

2. Mix together the sesame oil, mustard, sour cream, onion, and garlic in a small bowl. Brush the sour cream mixture on both sides of each breast with a pastry brush.

3. Sprinkle the chicken with paprika and black pepper and bake for about 30 minutes.

4. To microwave, cover the baking dish loosely with plastic wrap. Microwave for 6-8 minutes on high or until the juices run clear. Be sure to rotate the dish halfway through the cooking time for even cooking.

Crusted Chicken Breast

Berta Scott
Founder and Co-Owner Southern
Supreme

2 boneless skinless chicken breast halves

Blend 2 egg whites, 2 teaspoons cornstarch and juice of ½ lemon.

Combine:
1 cup coarse dry bread crumbs
1 teaspoon chopped fresh parsley
1 teaspoon salt
½ tablespoon ground black pepper
Zest of 1 lemon

Sauté chicken in 3 tablespoons olive oil

Trim excess fat from chicken, slice lengthwise down the center. Lightly pound each piece (use plastic bag). Blend egg whites, cornstarch and lemon juice in a shallow dish. Add breadcrumbs, lemon juice, salt and pepper in second dish. (Make crumbs fine dry in baking sheet for best results). Dip chicken in prepared egg whites, cornstarch mixture; then to crumb dish pat crumbs on both sides. In nonstick pan, heat the oil. Sauté chicken on both sides for about 3 or 4 minutes each side until brown. Roast chicken in the same pan. Put in oven 8-10 minutes on 400°.

Moravian Chicken Pie

Audrey Poe
Bear Creek, NC

Pastry:
2 cups sifted all-purpose flour
1 teaspoon salt
¾ cup Crisco
6 to 8 tablespoons cold water

Filling:
3 cups finely chopped chicken
¼ cup flour
1 ¼ cup diluted chicken broth
Salt and pepper to taste

For the pastry: mix flour, salt, Crisco and water into soft dough. Handle as little as possible. Roll out half the dough to fit a greased 10 inch pie plate. Mix chicken, flour, chicken broth, salt, and pepper. Place filling in the shell. Cover with top crust made from other half of dough. Pinch edges of crust together to seal. Flute around the edges. Bake at 375-400° for 45-60 minutes.

Chicken Divan

Audrey Poe
Bear Creek, NC

1 (10-ounce) package frozen broccoli cooked and drained
⅓ cup milk
3 to 4 servings of cooked chicken
1 can cream of chicken soup
½ cup shredded cheddar cheese

Arrange broccoli in 1 ½ quart shallow baking dish; top with chicken. Blend soup and milk together then pour over above. Sprinkle with cheese; bake at 450° for 15 minutes or until hot. Yield: 3-4 servings

Easy Baked Chicken Breast

Gail Scott
Bear Creek, NC
Co-owner

1 ⅓ cup French fried Onions
1 pound boneless skinless chicken breast
1 egg, beaten

Crush onions in plastic bag. Dip chicken into egg then coat in onion crumbs. Bake 20 minutes in 400° oven until cooked through.

Can Chicken Pie

Dottie Josey
Employee
Bear Creek, NC

2 cans white chicken chunks (drained)
1 large can cream of chicken soup
1 large can mixed vegetables drained
(optional)

Topping: 1 cup self rising flour and 1 cup
milk

Mix first three ingredients and put in
casserole dish. Mix topping and pour
over top. Bake in preheated 350˚ oven
until top is brown.

Parmesan Chicken Cutlets

Dottie Josey
Employee
Bear Creek, NC

¼ cup grated Parmesan cheese
2 tablespoons Italian-style breadcrumbs
⅛ teaspoon paprika
4 skinless, boneless chicken breasts

Preheat oven to 400˚. In a resealable
plastic bag, combine cheese, crumbs,
and paprika, shake well. Transfer
mixture to plate; dip each chicken breast
in cheese mixture, turning to coat all
sides. Arrange on nonstick baking sheet;
bake until chicken cooks thoroughly,
approximately 20-25 minutes.

My Favorite Chicken Pie

Mary John Resch
Siler City, NC
Food Editor
Chatham News

2 cups all purpose flour
1 teaspoon salt
⅔ cup Crisco
Several tablespoons of ice water

1 (3 pound) fryer
½ cup all purpose flour
1 (5 ounce) Can of evaporated milk
½ cup margarine
2 cups chicken broth
Salt, pepper, and lemon juice to taste

Stew fryer in salted water until tender. Remove meat from bone and tear into bite sized pieces, discarding skin.

Melt margarine and add ½ cup flour, stirring to make a roux. Add chicken broth. Taste and add salt, pepper, and lemon juice to taste. Stirring constantly, cook until thickened; remove from heat and add evaporated milk. Stir in chicken. Taste again and add more seasonings if necessary.

Prepare crust:
Sift flour with salt. Cut in Crisco. Add ice water until proper consistency to roll out. If you prefer use a refrigerated crust. Divide crust and place half in bottom of 8x8 casserole. Fill with chicken mixture. Top with remaining crust. Prick several times with a fork so steam can escape. Bake at 350° for 45 minutes or until golden brown and bubbly. Serves 6

You can make this without the bottom crust if you prefer.

Chicken Italiano

Wendy Paschal
Siler City, NC

2 tablespoons butter, melted
1 ½ teaspoons Italian dressing mix (I use Good Seasons mix)
4 boneless chicken breasts
1 can cream of mushroom soup
3 ounces softened cream cheese
4 ounce can mushrooms, (undrained)
½ cup white wine

Mix butter and dressing mix, sauté chicken in the seasoned butter, turning once. Place chicken in baking dish. Combine soup with cream cheese, mushrooms and wine; pour over chicken. Bake at 350° until done, approximately 50 minutes.

No Peak Chicken

Frankie Meuller
Siler City, NC
Special Hairdresser friend of Berta

1 can cream of mushroom soup
1 can cream of celery soup
1 can water
1 box "Uncle Ben's" original wild rice
1 can milk
1 envelope "Lipton" French onion soup
4-6 boneless, skinless chicken breasts

Preheat oven to 400°. Spray baking dish with "Pam" or olive oil.

Mix can soups, wild rice with its flavor packet with the water and milk. Pour into baking dish. Place chicken into dish on top of mixture.

Sprinkle the top with the envelope of "Lipton" French onion soup.

Cover with aluminum foil and bake for 2 hours. (No Peaking!)

After 2 hours remove from oven and serve with garlic bread and salad.

Creamy Chicken Enchiladas

Wendy Paschal
Siler City, NC

1 medium onion, chopped
1 (4 ½ ounce) can chopped green chilies
1 (8 ounce) package cream cheese (cubed)
1 teaspoon butter
3 ½ cups cooked chicken, cubed, season to taste
2 (8 ounce) packages Monterey Jack cheese (grated)
2 cups heavy whipping cream

Melt butter and sauté onion 5 minutes; add green chilies and sauté 1 minute. Add chicken and cubed cream cheese stirring constantly until cream cheese melts. Put 2-3 tablespoons of chicken mixture in center of tortilla; wrap and place seam side down in 9x13 (or larger) baking dish. Put cheese on top and drizzle with whipping cream. Bake at 350° for approximately 45 minutes.

Garlic Chicken with Sweet Roasted Pepper

Sandy Brown
Sandy & Co.
Bear Creek, NC

4 boneless, skinless chicken breast
Salt and Pepper
2 tablespoons vegetable oil
1 small onion, sliced thin
6 garlic cloves, sliced thin
1 (12 ounce) can roasted peppers
2 teaspoons sugar
1 ½ cups low-sodium chicken broth
¼ cup chopped fresh basil
2 tablespoons unsalted butter

Pat chicken dry, season with salt and pepper; heat oil in large pan over medium heat. Cook chicken until brown, remove from heat. Remove chicken from pan and set aside. Add onions to fat in pan and cook until brown. Stir in garlic and cook until tender, add peppers, sugar, broth and place browned chicken back into pan and bring all to boil. Reduce heat to medium and simmer until chicken is cooked. Remove chicken and place on serving dish. Simmer remaining mixture until thickened. Pour over chicken and serve.

Chicken Breast in Wine Sauce

Carl Horst
Niagara Falls, NY

4 boneless skinless chicken breast cut into cubes
1 teaspoon salt
1 tablespoon paprika
⅛ teaspoon pepper
1 tablespoon butter
Dash of rosemary
1 chicken bouillon cube dissolved in 2-tablespoons of hot water
1 cup Rose' wine ("Canei Mellow Rose' Wine)
2 teaspoons chopped onions
1 tablespoon cold water
1 tablespoon cornstarch

Shake chicken pieces in a bag with salt, paprika, and pepper. Sauté' chicken in butter in skillet: browning slowly. Sprinkle with rosemary. Add bouillon with water, wine, and onion to skillet. Cover and simmer (low heat) until chicken is cooked and tender about (20 minutes). Blend water with cornstarch, stir into liquid in skillet. Cook, stirring gently until sauce boils and thickens. Serve over rice or noodles.

The clock of life is wound
but once

And no man can tell what day
or hour

The hands will stop.

Now is the only time
you have left,

So live it with a will

Don't wait until tomorrow.

The hands may then be still.

Old-Fashioned Chicken Pot Pie

Elmo Phillips
Bear Creek
Kitchen Staff

⅓ cup butter or margarine
⅓ cup all-purpose flour
1 garlic clove, minced
½ teaspoon salt
¼ teaspoon pepper
1 ½ cups water
⅔ cup milk
2 teaspoon chicken bouillon granules
2 cups cubed cooked chicken
1 cup frozen mixed vegetables
Pastry:
1 ⅔ cups all-purpose flour
2 teaspoons celery seed
1 package (8 ounce) cream cheese, cubed
⅓ cup cold butter or margarine

In a saucepan, melt butter. Stir in flour, garlic, salt and pepper until blended. Gradually stir in water, milk and bouillon. Bring to boil; boil and stir for 2 minutes. Remove from the heat. Stir in chicken and vegetables; set aside. For pastry, combine flour and celery seed in a bowl. Cut in cream cheese and butter until crumbly. Work mixture by hand until dough forms a ball. On a lightly floured surface, roll ⅔ of dough into a 12 inch square. Transfer to an 8 inch square baking dish. Pour filling into crust. Roll remaining dough into a 9 inch square; place over filling. Trim, seal and flute edges. Cut slits in pastry. Bake at 425° for 30-35 minutes or until crust is golden brown and filling is bubbly. Yield: 6 servings.

Never Fail Chicken & Dumplings

Marilyn Sehen
Sanford, NC

1 ½ cups all-purpose flour

½ teaspoon of salt

3 tablespoons shortening

1 large egg lightly beaten

5 tablespoons cold water

½ teaspoon black pepper

Broth from one chicken or 3 cans chicken broth

1 can cream of chicken soup

1 roasted chicken from deli (remove meat from bone)

Combine flour and salt, cut in shortening with pastry blender until mixture is crumbly. Gently stir in egg and cold water. Form dough into ball and knead 3-4 times.

Combine broth and black pepper together in pot. Bring to a rolling boil over medium heat. Add chicken soup.

Meanwhile roll dough to ¼ inch thickness on floured surface. Cut dough into 2 x 3 or 4-inch strips, drop several dough strips at a time into boiling broth. Reduce heat to medium and cook uncovered for 7 minutes. Add chicken and cook 4-6 minutes or until dumplings are tender and chicken is heated, stirring occasionally. Yield 4 serving.

Pork

Pork Tenderloin with Southern Supreme Red Pepper Jelly

Berta Scott
Southern Supreme Co-owner
Bear Creek, NC

This pork dish is very easy and delicious!

2-3 pound pork Tenderloin
1 jar Southern Supreme Hot Pepper Jelly

Pour over the pork tenderloin the hot pepper jelly; completely cover with at least ⅔ of the jar. Place in plastic bag and refridge over night. Heat oven to 350°, wrap roast in tin foil and bake until tender. Usually about 1 ½ hours. The last 30 to 40 minutes baste with the hot pepper jelly and remove the tin foil and return to heat and let brown. The jelly will give the roast enough salt and seasoning.

Pork Chops And Rice

Karen Zimmerman
Bear Creek, NC

1 can cream of mushroom soup
1 can cream of celery soup
1 can cream of chicken soup
2 ½ to 3 cups Minute Rice, uncooked
1 can mushrooms, optional
4-6 pork chops

Preheat the oven to 450°. In a large skillet brown the chops on both sides. Remove from heat and drain excess fat. Place the chops in a 9x13x2 inch baking pan. In a bowl combine the soups, rice and mushrooms together. Mix well. Pour the mixture over the chops. Bake uncovered, for 30-45 minutes or until the rice is tender. Let stand for 10 minutes. Serve warm

Grilled Pork Chops

Mae Maness
Snow Camp, NC

1" thick boneless pork chops
Accent'
meat tenderizer
Salt & pepper to taste

Lightly charcoal 30 minutes before ready to cook. Sprinkle pork chops with Accent'. Put meat tenderizer, salt and pepper. Let sit 20 minutes. Cook until done. This is delicious!

Stuffed Porkchops

Olga Phillips
Bear Creek, NC

6 thick pork chops with pockets
4 slices of crisp toast (cubed)
1 stalk of celery (diced)
8 pimiento stuffed green olives (diced)
1 small onion
1 teaspoon garlic salt
½ teaspoon parsley
1 teaspoon pepper
½ teaspoon basil
1 can tomato soup

Slice pork chops to form pockets. Brown pork chops in the skillet.

Mix toast, celery, olives, onions, garlic salt and pepper. Secure pork chops with toothpicks.

In a large pot or pressure cooker, combine tomato soup, 2 cups of water and any remaining seasonings.

Add pork chops. You may wish to add potatoes and carrots.

Cook over medium heat for 1 hour. Serve over white rice or mashed potatoes.

Grilled Mustard-Glazed Pork Loin

Allen Zimmerman
Bear Creek, NC
Show Staff

Dijon and yellow mustard also works well in the glaze, but make certain to use apple jelly (not apple butter). Look for a pork roast with about ¼- inch fat on top and tie roast at 1-inch intervals to ensure an even shape.

½ cup mustard
6 tablespoons apple jelly
2 tablespoons dark brown sugar
2 tablespoons extra virgin olive oil
1 large garlic clove minced
2 teaspoons minced fresh thyme
½ teaspoon salt
¾ teaspoon salt
¾ teaspoon pepper

1 boneless pork loin roast (2 ½ to 3 pounds)

Heat all burners on high, covered for 15 minutes. Prepare glaze and save ½ of glaze for serving. Rub ½ into pork; oil cooking grate. Place roast on grill and brown 15 to 20 minutes. Turn fat-side of roast and keep on brushing with glaze. Close cover to grill. Lift to brush glaze on every 10 minutes. Cook about 35 to 50 minutes and let rest for 15 to 30 minutes. When sliced, spoon the reserved mixture over top. (Could cook in oven) at 350°, cook or time according to size. Cover with tin foil; take off to brown last few minutes.

185

Orange-Ginger Glaze

Randy Scott
Bear Creek, NC

4 bone-in center-cut pork chops, about
1-inch thick salt and pepper
2 tablespoons vegetable oil
½ small onion, chopped fine
½ teaspoon ground ginger
1 cup juice plus 2-strips zest from 3 or 4 oranges
½ cup low-sodium chicken broth
¼ cup packed dark brown sugar
1 tablespoon hot sauce
1 tablespoon unsalted butter

1.Pat chops dry with paper towels and season with salt and pepper. Over medium high heat, heat 1tablespoon oil in a large skillet. Heat until oil starts to smoke. Add chops and cook until well browned, about 4 minutes per side.

Transfer to plate.

2.Add remaining oil and onion to skillet and cook until lightly brown, about 3 minutes. Stir in ginger and cook until fragrant, about 30 seconds. Stir in juice, zest, broth, sugar, and hot sauce, scraping up any browned bits from bottom of pan. Cook until sauce thickens slightly, about 3 minutes.

3.Return chops and any accumulated juices to skillet. Simmer, turning once or twice, until sauce glazes chops and meat registers 145°, for 3 to 5 minutes. Transfer chops to platter. Off heat, whisk butter into glaze and season with salt and pepper. Spoon glaze over the chops. Serves 4

Fish

Tuna Confetti

Lisa Scott
Bear Creek, NC

2 cans tuna in spring water
½ cup grated apple
¼ cup grated carrot
¼ cup chopped zucchini
¼ cup chopped red and green bell peppers
¼ cup chopped onion
¼ cup chopped tomato
¼ cup frozen green peas
2 boiled egg whites, grated
Mayo to taste

Squeeze out as much water as possible from tuna before breaking it up. Add rest of ingredients and toss with the mayo.

Grilled Salmon

Eric Wilson
Bear Creek, NC
Nephew's Son of Lisa Scott

8 ounce salmon filet
¼ cup Italian dressing
½ cup 'Lawry's' 30-minute marinade
¼ cup lemon juice

Put salmon in zip lock bag. Combine dressing, marinade and lemon juice. Pour over salmon and seal. Let marinade for at least 4 hours. Grill at 350° and cook until desired doneness.

Crispy Almond/ Parmesan Tilapia

Kate Henry
Charleston, SC

1 pound tilapia
⅔ cup Italian bread crumbs
1 cup slivered almonds
½ teaspoon paprika
¼ cup milk
1 egg
¼ cup garlic flavored parmesan cheese
¼ cup olive oil
Salt to taste

Preheat olive oil in skillet on medium heat. Mix together bread crumbs, paprika and parmesan. In a separate bowl, mix milk and egg. Scatter almonds on a plate. Dip tilapia in milk/egg mixture then coat with crumb mixture and roll in almonds. Increase skillet heat to medium-high. Place 'tilapia' in skillet and sauté for 5 minutes on each side.

Crunchy Catfish

Ricky Scott
Son of Hoyt and Berta Scott
Husband of Gail Scott

½ cup Miracle Whip salad dressing
1 ½ teaspoons dried Italian seasoning
4 large catfish fillets
2 cups crushed potato chips

Combine salad dressing and seasoning blend.

Spread mixture on both sides of fish.

Dredge in crushed chips.

Bake at 350° for 30 minutes or until fish flakes easily with a fork.

Thought For Today

Watch your thoughts; they become words.

Watch your words; they become actions.

Watch your actions; they become habits.

Watch your habits; they become character.

Watch your character; it becomes your destiny.

--- Frank Outlaw

Breads & Breakfast

6 Week Bran Muffins

Berta Scott
Bear Creek, NC

1 box Raisin Bran cereal (15 ounces or 8 cups)
1 quart buttermilk
1 cup vegetable oil
2 ½ cups sugar
5 cups flour plus 5 teaspoons baking powder
4 slightly beaten eggs
2 teaspoons salt

Combine all. Cover and refrigerate at least 6 hours before using. Fill muffin tins ⅔ full. Bake at 375° for 15-20 minutes. Mixture will keep in fridge 6 weeks. Makes 6 dozen.

Cornbread

Ethelda Stumpf
Co-owner
Bear Creek, NC

1 cup self rising cornmeal
¼ cup self-rising flour
1 teaspoon salt
1 tablespoon sugar
¼ teaspoon baking soda
2 eggs
2 tablespoons canola oil
1 cup buttermilk

Mix cornmeal, flour, salt, sugar and baking soda in mixing bowl. Add eggs, buttermilk, and canola oil.

To prepare in iron skillet, heat on top of stove. Add 3 tablespoons canola oil and sprinkle with flour. Pour cornbread batter in skillet and bake 400° approximately 30 minutes.

Everlasting Apple Muffins

Elmo Phillips
Employee
Bear Creek, NC

1 cup butter or margarine

2 cups sugar

2 eggs

1 cup chopped nuts

3 teaspoons cinnamon

2 teaspoons baking soda

1 teaspoon allspice

½ teaspoon salt

4 cups flour

2 cups applesauce

Cream together the butter and sugar. Add eggs, nuts (if desired), cinnamon, soda, allspice and salt. Mix well. Add flour and applesauce, mixing thoroughly. Fill greased muffin pans about half full. Bake 325° until done for 10-15 minutes. The batter will keep for six weeks in the refrigerator and used as needed, or all muffins may be baked and frozen. This recipe will make 40-50 muffins.

Sweeter Muffins

Joanne Diggs
Gastonia, NC

1 egg

½ cup milk

¼ cup oil

1 ½ cup plain flour

½ cup sugar

2 teaspoons baking powder

½ teaspoon salt

Grease muffin cups. Beat egg with fork. Stir in milk and oil. Add flour, sugar, baking powder and salt. Stir to moisten. Fill cup ⅔ full. Bake 20-25 minutes at 400°. Serves 12.

Monkey Bread

Pam Fields
Bear Creek, NC

3 cans Hungry Jack Biscuits

1 cup sugar

2 teaspoons cinnamon

Put sugar and cinnamon in 'Ziploc' bag. Cut biscuits into quarters and put in bag with mixture. Shake, coating all biscuits. Put in 'Bundt' pan sprayed with 'Pam'. Melt 1 stick of margarine and 1 cup brown sugar in saucepan. Boil 1 minute. Pour over biscuits. Cook 350° for 35-40 minutes. Let sit in pan for 15 minutes; turn out on platter. Pinch and eat.

Cream Cheese Carrot Bread

Frances Brewer
Asheboro, NC

2 (3 ounce) packages cream cheese
softened
¼ cup sugar
1 large egg
1 teaspoon grated orange rind
1 (15.6 ounce) package carrot bread mix
¾ cup water
¼ cup orange juice
3 tablespoons oil
1 large egg
⅓ cup sliced almonds
3 tablespoons orange marmalade

Beat first four ingredients at medium
speed with an electric mixer until smooth.

Combine bread mix and next four
ingredients, stirring just until moistened.
Pour half into a greased and floured 9x5
inch loaf pan. Spoon the cream cheese
mixture evenly over batter, top with
remaining batter. Sprinkle with almonds.

Bake at 350° for 60-65 minutes or
until wooden pick inserted in center
comes clean. Cool in pan or wire rack
15 minutes, remove from pan and cool
on wire rack. Stir marmalade in a small
saucepan over medium heat until melted.
Brush over top as desired. Yield 1 (9 inch)
loaf.

Mexican Corn Bread

Sue Farlow
Raleigh, NC

1 ½ cups self rising corn meal
2 eggs (may use egg substitute for one
egg)
½ cup oil
1 cup cream style corn (small can)
⅔ cup sour cream
½ cup finely chopped onions
1 cup grated cheddar cheese
Dash hot sauce

Mix all ingredients together well and
pour into a hot greased pan (8x8x1 ½).

Bake 45-50 minutes in 350° oven.

Pumpkin Bread Pudding

Coastal Development & Realty
Holden Beach, NC

1 (15 ounce) can pumpkin pie mix

2 cups half-and-half

⅓ cup dark brown sugar

2 large eggs

10 ounces of egg bread (cut into cubes)

½ cup raisins (golden/black)

½ cup caramel sauce

3 tablespoons powdered sugar

In a bowl, whisk together the first four ingredients. Fold in bread and raisins. Transfer to baking dish and let bread soak for 15 minutes. Bake at 350° for approximately 40 minutes. Remove. Dust with powdered sugar. Serve warm with caramel sauce or whipped cream. Serves 6.

K&W Biscuits

Evelyn Cheek
Asheboro, NC

5 cups self-rising flour

1 cup "Crisco"

3 tablespoons sugar

2 packages of yeast dissolved in 6-tablespoons warm water

1 ½ cup buttermilk

Mix well and refrigerate. Make and bake as regular biscuits. Keep in the refrigerator. Take out and make biscuits as needed

Angel Biscuits

In memory of Allene Watts
Sister of Berta and Ethelda
Siler City, NC

5 cups self rising flour, unsifted

¼ cup sugar

1 cup shortening

1 package dry yeast

2 tablespoons warm water

2 cups buttermilk

Mix sugar and flour, cut in shortening. Dissolve yeast in warm water. Add with buttermilk to flour mixture. Mix well; turn out on floured board, if needed. Add more flour to make 5 quarts dough. Roll out and cut. Bake at 400° for 20 minutes or until done. Keep dough in refrigerator for 2 weeks.

Zucchini Bread

Gail Scott
Bear Creek, NC

3 eggs
1 cup oil
2 cups grated zucchini
2 teaspoons vanilla
3 cups flour
2 cups sugar
1 teaspoon salt
1 teaspoon baking soda
1 teaspoon cinnamon
¼ teaspoon baking powder
1 cup chopped nuts

Mix together eggs, oil, zucchini and vanilla. Set aside. Mix together remaining ingredients; add egg mixture. Bake at 350° for 1 hour for 2 large loaves or 35-45 minutes for 3-4 small loaves.

Helpful Hint

When in doubt, always sift flour before measuring.

Cheddar Cheese Biscuits

Deborah Pickard Stephenson
Carthage, NC
Showroom Employee

2 cups all purpose flour
1 tablespoon baking powder
½ teaspoon salt
¼ cup shortening
1 egg beaten
¾ cup milk
½ cup shredded sharp cheddar cheese
1 tablespoon melted butter
Poppy seeds

In medium bowl, stir together flour, baking powder and salt. Cut in shortening until it resembles coarse crumbs. Make a well in center. In a small bowl combine egg and milk, then add all at once to dry mixture; add cheese. Stir just until dough clings together. Knead gently on lightly floured surface for 10-12 strokes. Roll dough to ½ inch thickness. Cut with a 2 ½ inch biscuit cutter; dipping cutter in flour between cuts. Place on ungreased baking sheet. Brush the tops with melted butter and sprinkle with poppy seeds. Bake 450° for 10-12 minutes or until golden. Makes 10 biscuits.

Sour Dough Bread

Denise Holt
Showroom Staff
Bear Creek, NC

STARTER:

1 teaspoon yeast in cup warm water

2 teaspoons sugar

2 cups warm water

2 ½ cups flour

Cover with damp cloth and leave at room temperature for 5 days, then store in glass container in refrigerator. Each time you use the starter, add to the jar:

1 cup flour, ⅓ cup sugar, 1 cup milk

Stir, replace in refrigerator. Stir every day; if you use, remember to feed; add the above.

Sour Dough Bread:

1 cup sour dough starter

4 tablespoons oil

1 package yeast in ½ cup water

2 cups warm water

2 cups flour

½ tablespoon salt

Monkey Bread Coffee Cake

Gail Scott
Co-owner
Bear Creek, NC

2 large 'Grand' canned biscuit dough

¾ cup granulated sugar

2 ½ tablespoons cinnamon

¾ cup butter

½ cup granulated sugar

½ cup packed brown sugar

1 cup nuts

Cut biscuit into quarters. Combine ¾ cup granulated sugar, 2 ½ tablespoons cinnamon in bowl. Roll dough in mixture and place in greased pan. Combine balance of ingredients and bring to boil, pour over biscuit dough. Bake 350° for 35-40 minutes.

Jalapeno Corn Muffins

Sara Scott
Employee

Room temperature 2 sticks butter
1 cup all-purpose flour
1 cup yellow cornmeal
¼ cup sugar
1 tablespoon baking powder
1 teaspoon salt
4 large eggs
¾ cups whole milk
¼ cup corn oil
2 tablespoons minced seeded jalapeno chilies
2 cups fresh corn kernels or frozen thawed (about 9 ounces)

Mix all ingredients well. Pour in a skillet. Bake at 420° for 25 minutes.

I enjoy cooking this for my family.

Best-Ever Bread

Dawn Stumpf
Bear Creek, NC

1 cup water
⅓ cup oil
⅓ cup sugar
1 egg, slightly beaten
1 teaspoon salt
3 cups bread flour
1 package rapid rise yeast
2 tablespoons dry milk

Put each ingredient into a bread machine in the order given and set machine for at least 3 hours to make and bake using a light crust setting. Can be hand mixed to make the best rolls ever by mixing, letting it rise, punch down and form rolls. Let rolls rise and bake 350° for about 25 minutes.

Raisin Bran Muffins

Ethelda Stumpf
Co-owner
Bear Creek, NC

3 cups Raisin Bran cereal
⅔ cup sugar
1 ⅔ cup plain flour
1 ⅔ teaspoons baking soda
⅔ teaspoon salt
⅓ cup cooking oil
1 ⅓ cup buttermilk
2 eggs

Mix dry ingredients and oil. Add eggs and buttermilk. Spoon into greased; muffin tins. Bake at 375° for 20 minutes.

Banana Muffins

Ethelda Stumpf
Co-owner
Bear Creek, NC

1 ¾ cup plain flour
¾ cup sugar
1 ½ teaspoons cream of tarter
¾ teaspoon baking soda
½ teaspoon salt
2 ripe bananas-mashed
2 eggs beaten
½ cup vegetable oil
¾ cup pecans, chopped fine

Combine dry ingredients. Make a well in the middle. Combine rest of ingredients. Add liquid ingredients. Mix only enough to moisten dry ingredients. Spoon into greased muffin tins or muffin papers. Bake 400° for 15 minutes.
Yield: 12-18 muffins

Applesauce Walnut Bread

Faye Oldham
Robbins, NC

6 cups flour-approximate
1 cup whole bran cereal
1 cup firmly packed brown sugar
½ teaspoon salt
1 teaspoon cinnamon
2 packages yeast
½ cup milk
⅓ cup water
⅓ cup oleo
1 cup applesauce-room temperature
2 eggs-room temperature
1 cup walnuts

Mix 1 cup flour, cereal, brown sugar, salt, baking soda, cinnamon and dissolved yeast. Heat milk, water and oleo to 120-130°, add to dry ingredients and beat 2 minutes at medium speed. Add applesauce, eggs and 1 cup flour. Beat at high speed 2 minutes. Stir in walnuts and enough additional flour to make soft dough. Cover, let rise in warm place until doubled, about 1 hour.

Stir batter down, divide equally between two well-greased 1 ¼ quart casseroles. Cover, let rise until double in bulk, about 1 hour. Bake at 350° for 35 minutes or until done. Remove from casseroles and cool.

Banana Bread

Karen Zimmerman
Bear Creek, NC

1 stick unsalted butter
1 ⅓ cups dark brown sugar
3 large eggs beaten
1 teaspoon vanilla extract
1 teaspoon baking soda
¼ cup sour cream
¾ cup whole-wheat flour
¾ cup all-purpose flour
¼ teaspoon salt
3 overripe mashed bananas

Pre-heat oven to 350° Grease a 9x5x3 ½ inch loaf pan. Cream butter and sugar; add eggs and vanilla and beat until light. Stir in baking soda and sour cream. Mix together flours and salt. Add to batter and mix. Add bananas and mix well. Pour into loaf pan. Bake about one hour until a tester inserted into the middle comes out clean.

Cheese Biscuits

Gail Scott
Co-Owner
Bear Creek, NC

Easy to Make:

1 cup of butter
8 ounces sharp cheddar cheese, grated
1 cup sour cream
2 cups of self-rising flour

Melt butter and add grated cheese. Stir; cook 2-3 minutes. Add sour cream and mix well. Stir in flour; fill greased miniature muffin pan ⅔ full. Bake at 350° for 20-25 minutes. Serve hot.

Helpful Hint

To keep boiled syrup from crystallizing add a pinch of baking soda.

Banana Zucchini Bread

Katherine Frazier
Liberty, NC
Showroom Employee

2 cups mashed bananas

3 eggs, beaten

2 cups sugar

1 cup vegetable oil

1 teaspoon vanilla

2 cups grated zucchini

3 ½ cups self rising flour

1 teaspoon cinnamon

1 cup chopped pecans

Preheat oven to 350°. Grease two 9x5x3 inch loaf pans and set aside.

In a large mixing bowl, combine eggs, sugar, oil and vanilla. Using a wire whisk, blend well. Stir in zucchini until well blended into the egg mixture. Slowly add flour, stirring into the liquids until all is incorporated. Add cinnamon, pecans and mashed bananas. Gently fold into the batter and, when thoroughly mixed, spoon into the loaf pan and bake for approximately 45 minutes or until thoroughly cooked. Cool in pans for 5 minutes then remove to a wire rack. For best flavor, serve warm.

You may also cook in muffin tins.

Cream Biscuits

Sandy Brown
Sandy & Company
Daughter of Berta and Hoyt Scott
Bear Creek, NC

3 cups sifted flour
6 teaspoons baking powder
¾ teaspoon salt
1 cup heavy cream

Sift flour, baking powder and salt together and cream, stirring just enough to dampen all the flour. On a board, knead lightly for a few seconds, using as little flour as possible. Roll to ½ inch thickness and cut with floured cutter. Place on greased baking sheet. Bake in hot oven 425° for 12-15 minutes.

Second choice: Sour cream: use 2 tablespoons sour cream. Use only 4 ½ teaspoons baking powder and add ½ teaspoon baking soda. Delicious!

Farmhouse Barbeque Muffins

Jamie Brady
Daughter of Ethelda
Bennett, NC

1 tube (10 ounces) refrigerated buttermilk biscuits
1 pound ground beef
½ cup ketchup
3 tablespoons brown sugar
1 tablespoon cider vinegar
½ teaspoon chili powder
1 cup (4 ounces) shredded cheddar cheese

Separate dough into 10 biscuits; flatten into 5-inch circles. Press each into the bottom and up the sides of a greased muffin cup; set aside. In a skillet, brown ground beef; drain. In a small bowl, mix ketchup, brown sugar, vinegar and chili powder; stir until smooth. Add to meat and mix well. Divide the meat mixture among biscuit-lined muffin cups, using about ¼ cup for each. Sprinkle with cheese. Bake 375° for 18-20 minutes or until golden brown. Cool for 5 minutes before removing from tin and serving. Yield: 10 servings

Basic Buttermilk Biscuits

Bonnie Reynolds
Daughter of Ethelda Co-owner
Carthage, NC

⅓ cup butter
2 cups self-rising soft wheat flour (we use Martha White)
¾ cup buttermilk
melted butter

Cut ⅓ cup butter into flour until mixture is crumbly. Add buttermilk stirring until all dry ingredients are moist. Turn dough out onto a lightly floured surface and knead 3-4 times. Roll dough to ¾ inch thickness. Cut with a 2 ½ inch biscuit cutter. Place on lightly greased baking sheet. Bake at 425° for 12-14 minutes. Brush biscuits with melted butter.

Corn Bread Dressing

In Memory of June Holt
Hoyt's sister and Lorrie's Mother

⅔ cup chopped onion
2 cups chopped celery
2 quarts (8 cups) day-old grated corn bread
1 quart (4 cups) day-old grated biscuits
¼ cup dried parsley flakes
2 teaspoons poultry seasoning
2 teaspoons ground sage
1 teaspoon coarse ground pepper
1 stick butter, melted
1 quart plus 1(14 ounce) can chicken broth

Preheat oven to 400°.

Mix onion, celery, corn bread, biscuits, parsley, poultry seasoning, sage and pepper in a large mixing bowl. Add melted butter and blend well. Add chicken broth to dry ingredients and mix well. The dressing should have a wet but not soupy consistency like a quick bread batter. Divide mixture evenly into two 8 inch pans sprayed with nonstick spray. Bake uncovered for 1 hour or until lightly brown on the top. Makes 16 servings.

Sausage and Cheese Cornbread

Wyanne L. Caviness
Bennett, NC
First Bank

1 pound sausage
1 large onion (chopped)
2 eggs (slightly beaten)
1 ½ cups self-rising cornmeal
1 (17 ounce) can cream style corn
¾ cup milk
¼ cup vegetable oil
2 cups grated cheese

Brown sausage and onion. Drain well. Combine eggs, cornmeal, corn, milk, and oil. Pour half of cornmeal mixture into a greased 10 ½ inch iron skillet. Sprinkle with sausage mixture and cheese. Pour remaining batter over top. Bake in preheated oven at 425° 30-40 minutes or until done.

Helpful Hint

Wipe down cutting boards with vinegar to clean, cuts grease and absorbs the smell.

Nana's Banana Bread

Elmo Phillips
Kitchen Staff
Bear Creek. NC

5 tablespoons butter

½ cup granulated sugar

½ cup firmly packed light brown sugar

1 large egg

2 egg whites

1 teaspoon vanilla extract

1 ½ cups mashed, very ripe bananas

1 ¾ cups all-purpose flour

1 teaspoon baking soda

½ teaspoon salt

¼ teaspoon baking powder

½ cup heavy cream

⅓ cup chopped walnuts

Preheat oven to 350˚. Spray bottom only of 9x5x3-inch loaf pan with nonstick cooking spray.

Beat butter in large bowl with an electric mixer set at medium speed until light and fluffy. Add granulated sugar and brown sugar; beat well. Add egg, egg whites and vanilla; beat until well blended. Add mashed banana, and beat on high speed 30 seconds.

Combine flour, baking soda, salt and baking powder in medium bowl. Add flour mixture to butter mixture alternately with cream, ending with flour mixture. Add walnuts to batter; mix well.

Pour batter evenly into prepared loaf pan. Bake until browned and toothpick inserted near center comes out clean, about 1 hour 15 minutes.

Cool bread in pan on wire rack 10 minutes. Remove bread from pan; cool completely on wire rack. Slice and serve with butter and jam.

Helpful Hint

Add a little vinegar to the water when an egg cracks during boiling. It will help seal the egg.

Streusel Coffeecake Muffins

Berta Scott
Co-Owner
Bear Creek, NC

Streusel:

8 tablespoons granulated sugar

⅓ cup packed light brown sugar

⅓ cup all-purpose flour

1 tablespoon ground cinnamon

4 tablespoons unsalted butter (cut into ½-inch pieces and chilled)

½ cup pecans

Muffins:

2 large eggs

1 cup sour cream

1 ½ teaspoons vanilla extract

1 ¾ cups all-purpose flour

½ cup granulated sugar

1 tablespoon baking powder

¼ teaspoon salt

5 tablespoons unsalted butter, cut into chunks and softened

For the streusel: Pulse 5 tablespoons granulated sugar, brown sugar, flour, cinnamon and butter in food processor until just combined. Reserve ¾ cup sugar mixture for cinnamon filling. Add pecans and remaining granulated sugar to food processor with remaining sugar mixture and pulse until nuts are coarsely ground. Transfer to bowl and set aside for streusel topping. Do not wash food processor.

For the muffins: Adjust oven rack to middle position and heat oven to 375 350°. Grease muffin tin with cooking spray and line with paper liners. Whisk eggs, sour cream and vanilla in bowl. Pulse flour, sugar, baking powder, salt and butter in food processor until mixture resembles wet sand. Transfer to large bowl. Using rubber spatula, gradually fold in egg mixture until just combined. Place 1 tablespoon batter in each muffin cup and top with 1 tablespoon cinnamon filling. Using back of spoon, press cinnamon filling lightly into batter, then top with remaining batter. Sprinkle streusel topping evenly over batter.

Bake until muffins are light golden brown and toothpick inserted into center comes out with a few dry crumbs attached, 22-28 minutes. Cool muffins in tin for 30 minutes, then transfer to rack to cool. Serve.

Breakfast

Breakfast Pizza

Jo Ellis
Durham, NC

1 pound regular sausage
1 can (8 ½ ounces) crescent rolls
1 cup hash brown frozen potatoes, thawed
1 cup (40 ounces) shredded sharp cheese
3 eggs, lightly beaten*
3 tablespoons milk*
½ teaspoon salt and 1 teaspoon black pepper*
3 tablespoons diced red and yellow peppers
¼ cup thinly sliced green onions
2 tablespoons grated Parmesan cheese

Cook sausage until no longer pink. Separate rolls to make 8 triangles. Place on ungreased 12" pizza pan with points together to make a circle. Top the circle with potatoes, shredded cheese and vegetables. Combine * items and pour over the cheese. Sprinkle the Parmesan cheese. Bake at 375° approximately 20 minutes until mixture is set.

Breakfast Casserole

Dawn Kidd
High Falls, NC

6 slices of buttered loaf bread
1 pound sausage
1 ½ cups shredded sharp cheese
6-8 eggs
1 teaspoon salt
2 cups "half & half"

Line the baking pan with buttered loaf bread. Cook sausage until done and drain well. Sprinkle over bread. Cover with shredded cheese. Beat eggs adding salt and "half & half" together. Pour over cheese and sausage.

Cover and refrigerate over night.

Remove from refrigerator, uncover and let stand at room temperature for 15 minutes.

Bake 45 minutes in 350° oven.

Sawmill Gravy Or Dobbin' Gravy

Deborah Pickard Stephenson
Carthage, NC
Showroom Employee

½ pound ground pork sausage

¼ cup butter

⅓ cup all purpose flour

3 ¼ cups milk

½ teaspoon salt

¾ teaspoon pepper

Cook sausage in large skillet over medium heat stirring until it crumbles and no longer pink. Remove sausage and drain on paper towel. Wipe skillet clean.

Melt butter in skillet over low heat. After the butter is melted add the flour, salt and pepper to make a rouge and gradually add the milk stirring with a whisk constantly over medium heat about 10-12 minutes or until thickened and bubbly. Stir in sausage, salt and pepper. Makes 3 ¾ cups

This was a favorite of my late husband William David "Bill" Pickard.

Cheese-Sausage Casserole

Elmo Phillips
Employee
Bear Creek, NC

9 boiled eggs-quartered

1 pound sausage (or more) browned and drained. Layer sausage on eggs

Spread 1 pint sour cream on that. Top with grated cheese mixed with breadcrumbs. Bake until bubbly, approximately 29 minutes. A good Easter dish.

Breakfast Casserole

Deborah Pickard Stephenson
Showroom Employee

6 slices bread (diced)

2 cups grated sharp cheddar cheese

5 eggs (beaten)

2 cups milk

1 teaspoon salt

1 pound sausage, cooked and drained

Spray or grease a 9x13 inch casserole dish. Layer bread, sausage, cheese, twice in that order; mix together eggs, milk and salt. Pour over layers. Bake at 350° for 1 hour. (Also may refrigerate and cooked the next morning).

Desserts

Cherry Crisp

Jo Ellis
Durham, NC

1 can (21 ounces) cherry pie filling
⅔ cup brown sugar
½ cup quick cooking oats
½ cup flour
1 teaspoon vanilla
⅓ cup butter, softened

Lightly butter a 3 ½ quart slow cooker. Place cherry pie filling in the slow cooker. Combine dry ingredients with vanilla and mix well. Cut in butter with a pastry cutter or fork. Sprinkle crumbs over the cherry pie filling. Cook for five hours on low.

Straw-ba-nut Ice Cream

Tina Brady
Bennett, NC

1 pint strawberries (mashed)
2 bananas (mashed)
1 cup chopped pecans
1 8 ounce container of Cool Whip
1 can sweetened condensed milk
¾ cup sugar
2 tablespoon vanilla (or to taste)
4 beaten eggs

Mix together. Pour into freezer and finish filling with regular milk. Follow instructions on freezer.

Apple Dumpling Pie

Thelma Branson
Bennett, NC

Crust:

1 ½ cups all-purpose flour

1 ½ tablespoons sugar

1 teaspoon salt

½ cup cooking oil

2 tablespoons milk

Preheat oven to 425°. Combine flour, sugar, salt, oil and milk. Press into an 8 inch deep-dish pie pan.

Filling:

1 cup sugar

2 tablespoons all-purpose flour

8 cups thinly sliced, peeled, tart baking apples (about 7 apples)

3 tablespoons butter or margarine

Toss apples in sugar and flour. Place in pie crust and dot with the butter.

Topping:

1 cup all-purpose flour

½ cup sugar

½ cup butter

Combine flour and sugar, and then cut in butter until mixture resembles coarse meal. Spread evenly over apples. Cover pie lightly with aluminum foil and bake for 40 to 50 minutes. Remove foil for the last 15 minutes of baking.

Not Your Mama's Banana Pudding

Mae Maness
Snow Camp, NC

1 large box instant vanilla pudding mix (mix as directed on box)

1 can "Eagle Brand" sweetened condensed milk

1 (8 ounce) package cream cheese

1 (8 ounce) container Cool Whip

2 bags "Pepperidge Farm" Chessman cookies

8 bananas

Fold first 4 items together. Line cookies in bottom of a 9x13 inch dish. Cut up bananas and place on top of the cookies. Pour pudding mixture over bananas, place more cookies on top of pudding. Chill.

Fall Fritters

Dawn Kidd
Employee
Robbins, NC

1 cup flour
1 ½ teaspoons baking powder
3 tablespoon sugar
¼ teaspoon salt
1 egg, beaten
⅓ cup milk
1 cup apples, diced
1 cup cooking oil
Confectioners sugar-for dusting

Measure and sift all dry ingredients. Beat eggs and milk together, slowly incorporating the dry ingredients. Add the chopped apples. In a heavy skillet on the stovetop, heat cooking oil over medium-high heat. Drop teaspoon full of apple butter into hot oil and fry until golden brown in color 3-4 minutes on each side. Remove from oil and drain on brown paper. Cool and sprinkle with powdered sugar. Yield: 12 small fritters.

Lemon Sponge Pie

Chaplain Larry E Small
Asheville, NC

2 graham cracker pie shells
2 large egg whites
2 tablespoons plus ¾ cups-granulated sugar
3 tablespoons butter or margarine at room temperature
3 tablespoons, all-purpose flour
1 cup milk
2 teaspoons grated lemon peel
¼ cup fresh lemon juice (for more lemon flavor increase the lemon juice to ⅓ cup)

In a medium bowl beat the egg whites until foamy. Gradually add in 2 teaspoons of sugar until stiff peaks form when you lift out the beaters. In another medium size bowl beat the yolks, remaining ¾ cup of sugar, butter, and flour until blended and smooth. Turn mixer to low speed and gradually add in the milk, lemon peel, and lemon juice just until blended. With a rubber spatula, gently fold the egg whites into the yolk mixture until no white streaks remain. Pour into the pie shells. Bake in a pre-heated 350° oven for 50 to 55 minutes or until the top is a golden brown and a toothpick inserted near the center comes out clean. Set on wire racks to cool, then ice with chocolate icing if you care to. Makes 2 9 inch pies

Hawaiian Pudding

Chaplain Larry E Small
Asheville, NC

In a 10" square pan, mix together crust:

2 cups vanilla wafer crumbs

1 stick melted butter

Line pan in the following order:

1 banana sliced

2 cans eagle brand milk

¼ cup lemon juice

1 small carton of Cool Whip

1 small can crushed pineapple (drained),

1 small can coconut

½ cup chopped nut pecans

whole maraschino cherries-place on top

Chill 2-3 hours.

Peach Dumplings

Ruby Brady
Bennett, NC

2 large peaches

8 crescent rolls

1 cup sugar

1 cup water

1 stick butter

Topping: ½ teaspoon cinnamon, 1 teaspoon sugar

Peel peaches and cut into quarters. Roll peaches up in crescent rolls and put into a baking dish. Bring sugar, water, and butter to a boil. Pour mixture over peach rolls. Sprinkle rolls with topping and bake 30 minutes in 350° oven.

Pecan Tarts

Linda Hamrick

4 ounces cream cheese

½ cup margarine

1 cup flour

1 egg

¾ cup brown sugar

1 tablespoon soft margarine

1 teaspoon vanilla

⅔ cup chopped pecans

Dash of salt

Let margarine and cream cheese soften at room temperature. Blend and stir in flour. Chill for 1 hour. Press into a muffin tin. Beat egg, sugar and margarine until smooth. Add other ingredients. Fill crust in muffin tin. Bake 325° for 25 minutes. Makes 6 large or 12 small tarts.

Apple Dumplins

Marilyn Sehen
Sanford, NC

5 Red Delicious apples
1 can Hungry Jack biscuits
2 sticks margarine
2 cups sugar
1 cup water
Dash of salt
1 teaspoon ground cinnamon
1 cup orange juice
½ teaspoon apple pie spice

Peel and quarter apples. Cut biscuit in half. Roll thin. Wrap around ¼ of the apple. Continue this until you have 20 wrapped apple pieces. Melt margarine in oblong baking dish. Place apple parts in margarine. Bring sugar, water, salt, cinnamon, orange juice, and apple pie spice to a boil. Pour over apples placed in dish. Bake at 350° for 45 minutes. Halfway through baking; take out of oven and spoon juices over apples. Return to oven. At end of baking, spoon juices over apples again.

Banana Split Cheese-Cake Squares

Barbara Lloyd
Vonore, TN

2 cups crushed graham crackers (about 14 whole crackers)
⅓ cup butter, melted
1 cup sugar
3 (8 ounce) packages cream cheese
1 teaspoon vanilla
¾ cup egg substitute
½ cup mashed banana
1 cup halved strawberries
1 banana, sliced, tossed with 1 teaspoon lemon juice
1 (8 ounce) can pineapple chunks (drained)

Mix crushed graham cracker crumbs, butter and ¼ cup sugar. Press into bottom of a 9x13 baking dish. Mix cream cheese, remaining ¾ cup sugar and vanilla with mixer until well blended. Add egg product and mix until blended. Stir in mashed banana. Pour into crust. Bake at 350° for 40 minutes until center is almost set. Cool, refrigerate 3 hours or overnight. Top with strawberries, sliced bananas and pineapple. Sprinkle with nuts. If desired you can drizzle with melted semi-sweet baking chocolate. Cut into squares.

213

Chocolate Dream Dessert

Barbara Lloyd
Vonore, TN

Pastry:
1 heaping cup all-purpose flour
1 stick of butter (melted)
1 cup chopped pecans
Mix and spread in 9x13 baking dish.
Press down with hands or fork. Bake at
350°° for 20 minutes. Cool.

First, layer:
1 (8 ounce) package cream cheese
1 cup powdered sugar
1 cup "Cool Whip" (9 ounces)
Beat with mixer and spread over pastry.
Second layer:
1 box instant vanilla pudding (¾ ounce)
1 box instant chocolate pudding (¾ ounce)
2 cups cold milk

Beat all together with mixer and spread
over first layer. Cover with remaining
cup of Cool Whip and shave a "Hershey
Bar" over top.

Strawberry Heaven

Clara Hunsucker
Bennett, NC

1 Angel Food cake
1 (16 ounce) container Cool Whip
1 (8 ounce) package cream cheese
1 cup sugar (divided)
1 teaspoon vanilla extract
1 quart fresh strawberries (sliced)
¼ cup cornstarch
1 (3 ounce) package strawberry Jell-O
1 tablespoon lemon juice
1 cup water

Combine in medium sauce pan ½ cup of
sugar, cornstarch, Jell-O, lemon juice,
and water. Cook over medium heat,
stirring constantly, until mixture comes
to a boil and thickens. Set aside to cool
slightly. Stir in sliced strawberries. Tear
angel food cake into 1-inch pieces and
toss with 2 cups of the Cool Whip. Press
into 9x13 inch pan (I use glass so you can
see the pretty layers). Set Aside. Combine
cream cheese, ½ cup remaining sugar,
and vanilla extract in mixer bowl. Beat
until smooth. Stir in remaining Cool
Whip. Spread evenly over cake layer.
Pour cooled strawberry mixture over
cream cheese layer, spreading to cover
cake evenly. Refrigerate 2 to 3 hours
before serving. Serves about 15

Apple Crisp

Marjorie McManus
Bear Creek, NC
Neighbor of Southern Supreme

5-6 Wine sap or McIntosh apples
1 tablespoon lemon juice
½ cup white sugar
½ teaspoon cinnamon
¼ teaspoon nutmeg
⅓ cup flour
1 cup rolled oats
½ cup brown sugar
½ teaspoon salt
⅓ cup melted butter (oleo)

Peel, core, and slice apples. Sprinkle with lemon juice, mix with white sugar, cinnamon and nutmeg. Mix well. Turn into 8x8x2 baking dish. Combine flour, oats, butter, brown sugar and salt, spread over apples. Bake 375° for 30 minutes. Serve warm with whipped cream. 6-8 servings

Helpful Hint

Simmer ¼ cup vinegar in a pot of water to sweeten the air.

"Uncooked" Fruit Chocolate Bavarian Torte

Deborah Pickard Stephenson
Carthage, NC
Showroom Employee

1 package (18 ¼ ounces) devil's food cake mix without pudding
1 package (8 ounces) cream cheese, softened
⅔ cup packed brown sugar
1 teaspoon vanilla extract
⅛ teaspoon salt
2 cups whipping cream, whipped
2 tablespoons grated semi-sweet chocolate

Mix and bake cake according to package directions, using two 9 inch round pans. Cool for 15 minutes; remove from pans and cool completely on wire racks. In a mixing bowl, beat cream cheese, brown sugar, vanilla and salt until fluffy. Fold in cream. Split each cake into two horizontal layers; place one on a serving plate. Spread with a fourth of the cream mixture. Sprinkle with a fourth of the chocolate. Repeat layers. Cover and refrigerate for 8 hours or overnight. Yield: 12 servings

Cream Puff

Anne Millette
Franklinton, LA
Former Employee
Special Friend of Scott Family

Pastry:

1 cup margarine

1 cup water

Boil until melted. Remove from heat and stir in 1 cup flour (in one direction) until soft ball forms. Stir in 4 eggs one at a time until mixed well. Plop onto a Pam sprayed cookie sheet. Bake at 400° for 45-50 minutes-shut off oven-but leave in oven for about 10-15 minutes (do not open oven door-may cause pastry to fall). Remove from oven and cool. When completely cooled, cut in half.

Filling:

2 boxes of instant vanilla pudding

1 ½ cups milk

Mix and add in one (8 ounce) container of Cool Whip. Spoon filling into the pastry; cover with top. Microwave can of chocolate frosting-remove foil cover and cover with plastic lid-for about 30-35 seconds-pour over top of pastry and cool. This is REAL EASY-GOOD LUCK!

Blackberry Cobbler

Dawn Stumpf
Daughter of Ethelda Co-owner
Bear Creek, NC

5 cups fresh or 2 (14 ounce) package frozen blackberries thawed and drained

1 cup sugar

3 to 4 tablespoons all-purpose flour

1 tablespoon lemon juice

2 tablespoons butter or margarine melted

1 teaspoon sugar

Combine first four ingredients, mix well; spoon into lightly greased 8 or 9 inch square pan. Prepare crust and spoon 9 mounds over blackberries. Brush with melted butter and sprinkle with sugar. Bake uncovered 425° for 30 minutes or until browned and bubbly. Serve warm with ice cream or whipped cream if desired.

Strawberry Pizza

Elmo Phillips
Employee
Bear Creek, NC

Crust
1 ½ cups plain flour
½ cup pecans chopped fine
1 tablespoon sugar
Dash of salt
1 ½ sticks butter melted
Mix and spread in pan. Cook at 350°
until brown. Cool.

Layer
1 (8 ounce) package cream cheese
2 cups powdered sugar
2 cups "Cool Whip"

Mix cream cheese and powdered sugar,
fold in Cool Whip, spread over cool crust.
Slice 1 cup fresh strawberries and spread
over this layer.

Topping
1 pint crushed strawberries
¾ cup sugar
⅓ cup cold water
2 tablespoons cornstarch

Cook topping until thick, cool and spread
over sliced berries in 9x13 pan.

Apricot Dessert

Peggy Fox
Asheboro, NC

1 cup melted butter
2 eggs, beaten
1 cup confectioner's sugar
Cook in double boiler until thick. Crush
vanilla wafers for crust, enough to cover
bottom of a large size Pyrex dish.

2 cups whipping cream, whipped with a
little sugar
2 can apricot halves
1 cup chopped pecans

Pack vanilla wafer crumbs in Pyrex
dish. Pour cooked filling over crumbs.
Let cool. Spread half the whipped cream
over filling, then layer apricots and nuts.
Cover with remaining whipped cream.
Sprinkle with a few wafer crumbs.
Refrigerate overnight.

"Deep River" Fluff

Crystal P Stubits
Sanford, NC

2 package Chips Ahoy cookies
1 carton 8 ounce Cool Whip
2 cup milk

Dip cookies in the milk and layer them in 8x8 inch dish. Layer the cookies with Cool Whip. Continue to layer cookies, then Cool Whip until top of the dish is reached. End with cool whip. Crumble a few cookies and sprinkle on top. Refrigerate 2 to 3 hours before serving. Serves 10-12.

Gooey Chocolate Butter Squares

Thelma Binkley
Goldston, NC
Gail Scott's Mother

Mix:

1 box chocolate cake mix
1 egg
1 stick butter
Spread in ungreased 13x9 pan
Combine:
1 (8 ounce) package cream cheese
1 box confectioner's sugar
2 tablespoons cocoa
1 stick butter
2 eggs
1 teaspoon vanilla flavoring

Add 1 one cup pecans if desired pour over cake mixture and bake at 350° for 30-35 minutes.

Persimmon Pudding

Evelyn Cheek
Asheboro, NC

2 cups persimmon pulp
3 eggs
1 ¾ cups milk
1 ¾ cups sugar
2 cups flour

¼ teaspoon soda
1 teaspoon vanilla

Mix all ingredients together. Melt 1 stick butter in pan combine with mixture. Bake 300° for 1 hour.

Apricot Casserole

Wendy Paschal
Siler City, NC

2 (15 ounce) cans apricots, drained
½ cup brown sugar
1 tablespoon cornstarch
1 stick butter
15 to 20 Ritz crackers, crumbled

Place drained apricots in casserole dish. Mix sugar and cornstarch then sprinkle over apricots; dot with butter. Bake 25-30 minutes at 450°. Remove from oven and crumble Ritz crackers over apricots; place back in oven at 350° for 10 minutes.

Jeanie's Apple Crisp

Jeanie Scott
Siler City, NC

4 cups sliced apples
1 cup flour
1 stick margarine
½ cup water
¼ teaspoon cinnamon
¾ cup sugar
½ cup brown sugar

Toss apples in water. Toss moist apples in sugar and cinnamon mixture. Place in a 9x13 inch dish.

Mix last three ingredients together until crumbly. Pour over apples covering well and bake at 350° for 45 minutes.

Persimmon Pudding

In loving memory of Sue Wilson,
By Lisa Scott
Bear Creek, NC
Co-owner

2 cups self-rising flour
2 cups persimmon pulp
1 ½ cups milk
3 eggs
1 ½ cups sugar
½ stick margarine
½ teaspoon baking powder

Mix together persimmon pulp, milk, eggs and margarine. Then add dry ingredients to it. Cook at 300° for 1 hour. Cool and cut in desired pieces.

Sweet Potato Cobbler

Nellie Brewer
Bennett, NC
Sample Bar Staff

Slice about ¼ inch thick sweet potatoes and boil until crisp and tender, about 10 minutes. Mix together 1 ½ cups sweet milk, 1 ½ cups of sugar, 3 tablespoons of flour, ½ teaspoon cinnamon, ¼ teaspoon nutmeg, ¼ teaspoon salt and ½ cup melted butter. Mix well. Pour over layers of sweet potatoes and top with lattice pie crust. Bake at 400° for 30 minutes. Top should be golden brown.

Peach Dumplings

Mary Lois Thomas
(Moosie)
Sanford, NC

2 large peaches (or canned peaches and use the juice for the water)
8 canned Pillsbury crescent rolls
1 cup sugar
1 cup water
1 stick butter
Topping:
1 teaspoon sugar
½ teaspoon cinnamon

Preheat oven to 350°. Peel and cut peaches into quarters. (canned peach halves, cut in half can be used.) Roll each peach quarter inside a crescent roll and place in a baking dish. Bring sugar water and butter to a boil. Pour mixture over crescent rolls. Combine topping ingredients and sprinkle over rolls. Bake for 30 minutes. Top with vanilla ice cream or whipped topping.

Easy Old-Fashioned Rice Pudding

In Memory of
Mrs. Nannie Phillips

½ cup rice
½ teaspoon salt
1 ½ cups sweetened condensed milk
Cinnamon or nutmeg, as desired

Cover rice with water and cook slowly until done. Put into baking dish with milk. Add cinnamon or nutmeg. Bake 30 minutes in 350° oven.

Creamy Dutch Apple Delight

Pat Brown

Crust:

Mix 1 ½ cups graham cracker crumbs with ½ cup butter and line a 7X11 inch dish with the crumbs.

Filling:

Mix and pour the following over the crust:

1 can Eagle Brand sweetened condensed milk

8 ounces sour cream

¼ cup lemon juice

Carefully spread 1 can of Apple pie filling over this. Bake for 20 minutes at 350°. After removing from oven, sprinkle with cinnamon and walnuts.

Apple Crisp

Frankie Meuller
Siler City, NC
Special Hairdresser friend to Berta

1 quart of sliced apples (5 or 6 apples)

Sift together:

¾ cup flour

1 cup sugar

1 teaspoon cinnamon

½ cup butter

½ cup water

Butter a shallow baking dish. Add cinnamon to apples and flour into baking dish. Add ½ cup water to apples, add butter to sifted flour and sugar and work together until crumbly. Spread over apples and bake uncovered for 45 minutes to 1 hour. Serve with whipped cream.

Bread Pudding With Lemon Sauce

Carolyn Brewer
Eagle Springs, NC

2 cups milk

4 eggs

½ cup sugar

5 slices white bread, cut into 1-inch cubes

⅓ cup semisweet chocolate chips

⅛ teaspoon ground cinnamon

LEMON SAUCE:

1 cup sugar

½ cup butter, melted

¼ cup water

2 tablespoons lemon juice

1 egg yolk

1 teaspoon grated lemon peel

In a large bowl, combine the milk, eggs and sugar. Stir in bread cubes; let stand for 5 minutes, stirring occasionally. Pour into a greased 1 ½ quart baking dish. Sprinkle with chocolate chips and cinnamon. Bake at 350° for 55-60 minutes or until a knife inserted near the center comes out clean.

For sauce, combine the sugar, butter, water and lemon juice in a saucepan. Whisk in egg yolk. Bring to a boil over medium heat, stirring constantly. Cook and stir for 1 minute. Remove from the heat; stir in lemon peel. Serve over pudding. Yield: Eight servings

Delicious Ice Cream Dessert

Berta Scott
Founder of Southern Supreme
and Co-owner
Bear Creek, NC

12 ice cream sandwiches

1 can chocolate syrup

1 cup of roasted pecan pieces

1 large carton Cool Whip

Take dish about 9x9 and lay six ice cream sandwiches in bottom. Layer with Cool

Whip and sprinkle half of nuts over the cool whip. Lay six more sandwiches, layer the top with Cool Whip, pour chocolate syrup over top (might not use whole can). Layer the rest of nuts on top with syrup. Place in refrigerator until frozen, slice in squares to serve.

Chocolate Bowl Delight

Kristy Cheek
Employee
Robbins, NC

1 Box 'Duncan Hines' Brownie mix with syrup
3 (small packages) chocolate instant pudding
4 cups milk
1 (6 ounce) Cool Whip
Heath bars or Hershey bars

Prepare brownies (fudge style) and let cool. Cut or crumble into small chunks. Use ½ of brownie chunks for first layer. Mix milk with pudding mix. Use ½ of pudding for next layer. Use ½ of Cool Whip for next layer. Top with crushed candy bars. Repeat layers. Refrigerate.

Vanilla Ice Cream

Keith & Cindy Dixon
Bear Creek, NC
Family of Lisa Scott

4 eggs
1 cup sugar
⅛ teaspoon salt
2 teaspoons vanilla
2 (14 ounce) cans Eagle Brand sweetened condensed milk
1 ½ quart milk

Combine eggs, sugar, salt and vanilla in bowl and mix well with mixer. Pour into ice cream freezer. Add Eagle Brand milk and mix well. Add milk to fill line on can and freeze per instructions on freezer.

Hot Fudge Sauce

Wendy Paschal
Siler City, NC

1 cup sugar
⅓ cup evaporated milk
1 stick margarine
⅓ cup chocolate chips
1 teaspoon vanilla

Put sugar, evaporated milk and margarine in pot and cook 1-2 minutes over medium heat (until bubbly). Remove from heat and add the chocolate chips and 1 teaspoon vanilla. Stir until chips melt; spoon over ice cream while warm. Store one or two days in the refrigerator in an airtight container. Reheat sauce as needed.

Rich Chocolate Sauce

Sandy Brown
Sandy & Company
Daughter of Hoyt and Berta Scott
Bear Creek, NC

This is good for topping for ice cream and for fruit. Also, warm over brownies.

6 ounces fine quality bittersweet chocolate
½ cup heavy cream
1 tablespoon sugar

Chop chocolate and transfer to a bowl in a small saucepan. Bring cream with sugar just to a simmer, stirring until sugar dissolves and pour over chocolate. Stir mixture until chocolate completely melts. Sauce may be kept chilled in an airtight container (can reheat stirring occasionally over saucepan with simmering water). Great warm over Brownies.

Chocolate Ice Cream

Gail Scott
Co-owner
Bear Creek, NC

1 can 'Eagle Brand' sweetened condensed milk
1 (12 ounce) container Cool Whip
½ gallon chocolate milk
A few squirts of chocolate syrup

Combine Eagle Brand Milk and Cool Whip. Gradually stir in chocolate milk, add chocolate syrup to taste. Freeze.

Cakes

Swiss Chocolate Cake

Nancy Hogan
Siler City, NC

1 box Swiss chocolate cake mix (Duncan Hines)
1 regular size box vanilla instant pudding
3 eggs
1 ½ cups milk
1 cup oil
Bake at 300° to 325° for approximately 25 minutes.
Icing:
8 ounces softened cream cheese
1 cup confectionary sugar (heaping)
⅔ cup sugar
¾ cup chopped pecans

Stir in 12 to 16 ounces 'cool whip'. Put ½ bag of the chocolate chips in food processor and crumble.

Chocolate Fudge Icing

Dick Carswell

6 squares unsweetened chocolates
2 ½ cups brown sugar
½ teaspoon salt
1 cup plus 2 tablespoons water
1 ½ teaspoons vanilla
1 ½ sticks butter

Cut unsweetened chocolate in small pieces. Mix sugar, salt, water and butter in pan. Add chocolate and bring to a boil on medium high for 5 minutes, stirring as it boils. Remove from heat, cool to lukewarm stirring as it cools. Beat in vanilla. Add enough confectioners sugar to make spreading consistency.

Note: you will have plenty icing left over. Spread it on a plate and put it in the refrigerator. This icing makes good fudge.

Hawaiian Sunset Cake

Ms. Faye Parrish
Stedman, NC

4 eggs
½ cup oil
1 ½ cup milk
1 box orange supreme cake mix
3 ounce box instant vanilla pudding mix
3 ounce box orange gelatin mix

Mix all ingredients together. Beat 3 minutes on medium speed. Pour into three 9 inch greased and floured cake pans. Bake at 350° for 30 minutes. Cool layers before adding filling and topping.

Filling:
15 ounce can crush pineapple, drained well
12 ounces frozen coconut
8 ounces sour cream
2 cups sugar

Drain as much liquid as possible from pineapple. Mix all ingredients. Take out 1 cup of this mixture and reserve for topping recipe. Spread filling between layers and on top of cake.

Topping:
Mix together reserved 1 cup filling mixture and whipped topping. Spread on sides and top of cake. (Filling already should be on the top of the cake).

Lemon Poppy Seed Upside Down Cake

Jo Ellis
Durham, NC

1 package lemon poppy-seed bread mix
1 egg
1 (8 ounce) light sour cream
½ cup water
Sauce:
1 tablespoon butter
¾ cup water
½ cup sugar
Juice from one lemon (approximately ¼ cup)

Mix the first four ingredients together until well moistened. Spread batter in a lightly greased 3 ½ quart slow cooker. Combine sauce ingredients in a small saucepan. Bring to a boil. Pour boiling mixture over the batter; cover and cook on high for 2 to 2 ½ hours. Edges will be slightly brown. Turn heat off and leave in the pot for about 30 minutes with cover slightly ajar. When cool enough to handle, hold a large plate over the top of the pot and then invert.

Sour Cream Pound Cake

Joanne Diggs
Gastonia, NC

3 sticks butter
3 cups flour (plain)
3 cups sugar
6 eggs
1 cup sour cream (8 ounces)
1 teaspoon vanilla
1 teaspoon lemon extract (optional)

Cream butter and sugar in mixer until fluffy; add eggs one at a time blending well. Add flour alternately with sour cream; mix well until smooth. Blend in flavoring. Bake at 325° in greased and floured tube pan for 1 hour and 25 minutes.

Chocolate Pound Cake

Joanne Diggs
Gastonia, NC

3 cups sugar
½ pound butter
½ cup "Crisco"
½ cup cocoa
Dash of salt
1 ⅛ cups milk
3 cups plain flour
6 eggs
½ teaspoon baking powder

Cream together the butter, shortening and sugar. Add flour and milk alternately. Add eggs and blend. Add rest of ingredients and mix. Grease tube pan. Bake 1 ½ hours at 350°.

Leona's Pound Cake

Nellie Brewer
Bennett, NC

3 ½ cups cake flour
3 cups sugar
1 cup milk
1 cup "Crisco"
1 ½ sticks butter
6 eggs separated
1 tablespoons vanilla flavoring

Preheat oven 325°. Beat egg whites first, add last. Cream butter and sugar, add egg yolks one at a time; beating well after each addition. Add milk and flour alternately, add flavoring. Fold in beaten egg whites last. Place in preheated oven for 1 hour and 20 minutes.

Tropical Ambrosia Delight Cake

Chaplain Larry E Small
Asheville, NC

1 box yellow cake mix
1 box instant banana pudding
1 large bowl "cool whip"
½ cup flake coconut
¼ cup of chopped fruit (pineapples, kiwis, strawberries)

For top of cake enough of whole strawberries, kiwis and pineapples to decorate the top of cake.

Bake cake according to directions on the box in a 9 ½ inch pan. Cool on wire rack and using a piece of waxed dental floss cut cake into two tiers thru the middle the long way. Mix the pudding according to the box and add the ¼ cup of chopped fruit to the pudding. Spread the pudding on the bottom layer of cake. Cover with the top layer of cake and iced all over with the "cool whip". Decorate with "whole" fresh fruits on top and sprinkle with the flake coconut.

Pumpkin Cake

Carolyn Savina
Sanford, NC

2 cups pumpkin
1 cup oil
3 cups sugar
3 cups flour
1 teaspoon cinnamon
1 teaspoon nutmeg
1 teaspoon salt
1 teaspoon baking soda
1 teaspoon baking powder
½ teaspoon cloves

Mix pumpkin, oil and sugar together. Add spices to flour and mix with pumpkin mixture until thoroughly combined. Bake cake in either a loaf or pound cake pan. Bake 350° for 1 hour.

Lou's Pound Cake

Judy Davison
Raleigh, NC

1 box "Duncan Hines Butter Cake Mix"
4 eggs
½ cup sugar
½ cup salad oil
1 teaspoon vanilla
1 (8 ounce) container sour cream

Beat for ten minutes this is the secret of the cake. Bake at 325° for 1 hour.

Chocolate Walnut Fruitcake

Ann Perry
Burlington, NC

2 cups sifted flour

1 ½ cups sugar

½ cup unsweetened cocoa

1 teaspoon baking soda

1 teaspoon salt

1 ½ cups walnuts coarsely chopped *

2 cups diced mixed candied fruit **

1 cup raisins

1 cup thinly sliced pitted dates

2 eggs

1 cup commercial sour cream

1 teaspoon vanilla

¼ cup butter melted

On waxed paper, sift together the flour, sugar, cocoa, baking soda, and salt. On another sheet of wax paper, mix together the walnuts, candied fruit, raisins and dates. In a large mixing bowl, beat eggs, sour cream and vanilla until well blended. Add butter, then flour mixture and blend well. Beat with electric mixer at medium speed for one minute, or vigorously by hand until well blended.

Add walnut-fruit mixture and fold in until well distributed. Turn into prepared tube pan. Bake in a preheated 300° oven with a shallow pan of water on the floor of oven until a cake tester inserted in center comes out clean-about 1 ¾ hours. Cool in pan, placed on wire rack, for 10 minutes. With a small metal spatula loosen edges and around the tube. Turn on a wire rack and cool completely.

If serving the cake shortly after baking, you will need to cut in thicker slices and it will not have the traditional fruitcake texture. To obtain the traditional texture, wrap securely in plastic wrap, and store in refrigerator for about 2 weeks.

*Use the walnut that best suits your taste. I personally prefer the English walnut.

**You can use the candied fruit mixture as purchased or make your own mixture to suit your taste. I prefer the pineapple, orange and cherry mix.

Black Walnut Cake

Pearl Miller, Lella Cook Loftin,
Garnet Cook

3 eggs, separated
3 cups sugar
¾ cup milk
1 cup margarine
1 cup black walnuts, chopped
2 ½ cups flour
4 tablespoons cocoa
2 teaspoons baking powder
1 teaspoon vanilla
1 cup Irish potatoes, mashed

Cream margarine and sugar; add beaten egg yolks. Mix flour, baking powder and cocoa; add alternately with milk. Add walnuts and potatoes; fold in beaten egg whites, last. Bake at 350° until done.

Icing:
1 box 10x powdered sugar
6 tablespoons margarine
4 tablespoons cocoa
4 tablespoons coffee (brewed)

Beat well. Ice cooled cake.

This recipe as been handed down in the Cook family through Lella Cook Loflin, This cake is best if stored (covered) for a week in a cool place. Place fresh apple slices around the cake for moisture and enhanced flavor.

Plain Pound Cake

Mildred Jones
Bennett, NC

1 cup self-rising flour
3 cups cake flour
1 ½ cups "Crisco"
½ teaspoon baking powder
1 teaspoon vanilla
1 teaspoon lemon-optional
6 eggs
3 ¾ cups sugar
1 cup milk

Sift flour, sugar and baking powder together. Add milk, cut in 1 ½ cups "Crisco". Add flavoring, eggs and beat with mixer.

Start in cool oven. If you want coconut, add 1 cup of coconut to batter then cook. Cook 300° for 1 hour and 15 minutes.

Caramel Nut Pound Cake

Marilyn Sehen
Sanford, NC

2 sticks butter
½ cup "Crisco" shortening
1 pound box light brown sugar
1 cup white sugar
5 eggs
½ teaspoon baking powder
½ teaspoon salt
3 cups plain flour
1 cup milk
1 teaspoon vanilla
1 cup pecans chopped
Confectioners' sugar

Cream the butter, shortening, and brown sugar. Add white sugar and continue creaming. Add eggs one at a time, beating thoroughly after each addition. Combine baking powder, salt, and flour, add alternately with milk to creamed mixture. Add vanilla, and nuts; blend well. Pour batter into a well-greased and floured 10 inch tube pan. Bake 325°° for 1 ½ hours or until cake tests done. Dust with confectioner's sugar.

Fresh Apple Cake

Barbara Lloyd
Vonore, TN

Mix:
2 cups sugar
1 cup oil

Add in: 2 eggs

Sift and add: 3 cups flour
1 teaspoon soda
½ teaspoon salt
1 teaspoon cinnamon

Add:
2 teaspoons vanilla
3 cups apples chopped-any kind
1 cup nuts-broken into pieces

Start with a cold oven and bake at 350° until done.

Sweet Potato Layer Cake

Mrs. Brenda Howell
Siler City, NC

1 ½ cup vegetable oil

4 eggs separated

¼ cup water (hot)

1 teaspoon vanilla extract

2 ½ cups cake flour

1 teaspoon ground cinnamon

¼ teaspoon salt

2 cups sugar

1 ½ cup finely shredded sweet potato (uncooked)

3 teaspoons baking powder

1 teaspoon nutmeg

1 cup chopped nuts

Frosting

½ cup margarine

2 cans (5 ounces) each evaporated milk

1 cup chopped pecan

1 ⅓ cups sugar

4 egg yolks, beaten

2 ⅔ cup flaked coconut

2 teaspoon vanilla extract

In a mixing bowl, beat oil and sugar. Add egg yolks one at a time, beating well after each addition. Add sweet potato, water and vanilla, mix well. In a small mixing bowl, beat egg whites until stiff, fold into sweet potato mixture. Combine flour, baking powder, cinnamon, nutmeg and salt. Add to potato mixture. Stir in pecans. Pour into three greased 9 inch round pans. Bake for 22-27 minutes at 350° until done. Cool for 10 minutes.

For frosting, melt the margarine in a saucepan, whisk in sugar, milk, egg yolks until smooth. Cook and stir over medium heat for 10-12 minutes or until thickened. Remove from the heat. Stir in the coconut, pecans and vanilla, cool slightly. Place one cake layer on a serving plate, spread with ⅓ of the frosting. Repeat layers. Yield: 12-15 servings

Helpful Hint

When making a cake always add 2 tbsp of boiling water to the butter and sugar mixture. This makes a fine textured cake.

The Leach Family Cake

June Johnson
Greensboro, NC

11 box yellow cake mix "Duncan Hines Butter"
Follow instructions preparing 3 layers

FROSTING AND FILLING:
2 cups pecans chopped fine**
2 cups walnuts chopped fine**
2 cups Brazil nuts chopped fine**
1 box (15 ounces) raisins chopped fine**
⅓ cup light "Karo" syrup

1 pound box dark brown sugar
5 egg whites; beat until stiff

** Best when prepared in food processor

Bring syrup and sugar to a boil on medium heat, stirring constantly. Mixture is ready when a soft ball forms when dropped into a glass of cold water. While still hot, fold in egg whites, nuts and raisins. Spread between layers and on the sides and top. This cake is better, served cold.

Blueberry Pudding Cake

Nancy Meadows
Dry Fork, VA

2 cups fresh or frozen blueberries
1 teaspoon ground cinnamon
1 teaspoon lemon juice
1 cup all-purpose flour
¾ cup sugar
1 teaspoon baking powder
½ cup milk
3 tablespoons butter or margarine, melted

Topping
¾ cup sugar
1 tablespoon cornstarch
1 cup boiling water

Toss the blueberries with cinnamon and lemon juice; place in a greased 8 inch square baking dish. In a bowl, combine flour, ¾ cup sugar and baking powder; stir in milk and butter. Spoon over berries.

For the topping, combine ¾ cup sugar and cornstarch; sprinkle over batter. Slowly pour boiling water over all. Bake at 350° for 45-50 minutes or until the cake tests done. Yield: 9 servings.

Cheerwine Cake

Patricia Meadows
Siler City, NC

CAKE:
 1 box deviled food cake mix
1 (12 ounce) can "Cheer-wine" divided
1 teaspoon almond extract

FROSTING:

Use remaining "Cheer-wine" (⅓ cup)
½ cup margarine or butter
¼ cup unsweetened cocoa
2 ½ cups powdered sugar
¼ teaspoon almond extract
1 cup chopped nuts

Preheat oven to 350°. Prepare cake as directed on package, substituting 1 cup of Cheer-wine for the water and adding almond extract. Pour into pan and bake as directed. Make frosting while cake is baking. Frost cake immediately, using the "Cheer-wine" frosting.

In a saucepan, combine ⅓ cup Cheer-wine, margarine or butter and cocoa. Bring to a boil. Place powdered sugar in a bowl. Pour hot mixture over it and blend until smooth. Stir in almond extract and chopped nuts. Cool until lukewarm, about 20 minutes.

Key Lime Cake

Marilyn Sehen
Sanford, NC

1 box lemon cake mix
4 eggs
1 ⅓ cups oil
¾ cup orange juice
1 (3 ounce) box lime jell-o dry
3 limes
6 tablespoons powdered sugar
Mix first five ingredients together. Bake in 3 (9 inch) pan layers at 350° for 25-30 minutes. Mix juice of 3 limes and 6 tablespoons powdered sugar. Poke holes in cake layers with fork. Spoon over warm cake layers. Let cool.

Icing:
8 ounce cream cheese
1 box powdered sugar
1 stick softened margarine
1 teaspoon vanilla
1 cup chopped nuts

Mix cream cheese and margarine until well blended. Add sugar, vanilla, and half of nuts. Spread between layers and outside and top of cake. Sprinkle remaining nuts on top of cake.

Christmas Cake

Barbara Lloyd
Vonore, TN

2 ½ cups self-rising flour

1 cup buttermilk

1 ½ cups vegetable oil

1 teaspoon baking soda

1 teaspoon vanilla

2 bottles red food coloring

1 ½ cups sugar

1 teaspoon cocoa (unsweetened)

1 teaspoon white vinegar

2 large eggs

Preheat oven to 350°. Mix all ingredients with mixer. Spray three 9 inch round cake pans with non-stick coating. Pour batter equally into the pans and bake 20 minutes. Test for doneness with a toothpick. Cool layers in pans on wire racks for 10 minutes. Carefully remove layers from pans and cool completely.

FROSTING

1 ⅓ stick butter, softened

1 (8 ounce) package cream cheese, softened

1 box confectioners sugar

2 cups chopped pecans

Combine butter, cream cheese and confectioners sugar in a bowl. Beat with mixer until fluffy. Fold in 1 ½ cups pecans. Frost cake and decorate top with remaining ½ cup pecans. Refrigerate at least 1 hour before serving. Makes 10 to 15 servings

Cranberry Cake

Marilyn Sehen
Sanford, NC

1 box white cake mix

1 can cranberry sauce

½ cup orange juice

1 tablespoon grated orange zest

2 large eggs

½ cup confectioners sugar

Set aside ¼ cup of cranberry sauce for a glaze. Place remaining sauce, cake mix, orange juice, zest, and eggs in mixing bowl. Blend for 3 minutes. Pour batter into greased and floured tube pan. Bake 350° for 35 minutes or done.

Place reserved cranberry sauce and powdered sugar in mixing bowl. Blend with a fork until smooth. Spoon, glaze over cooled cake so it drizzles down the sides and into center.

Easy Bundt Cake

Dixie Holt
Wrapping Department

1 package (18 ¼ ounce) yellow cake mix
1 package (3.9 ounces) instant chocolate pudding mix
½ cup sugar
1 cup (8 ounce) sour cream
¾ cup vegetable oil
¾ cup water
4 eggs
1 cup (6 ounce) Semi-sweet chocolate chips
2 squares (1 ounce each) white baking chocolate

In large mixing bowl, combine the cake and pudding mixes, and sugar. Add the sour cream, oil and water, mix well, add eggs one at a time beating well after each addition. Stir in chocolate chips. Pour mixture in sprayed 'Bundt' pan and bake 350° for 50-55 minutes or until toothpick inserted near the center comes out clean. Cool cake for 10 minutes and remove from pan. In microwave or double boiler, melt the white chocolate, drizzle over cake. Yield: 12-16 servings

The "Best" Chocolate Cake

JoAnn Jones
Bennett, NC

1 box German chocolate cake mix
1(6 ounce) package chocolate chips
1 cup pecans chopped
4 eggs beaten
1 teaspoon vanilla
½ cup oil
1 (3 ½ ounce) package instant chocolate pudding
1 (8 ounce) carton sour cream

Toss chocolate chips and pecans in 1 tablespoon of dry cake mix. Beat the remaining ingredients together for three minutes. Fold in chips and pecans. Pour into a greased 'Bundt' pan and bake for 50 minutes at 350°. May also be used for chocolate bread.

Neapolitan Cake

Wanda Hunsucker
Robbins, NC

1 box "Duncan Hines" white cake mix
1 cup water
¼ cup vegetable oil
3 eggs
Food coloring
1 container fluffy white frosting

In a large mixing bowl, combine cake mix, water, oil and eggs. Beat on medium speed for 2 minutes. Divide batter into 3 equal portions. Pour one portion into greased and floured 'Bundt' or tube pan. Stir food coloring of your choice into other two portions; carefully spoon into pan. Do not swirl.

Bake at 350° for 37 minutes or until a toothpick comes out clean. Cool 10 minutes. Remove from pan. Frost; with fluffy white frosting when cool. I use "Betty Crocker".

Carrot Cake

Denise Holt
Bear Creek, NC

1 ¼ cup 'Wesson' oil
2 cups sugar
4 eggs
2 cups plain flour
1 teaspoon salt
1 teaspoon baking soda
2 teaspoons baking powder
2 teaspoons cinnamon
3 cups grated carrots
1 cup chopped pecans

Combine oil and sugar; mix well. Add eggs one at a time. Beat after each egg. Sift dry ingredients. Add ½ to egg mixture. Mix well and add remaining ½. Mix well. Add carrots and pecans mix well. Pour into greased and floured tube pan. Preheat oven to 325°. Bake 1 hour and 10 minutes or until done. Top with cream cheese frosting.

FROSTING:
1 (8 ounce) cream cheese
1 stick margarine
1 box confectioner's sugar
2 teaspoons vanilla

Combine all ingredients; mix well & frost carrot cake.

Mississippi Mud Cake

Lorrie Moore
Bonlee, NC

1 cup butter

4 eggs

1 cup flaked coconut

2 cups sugar

1 ½ cup sifted flour

⅓ cup cocoa

1 teaspoon vanilla

1 cup chopped walnuts or pecans

1 (13 ounce) marshmallow crème

FROSTING:

½ cup butter

6 tablespoons milk

⅓ cup cocoa

1 pound box confectioners' sugar

1 cup chopped walnuts or pecans

In large bowl, beat butter and sugar until creamy. Add eggs, 1 at a time, beating well. Add remaining ingredients, except marshmallow crème. Stir until well mixed. Spread batter in greased 13x9 pan. Bake in preheated 350° oven for 30-35 minutes. Remove from oven; spread marshmallow crème over hot cake. Cool 20 minutes; meanwhile make frosting. Mix all ingredients except nuts. Mix until smooth. Stir in ½ of nuts. Spread frosting on cake; swirling through marshmallow crème. Sprinkle with remaining nuts.

Pina Colada Cake

Ethelda Stumpf
Co-owner
Bear Creek, NC

1 yellow cake mix

1 can crushed pineapple drained

1 can (14 ounces) sweetened condensed milk

1 (8 ounce) carton whipped topping

⅔ cup coconut

Prepare cake mix as directed on back of package. Mix ½ can of pineapple into

batter. Bake according to directions on package. When done, poke holes with a fork in warm cake at 1 inch intervals. Pour sweetened condensed milk over cake; allow cake to cool. Spread whipped topping over the cake. Sprinkle the top with coconut and remaining pineapple. Delicious!

Gob Cake And Icing

Sharon Stumpf
Big Run, PA

1 chocolate cake mix
1 box instant chocolate pudding
1 ½ cups sugar
¾ cup margarine
1 teaspoon vanilla
3 eggs
¾ cup "Crisco"
¾ cup evaporated milk

ICING:
2 egg whites
¾ cup Crisco
1 ½ cup sugar
¾ cup margarine
¾ cup evaporated milk
1 teaspoon vanilla

Mix cake according to directions on box. Use one whole egg plus 2 egg yolks. Add pudding. Mix plus additional, ⅓ cup oil. Divide batter in half onto greased cookie sheets (2 sheets). Line one cookie sheet with waxed paper for easy removal. Bake at 350° for 10-15 minutes. Cool.

FOR ICING:
Beat 2 egg whites until stiff. Add 1 ½ cup white sugar, ¾ cup margarine, ¾ cup "Crisco" and ¾ cup evaporated milk. Heat milk to scalding before adding other ingredients in; beat until thick (may take awhile to thicken) add vanilla.

Put icing on one cake and top with other cake. Chill until ready to serve.

Mandarin Orange Cake & Icing

Eleanor Stumpf
Big Run, PA

1 yellow cake mix
4 eggs
½ cup oil
1 small can mandarin oranges and juice

ICING:
1 large crushed pineapple with juice
1 box instant vanilla pudding
1 (8 ounce) carton "Cool Whip"

Combine cake ingredients and beat with mixer. Bake in 9x13 pan for 35 minutes in 350° oven.

FOR ICING:
Combine ingredients and mix by hand. Refrigerate.

New York Style Cheesecake

Ethelda Stumpf
Co-Owner

CRUST:

2 cups graham cracker crumbs

3-4 tablespoons sugar

½ cup butter melted

Mix graham cracker crumbs, sugar and melted butter. Press mixture into spring form pan. (I use a 10 inch size)

FILLING:

3 (8 ounce) packages cream cheese softened

1 ½ cup sugar

4 eggs

3 teaspoons vanilla

Beat cream cheese and sugar for 5 minutes; add eggs one at a time. Add vanilla and beat 3-4 minutes. Pour into crust. Bake 350° for 50 minutes. Remove from oven. Cool for 10 minutes.

TOPPING:

¾ cup sour cream

4 teaspoons sugar

3 teaspoons vanilla

Berries of your choice to garnish

Mix sour cream, sugar, and vanilla. Stir and spread on top of cheesecake. Bake for additional 10 minutes. Cool, refrigerate, garnish with berries of your choice.

Easy "Pig Pickin" Cake

Denise Holt
Bear Creek, NC

1 box "Duncan Hines Butter Cake Mix"

4 eggs

½ cup oil

1 can mandarin oranges

Grease and flour 3 layer cake pans. Beat all ingredients together until batter is smooth and oranges are broken into small pieces. Pour into pans and bake 350° for 25 minutes or until done. Cool and ice cake.

ICING:

1 (20 ounce) can crushed pineapple, drained

1 small package instant vanilla pudding

1 (9 ounce) carton "Cool Whip"

Beat pineapple and pudding until thick. Then fold in "Cool Whip". Spread between layers and on top. Keep cake in refrigerator.

Lemon Cream Meringue Tarts

Berta Scott
Founder of Southern Supreme

4 large egg whites

¼ teaspoon cream of tarter

1 cup sugar

1 cup chilled whipping cream

5 large egg yolks

6 tablespoons sugar

⅓ cup fresh lemon juice

1 tablespoon grated lemon peel

½ tablespoon real vanilla

Meringues have to cook slowly to drying stage - 225°.

Line a large cookie or baking sheet with parchment paper. (Purchase at cooking store). Using electric mixer, beat egg whites and cream of tarter in large bowl until soft peaks form. Slowly add sugar, 1 tablespoon at a time and beat well until stiff and glossy, about 5-8 minutes. Take a small saucer and draw around it on the parchment. This will be your guideline. Take a cup or large spoon and fill ring spacing apart. Using back of spoon, make a 2½ inch wide indention in center of each meringue spreading to the ring. Bake 1½ hours and cool.

For Filling:
Bring ½ cup cream to simmer in heavy medium saucepan over medium heat. Remove from heat; cover and let sit for 30 minutes. Combine egg yolks, sugar, lemon juice and lemon peel in heavy medium saucepan. Stir constantly over med-low heat until sauce thickens, about 5-6 minutes. Transfer custard to glass bowl, whisk in cream. Refrigerate until cold, 1-2 hours. Take balance of cream (½ cup) in medium bowl; beat remaining until peak forms, fold into lemon juice; spoon filling into meringue shells.

I learned to make meringue when I attended the Culinary Institute in New York. They are delicious.

Cream Cheese Coffee Cake

Karen King
Sanford NC

CAKE BATTER:

2 sticks (1 cup) unsalted butter at room temperature

1 cup sugar

2 cups all-purpose flour

2 eggs

2 teaspoons baking powder

½ teaspoon salt

CAKE FILLING:

2 (8 ounces) cream cheese at room temperature

1 large egg yolk

½ cup sugar

1 teaspoon vanilla extract

CAKE TOPPING:

¼ cup sugar

¼ cup all-purpose flour

4 tablespoons unsalted butter at room temperature

Preheat oven 350°. Lightly grease 8x13 inch baking pan; set aside. Make the cake batter. In large bowl, cream butter and sugar with electric mixture until smooth. Add eggs one at a time, scraping the bowl after each addition. Sift flour, baking powder and salt together and add to butter mixture. Beat until flour is incorporated and batter is thick, pale and creamy; set aside.

For cake filling, in another mixing bowl using electric mixture combine all ingredients. Mix until sugar is dissolved and filling smooth. Make cake topping; combine sugar and flour in small mixing bowl. Using a pastry cutter or your fingertips, cut butter into sugar and flour until mixture is crumbly; set aside. Spread ⅔ of cake batter over bottom of baking pan. Spread the cake filling over the cake batter using a large spoon. Evenly distribute remaining cake batter over filling in dollops. Sprinkle entire cake surface with cake topping. Bake for 45 minutes.

Fresh Coconut Cake & Icing

Berta Scott
Founder of Southern Supreme and Co-Owner

3 cups cake flour sifted

2 teaspoons baking powder

¼ teaspoon salt

1 cup butter

1 box (1 pound) confectionary sugar

4 egg yolks, well beaten

1 cup milk

1 teaspoon vanilla

1 cup fresh coconut, grated

4 egg whites stiffly beaten

¾ cup coconut milk or skimmed milk

Sift flour with baking powder and salt. Cream the butter and sugar together until fluffy. Add egg yolks and beat 2 minutes. Add flour mixture with milk and stir. Add vanilla and coconut. Fold in beaten egg whites. Pour in three (9 inch) greased and floured cake pans.

Bake in 350° oven for 25 minutes or until cake test done. Turn layer on wire racks, sprinkle with coconut or skim milk.

FLUFFY SEVEN MINUTE FROSTING:

3 egg whites-unbeaten

½ cup water

2 ¼ cups sugar

2 teaspoons white corn syrup

1 ½ teaspoons vanilla

Fresh coconut grated

On top of double boiler, combine egg whites, water, sugar and corn syrup. Cook over boiling water beating constantly for 7 minutes or until it peaks. Remove from heat; add vanilla. Frost between layers, top and sides; coat with grated coconut.

Butter Pecan Cake

Sandy Brown
Bear Creek, NC

2 ⅔ cup pecans chopped
1 ¼ cup butter (no substitutes) softened and divided
2 cups sugar
4 eggs
3 cups all purpose flour
2 teaspoons baking powder
½ teaspoon salt
1 cup milk
2 teaspoons vanilla extract

Place pecans and ¼ cup butter in baking pan. Bake at 350° for 20-25 minutes or until toasted, stirring frequently. Set aside. In mixing bowl, cream sugar and remaining butter. Add eggs, one at a time beating well after each addition. Combine flour, baking powder and salt.

Add to creamed mixture alternately with milk. Stir in vanilla and 1 ⅓ cups toasted pecans. Pour into three greased and floured 9 inch round cake pans. Bake 350° for 25-30 minutes. Cool 10 minutes and remove from pan, cool on wire rack. Prepare frosting.

FROSTING:

1 cup butter (no substitute) softened
8 cups confectioner sugar
1 (5 ounce) can evaporated milk
2 teaspoons vanilla extract

Cream butter and sugar in mixing bowl. Add milk and vanilla; beat until smooth. Stir in remaining toasted pecans. Spread frosting between layers and top and side of cake.

"7-Up" Pound Cake

JoAnn Jones
Chocolate Kitchen
Bear Creek, NC

2 sticks butter
½ cup canola oil
5 eggs
3 cups sugar
3 cups plain flour
2 teaspoons vanilla extract or lemon juice
7 ounces of "7-up"

Cream butter and oil; add sugar gradually beating after each addition. Add eggs, one at a time then add sifted flour and alternate with "7-up" beating well. Add vanilla or lemon. Bake in greased and floured tube pan at 325°° for 1 ½ hours starting in cold oven.

Red Velvet Cake

In memory of Colene Scott
Bear Creek, NC

2 cups sugar
½ cup butter
3 eggs
1 tablespoon vinegar
1 tablespoon cocoa
2 ounces red food coloring
2 ½ cups cake flour
½ teaspoon salt
1 ½ teaspoons soda
¼ teaspoon baking powder
1 cup buttermilk
1 teaspoon vanilla flavoring

Frosting:
1 cup milk
3 tablespoons flour
1 cup sugar

1 cup butter
1 cup chopped pecans
1 can flaked coconut
1 teaspoon vanilla

Cream butter and sugar until light in color; add eggs one at a time. Make a paste of vinegar, cocoa and food coloring; add to creamed mixture. Sift together dry ingredients; add to mixture alternately with buttermilk. Add vanilla and blend thoroughly. Pour into three 10 inch pans and bake 350° for 30 minutes for the frosting. Cook milk and flour until thickened. Set aside to cool, cream butter and sugar add to cooled flour mixture and remaining ingredients mixing well. Stack layers, trim off excess if they do not stack even. Spoon the frosting between layers saving enough for top and side.

Directions to God's House

Make a right onto "Believeth Blvd." Keep straight and go through the green light, which is Jesus Christ. From there you must turn onto the "Bridge of Faith," which is over troubled water. When you get off the bridge, make a right turn and keep straight. You are on the "King's Highway" – Heaven-bound. Keep going for three miles: one for the Father, one for the Son, and one for the Holy Ghost. Then exit off onto "Grace Blvd." From there, make a right turn on "Gospel Lane." Keep straight and then make another right on "Prayer Blvd." As you go on your way, yield not to the traffic on "Temptation Ave." Also, avoid SIN STREET "Gossiping Lane," and Backbiting Blvd," but you have to go down "Long-suffering Lane," "Persecution Blvd.," and "Trials and Tribulations Ave." But that's all right, because "VICTORY Blvd." Is straight ahead! God bless you and Have a Wonderful Day!!
-- Tidbits from Pastor John

Pineapple-Upside Down Cake

In loving memory of Sue Wilson,
By Lisa Scott
Bear Creek, NC
Co-owner

2 tablespoons butter melted in large cast iron skillet
1 cup brown sugar
Slices of pineapple as desired
Jar of 'Maraschino' cherries

Place cherries in with pineapple. Spread chopped pecans around in skillet.

Batter:
2 eggs, well beaten
1 cup sugar
1 tablespoon warm water
1 cup self-rising flour, beaten in
2 teaspoons vinegar

Pour batter in skillet over other mixture. Bake in 375° oven until toothpick comes out clean in center. Flip skillet over on cake platter while warm.

Apple Cake

Hazel McMath
Employee

1 cup oil
2 cups sugar
3 eggs
2 ½ cups self-rising flour
3 peeled and diced apples
2 packages of black walnuts
1 small can of Baker's coconut
1 tablespoon vanilla

Caramel Glaze:
1 cup of light brown sugar
½ stick margarine, melted

Bring to a boil then add ¼ cup of can milk. Boil until it begins to thicken. Remove from heat and stir in 1 tablespoon of vanilla and spread over cake. Bake cake 350° for 1 hour.

Pixie Pound Cake

In loving memory of Sue Wilson
Cindy Dixon
Bear Creek, NC
Sister of Lisa Scott

1 cup Crisco
½ cup butter, softened
3 cups sugar
6 eggs
3 ¼ cups cake flour
1 teaspoon baking powder
½ teaspoon salt
1 cup milk
1 teaspoon vanilla flavoring
½ teaspoon lemon flavoring

Cream shortening, butter and sugar together. Add eggs one at a time, beating after each. Sift together flour, baking powder and salt. Add alternately with milk. Add flavoring. Pour into greased and floured tube pan; bake at 350° for 1 ½ to 2 hours, until golden brown.

Volcano Cake

Ruth Sapp Stamey
Bear Creek, NC

1 German Chocolate Cake Mix
1 cup chopped nuts
1 cup coconut
1 stick butter
1 box confectioners' sugar
1 (8 ounce) cream cheese
1 can Hershey's syrup
1 carton Cool Whip
1 chocolate candy bar

Grease 9x13 pan; put nuts and coconut in bottom of pan. Mix cake according to package directions. Pour over nuts and coconut. Mix butter, cream cheese, confectioners' sugar and pour over cake. Bake 350° until done. Pour Hershey's syrup over cake while hot; let cool. When cool spread Cool Whip over cake; sprinkle with shaved chocolate bar. Refrigerate.

Too Easy Apple Cake

Dawn Kidd
Employee
Robbins, NC

1 package yellow cake mix
1 can apple pie filling
3 eggs
3 teaspoons sugar
1 teaspoon cinnamon

Preheat oven to 350°. Lightly grease a 9x13 inch cake pan. Combine cake mix, apple pie filling and eggs, Beat 2 minutes with mixer at medium speed. Combine sugar and cinnamon. Spread half the batter into the pan, sprinkle with cinnamon sugar, pour over remaining batter and sprinkle with the remaining sugar mixture. Bake at 30-35 minutes or until a toothpick inserted in the center comes out clean. This recipe is great for a last minute dessert. If you want larger chunks of apple, just blend the ingredients with a spoon instead of mixer. I am thinking that adding chopped nuts with the cinnamon sugar mixture would be good too. Of course, whipped cream or ice cream on top would be perfect.

Chocolate Cake

Wyanne L. Caviness
Bennett, NC
First Bank

2 cups sugar
2 cups self-rising flour
4 tablespoons cocoa
1 teaspoon baking soda
1 teaspoon cinnamon
1 cup water
1 stick melted margarine
½ cup vegetable oil
½ cup buttermilk
2 eggs (slightly beaten)
1 teaspoon vanilla

Sift together sugar, flour, cocoa, soda and cinnamon. Bring to boil water, margarine, and oil. Pour over dry ingredients, mix well. Combine buttermilk, eggs and vanilla. Add to chocolate mixture. Pour into floured 9x13 pan. Bake at 400° for 20 minutes.

Icing:
1 stick margarine
4 tablespoons cocoa
6 tablespoons milk
1 box powdered sugar

Place first 3 ingredients in sauce pan and bring to boil. Remove from heat and add powdered sugar. Pour over cake while hot.

Candies

Potato Candy

Crystal P. Stubits
Sanford, NC

Peel and cook a medium Irish potato with a little salt until done, pour off water. Put potato in large dish and mash. Add powder sugar, mix. Add more powder sugar, and 1 teaspoon vanilla. Add more powder sugar until stiff mixture. Spread wax paper on counter. Pour 1 to 2 cups powder on paper. Roll out mixture on powder sugar. Spread with peanut butter. Roll-up like jelly roll. Cut into slices, put onto plate. Cover and refrigerate.

Depending on size of potato, it will take about 3 pounds of powdered sugar and 18 ounces peanut butter.

Million Dollar Fudge

Lois Ann Ramey
Pawleys Island, SC

2 large or 12 small Hershey bars
2 (6 ounce) packages chocolate chips
1 can evaporated milk
1 pint jar marshmallow crème
¼ pound margarine
4 ½ cups sugar

Break up candy bars, chocolate chips and marshmallow cream in large bowl. Mix in a saucepan sugar, evaporated milk and margarine. Bring to a boil. Boil mixture for 5 minutes and pour over candy bar mixture. Dissolve and mix well with a hand mixer. Pour into a buttered 9x13 pan. Set overnight or until firm.

(The more you beat the creamier the mixture). Add nuts if desired.

Chocoholic's Caramel Apples

Chaplain Larry E Small
Asheville, NC

8 apples
1 bag "Kraft" caramels
1 (16 ounce) package chocolate chips
1 (16 ounce) package white chocolate chips

Melt the caramels in a double boiler. Put the wooden skewers in the apples. Take each apple and dip it in the melted caramels. Cool the caramel apples until the caramel is set.

Taking one apple at a time, dip in the melted chocolate and let cool. Finally dip each one in the melted white chocolate mixture and cool until set. They are then ready to eat!!!!!!

Penuche

Submitted by Cheri Creed
For Great Grandmother Andrews
Aberdeen, NC

2 cups firmly packed brown sugar
⅔ cup whole milk
½ cup of peanut butter

In a 2 quart saucepan mix milk and brown sugar. Cook over medium heat until soft boil stage. Remove from heat; beat in peanut butter until it starts firming up. Pour into a buttered 8x8 pan.

Very easy and very good with either smooth or crunchy peanut butter.

Goochies

Dottie Croker
Atlanta, GA

1 stick margarine
½ cup sugar
¾ cup chopped pecans
1 stick butter
1 package graham crackers

Separate crackers. Place in a foil-lined pan (18x12x3) with edges of foil turned up. Place nuts on the crackers. Boil shortening and sugar for 2 minutes, spoon over the nuts and crackers. Bake at 325° for 10 minutes. Separate when cool.

Cinnamon Rock Candy

Brenda Howell
Siler City, NC

1 cup water

3 ¾ cups sugar

1 ¾ cups light corn syrup

1 teaspoon red food coloring

1 teaspoon cinnamon oil

⅓ cup confectioner sugar

Line a 15 x 10 x 1-inch baking pan with foil and butter the foil. Set aside. In a large saucepan, combine water, sugar, corn syrup and food coloring, bring to a boil over medium heat, stirring occasionally. Cover and cook for 3 minutes to dissolve sugar crystals. Uncover, cook on medium high heat, without stirring about 25 minutes.

Remove from the heat, stir in cinnamon oil; keep clear of mixture as odor is very strong; immediately pour into prepared pan. Cool completely about 45 minutes. Break into pieces using the edge of a metal mallet. Sprinkle both sides of candy with confectioners' sugar. Store in a airtight container.

Pumpkin Squares

Eleanor Stumpf
Big Run, PA

2 cups pumpkin

1 cup sugar

1 cup chopped pecans

36 ginger snaps crumbled

½ gallon vanilla ice cream softened

1 teaspoon ginger

1 teaspoon salt

1 teaspoon cinnamon

½ teaspoon nutmeg

Combine pumpkin, sugar, salt, ginger, cinnamon, nutmeg and pecans. In a chilled bowl, fold pumpkin mixture into softened ice cream. Line, 13x9x2 pan with ½ of the gingersnaps. Top with ice cream mixture. Cover layer with remaining gingersnaps then remaining ice cream mixture. Freeze until firm or when wanted to use. Before serving, top with whipped cream and pecan halves.

Mamie's Favorite Fudge

Jane Phillips
Bear Creek, NC

1 tall, can evaporated milk
2 tablespoons butter
4 ½ cups sugar
Dash salt
1 package (12 ounce size) semi-sweet chocolate pieces
3 bars (4 ounces) sweet cooking chocolate
1 pint marshmallow crème
2 cups chopped pecans

Combine milk, butter, sugar salt. Bring to a vigorous boil, stirring often; then reduce heat and simmer 6 minutes.

Meanwhile place remaining ingredients (except pecans) in a large bowl. Gradually pour boiling syrup over the chocolate-marshmallow mixture and beat until chocolate melts. Stir in nuts. Pour into buttered pans and store in cool place several hours to harden before cutting into squares.

Martha Washington Candy

Allene, Ethelda, Berta
Sue & Jane
The Phillips Sisters

2 boxes confectioners' sugar
¼ pound butter
1 can sweetened condensed milk
2 teaspoons vanilla
4 cups chopped pecans
1 (6 ounce bag) semi-sweet chocolate chips
2 tablespoons paraffin

Combine sugar, butter, milk and vanilla. Mix thoroughly and add nuts. Form mixture into balls. Melt chocolate and paraffin in top of double boiler. Dip balls in chocolate paraffin mixture. Refrigerate until set.

At Christmas this is one of the candies we sisters enjoyed making.

Our family enjoyed it very much!

Peanut Brittle

Dottie Josey
Employee
Bear Creek, NC

1 cup raw peanuts
1 cup sugar
½ cup white corn syrup
⅛ teaspoon salt
1 teaspoon vanilla
1 teaspoon butter
1 teaspoon baking soda

Butter a cookie sheet. Combine peanuts, sugar, syrup and salt. Cook on high 4 minutes. Stir. Cook 3 more minutes. Add vanilla and butter. Stir and cook 1 ½ minutes. Stir in baking soda and pour on cookie sheet. Spread thin. Break into pieces when cool.

Candy Cookies

Jamie Brady
Daughter of Ethelda Co-owner
Bennett, NC

1 (12 ounce) can sweetened condensed milk
16 large marshmallows
1 (6 ounce) package chocolate chips
2 cups crushed graham crackers

Put milk, marshmallows and chocolate chips into top of double boiler; heat until mixture melts. Remove from heat and add crushed graham crackers. Drop by teaspoonful onto wax paper cookie sheet. Allow to set overnight.

Pecan Kisses

Mary Lois Thomas
(Moosie)
Sanford, NC

2 egg whites
¾ cup light brown sugar
A pinch of salt
2 cups of pecan halves

Preheat oven to 250°. Beat egg whites until fluffy. Gently fold in brown sugar, salt and pecans. Drop by spoonfuls onto a cookie sheet sprayed with 'Pam'.

Bake 20 minutes and turn oven off. Leave in the oven for 20 minutes more Yield about 5 dozen.

Goo-Goo Clusters

Dawn Kidd
Employee
Robbins, NC

1 large bag miniature marshmallows
1 bag chocolate chips
2 cups dry roasted peanuts
1 can 'Eagle Brand' sweetened condensed milk
2 teaspoons butter

Mix marshmallows and peanuts in a large bowl. Set this aside.

Melt chocolate chips in pan with 'Eagle Brand' sweetened condensed milk. Pour melted mixture over nuts and marshmallows. Mix. Drop by spoonfuls.

Christmas Nut Roll

Jeanie Scott
Siler City, NC

1 box crushed vanilla wafers
1 cup chopped candied cherries (red or green)
3 cups chopped pecans
1 can Eagle Brand sweetened condensed milk
1 large package of frozen coconut (completely thawed)

Combine first four ingredients and mix well. Roll into 1½ x 6 inch logs. Roll each one in coconut and wrap in wax paper then in aluminum foil. Refrigerate until ready to serve. Cut into ¼ inch slices and serve on a platter.

Party Mints

Jeanie Scott
Siler City, NC

3 ounces of cream cheese (room temperature)
2 ½ cups confectionary sugar
¼ teaspoon peppermint oil
Choice of candy food coloring

Mix confectionary sugar and cream cheese together.

If mixture is too soft, add more sugar. Roll into small balls. Roll these balls in granulated sugar and fit into molds. Make each one individually and leave on wax paper uncovered over night. They will harden on the outside and stay soft on the inside. (Use thin molds). Mints do not pop out of thick molds easily. Store mints in an airtight container. Keep in the refrigerator.

Cookies

Peanut Butter Cookies

Terry Liles
Siler City NC
This recipe makes a large batch of cookies.

4 cups margarine

4 cups white sugar

4 cups brown sugar

8 eggs

4 cups peanut butter

4 teaspoons baking soda

2 teaspoons salt

4 teaspoons vanilla

8 cups flour

Cream together margarine and sugar; add eggs one at a time, beating well each time. Mix in peanut butter. Add vanilla, combine flour, salt, and baking soda in a large bowl. Add dry ingredients a little at a time to the creamed mixture. Dough will be very soft. Drop by teaspoonful onto cookie sheets. Flatten with fork tines dipped in sugar. Bake at 350° for approximately 10 minutes. Recipe makes approximately 3 dozen cookies.

Chewy Date Nut Bars

Amy Jordan, Kayle Jordan & Rebecca Jordan
Wayne and Belinda's granddaughters and daughter-in-law
Bear Creek,NC

1 package (18 ¼ ounce) of yellow cake mix

¾ cup packed brown sugar

¾ cup butter melted

2 eggs

2 cups chopped dates

2 cups chopped walnuts

Combine cake mix and brown sugar. Add butter and eggs; beat on medium speed for 2 minutes. Add dates and walnuts, batter will be stiff.

Spread into greased 13x9 inch pan. Bake 350° for 35-45 minutes. Cool in pan before loosening side. Cool completely before cutting.

Fruitcake Cookies

Beth Walker
Murray, UT

1 pound butter

1 pound light brown sugar

4 ½ cups self-rising flour

1 pound candied cherries (½ red ½ green)

2 pounds chopped dates (sugar coated)

18 to 24 ounces pineapple/apricot preserves

1 teaspoon baking soda

3 eggs

3 tablespoons milk

4 cups pecans

Cream the butter and sugar together. Add eggs. Beat slightly. Mix dry ingredients and hold 1 cup of flour to mix with chopped cherries and pecans. Fold dry mix and preserves into batter with milk. Batter will be too thick for a regular mixer. Use a big heavy spoon or a kitchen aide mixer to mix. Spoon batter into Teflon coated muffin tins. Bake at 300° for 10-12 minutes. Do not over-cook. Cookies will be too hard. Cool in tins approximately 10 minutes. Run a knife around edges to remove from tins. Lay out on a clean white cloth to cool completely before packing into an airtight container. Put wax paper between layers.

If you use a teaspoon to spoon out you will get approximately 12-15 dozen of cookies. If you use a tablespoon, you will have approximately 10 dozen cookies. Cookies will store well for approximately 1 month in an airtight container. Also freezes well.

Peanut Butter Kiss Cookies

Reba G Thomas
Pittsboro, NC

1 can sweetened condensed milk

¾ cup peanut butter

2 cups baking mix ("Bisquick")

1 tablespoon vanilla

¼ cup sugar chocolate kisses candy

Stir condensed milk, peanut butter, and vanilla until blended. Blend in baking mix. Shape mixture into 1-inch balls and roll in sugar. Bake on cookie sheet sprayed with Pam for 11 minutes at 350°. Do not overcook. Place chocolate kiss candy in center of each cookie -let cool.

Note: Fat free condensed milk and reduced fat baking mix work well.

Grammy's Molasses Cookies

Chaplain Larry E Small
Asheville, NC

¾ cup shortening

¾ cup molasses

¾ cup sour cream

1 tablespoon baking soda

1 tablespoon ground ginger

½ teaspoon cloves

¾ cup brown sugar

2 eggs

2 ½ cups flour (approximately)

1 teaspoon salt

1 teaspoon cinnamon

1 cup raisins

In a larger bowl with an electric mixer, cream Crisco and sugar together. Add molasses, eggs, and sour cream and beat to blend. Add ginger, cinnamon, cloves, salt, and baking soda and blend. Add enough flour to make soft dough. Stir in raisins. Chill dough thoroughly. Preheat oven to 350°. Grease cookie sheets. Drop dough by rounded teaspoonful to cookie sheets about 2-inches apart. Bake for 10 to 15 minutes. Cool for a few minutes on the cookie sheet. Remove and cool completely.

Grandmother's Sugar Cookies

Dawn Kidd
High Falls, NC

¼ cup buttermilk

¾ cup lard (shortening)

2 eggs

1 heaping cup sugar

3 cups self rising flour

Put ingredients in a bowl. Stir with a spoon until well mixed. Add flour gradually. Mix in flour and start to knead. Roll out and cut out your cookies. When done sprinkle with sugar on cookies. Cook 375° for 8 to 10 minutes until light brown. Grandmother cut her cookies out with a jar.

Chewy Fudge Brownies

Wanda Hunsucker
Robbins, NC

1 box "Betty Crocker Fudge Brownie Mix"

1 cup oatmeal

1 cup chocolate chips

Mix brownie mix according to package directions. Stir in oatmeal and chocolate chips. Pour in 13x9 pan. Bake at 350° for about 28-30 minutes.

Cut Out-Sugar Cookies

Marie Bibeau
White Bear Lake, MN

3 cups flour
½ teaspoon baking powder
½ teaspoon baking soda
1 cup butter
2 eggs
1 cup sugar

Cut batter in to the first 3 ingredients, as like pie crust. Beat eggs, add sugar in small bowl, and add to all the dry mix. Roll out, about ¼ inch thick on flour, cut and bake.

Bake 8-10 minutes in 375° oven. This is easy to do and so good....

Chocolate Cookies

Lisa Scott
Bear Creek, NC

2 packages (18 ¼ ounces) each, chocolate cake mix
5 eggs
⅔ cup vegetable oil
1 package vanilla or white chips
1 cup chopped pecans or walnuts

Combine all ingredients in large bowl. Last, add the chips and nuts. Drop by rounded tablespoons onto greased cookie sheet, 2-inches apart.

Bake 10-13 minutes 350°, tops will crack. Cool 5 minutes before removing.

Helpful Hint

Tin coffee cans make excellent freezer containers for cookies.

Secret Recipe
Chocolate Chip Cookies

Amy Bryant
Siler City, NC
Employee

½ cup rolled oats, regular or quick

2 ¼ cups all-purpose flour

1 ½ teaspoons baking soda

½ teaspoon salt

1 cup (2 sticks) butter, softened

¾ cup firmly packed brown sugar

¾ cup granulated sugar

2 teaspoons vanilla extract

1 teaspoon lemon juice

2 eggs

3 cups semisweet chocolate chips

1 ½ cups chopped walnuts

Preheat oven to 350°. Cover two baking sheets with parchment paper. Place rolled oats in blender or food processor and process until finely ground. Combine ground oats, flour, baking soda, salt and cinnamon in a mixing bowl.
In another bowl, cream sugars, vanilla and lemon juice together using an electric mixer. Add eggs and beat until fluffy.

Stir the flour mixture into egg mixture, blending well. Add the chocolate chips and nuts to the dough and mix well.

Using ¼ cup of dough for each cookie, scoop round balls with an ice-cream scoop and place 2 ½ inches apart on prepared baking sheets. Bake until cookies lightly brown, 16-18 minutes. Transfer to a wire rack to cool completely. Store in sealed container to keep them soft and chewy.

Chocolate Chunk Cookies

Joann Jones
Employee
Bennett, NC

Oatmeal keeps these cookies moist and flavorful. Traditional chips work just fine too.

1 cup all-purpose flour
1 cup whole-wheat flour
½ cup quick cooking oats
1 teaspoon baking soda
½ teaspoon salt
1 cup sugar
½ cup packed brown sugar
⅓ cup butter
2 egg whites
1 tablespoon 1% milk
1 teaspoon vanilla extract

1 package (6 ounces) semi-sweet chocolate pieces or morsels

Preheat oven to 375°, coat two baking sheets with non-stick spray. In large bowl, combine the all-purpose and whole-wheat flour, oats, baking soda and salt. In another bowl, combine sugar, brown sugar, butter, egg whites, milk and vanilla extract. Add flour mixture and stir until moistened. Stir in the chocolate pieces. Drop by rounded teaspoon 2-inches apart on baking sheets. Bake 10-12 minutes or until lightly browned around the edges. Remove cookies to rack to cool.

Helpful Hint

Keep the mixing of cookie dough to a minimum. Stir just until the flour disappears. Over mixing toughens the dough.

Key Lime Cookies

Kathryn Frazier
Liberty, NC
Showroom Employee

½ cup butter, softened

1 cup sugar

1 egg plus 1 egg yolk

1 ½ cups flour

1 teaspoon baking powder

½ teaspoon salt

¼ cup fresh lime juice

1 ½ teaspoon grated lime peel (green part only)

½ cup powdered sugar

Preheat oven to 350°. In a large bowl, mix butter, sugar, egg and egg yolk until creamy. Thoroughly mix in flour; baking powder, salt, lime juice and lime peel. Form dough into ½ inch balls, Place on greased cookie sheet and bake until lightly browned, 8-10 minutes. Remove to wire rack to cool. While still warm, sift powdered sugar over cookies.

Chocolate Caramel Pecan Cookies

Kathryn Frazier
Liberty, NC
Showroom Employee

1 cup margarine

¼ cup lightly packed brown sugar

½ cup granulated sugar

1 egg

1 ½ teaspoons vanilla

2 cups all-purpose flour

1 teaspoon baking soda

¼ teaspoon salt

6 squares semi-sweet chocolate-chopped

1 cup caramels, quartered

¼ cup coarsely chopped pecans

Preheat oven to 375°. Bake for 9-12 minutes, or until light golden. Makes about 36 cookies.

7 Layer Cookies

Rita Holt
Bear Creek, NC

1 stick butter or margarine
1 cup graham cracker crumbs
1 cup coconut
1 (6 ounce) package equals (1 cup)
chocolate chips
1 (6 ounce) package equals (1 cup)
butterscotch chips
1 ½ cups chopped walnuts
1 (14 ounce) can sweetened condensed
milk

Melt the stick of butter in a 9x13 cake
pan. Remove from heat and sprinkle the
next five ingredients in layers over the
butter. Drizzle sweetened condensed milk
over top. Bake at 350° for 25 minutes.
If using glass pan, reduce temperature
to 325°. The cookies will be light brown.
Allow to cool completely (about 2 hours)
before cutting.

Almond Butter Cookies With Cream Cheese

Deborah Pickard Stephenson
Carthage, NC
Showroom Employee

1½ cups sugar
1 cup butter
1 (8 ounce) package cream cheese
1 egg
1 teaspoon vanilla
1 teaspoon almond extract
4 cups all purpose flour
1 teaspoon baking powder

Cream the sugar, butter and cream
cheese until fluffy. Add egg and
flavorings. Beat until smooth. Add flour
and baking powder, mixing well. Drop
dough by spoonfuls onto ungreased
cookie sheets and flatten with a flat-
bottomed drinking glass dipped in sugar.
You can also force dough through a
cookie press. You can also chill dough 1 to
1 ½ hours and roll out on lightly floured
surface. Cut with cookie cutters. Bake
at 375° for 8-10 minutes, or slightly less
if you like a not-so-crispy cookie. These
cookies are best if not baked too brown.

Butterscotch Pecan Cookies

Rae Scott
Bear Creek, NC
These cookies are great; one would not think about them starting from cake mix and pudding mixes.

1 package "Pillsbury" (18 ¼ ounces) butter recipe cake mix
1 package (3 ¼ ounces) instant butterscotch pudding mix
¼ cup all-purpose flour
¾ cup vegetable oil
1 egg
1 cup chopped pecans

Combine the first five ingredients mix well, stir in pecans (dough will be crumbly). Roll in balls (use scoop spoon) on greased cookie sheets. Cook 10-12 minutes 350° °. Cool for 5 minutes before removing from pan.

Butterfinger Bars

Kathryn Frazier
Liberty, NC

1 cup flour
¼ cup brown sugar
1 (8 ounce) package cream cheese
1 cup "Cool Whip"
2 cups milk
1 cup coconut
½ cup butter
1 cup confectioners' sugar
1 cup miniature marshmallows
2 small boxes instant vanilla pudding
4 "Butterfinger" candy bars

Mix flour, coconut, brown sugar and butter until crumbly and pat into a 13x9 inch pan. Bake 12-15 minutes at 350°. Check frequently until brown. Cool. Cream together the cream cheese, powdered sugar, "Cool Whip" and miniature marshmallows. Put on top of crust. Mix the milk and pudding. Put on the cream cheese layer. Crumble 4 "Butterfinger" candy bars and sprinkle them on top of a layer of "Cool Whip" that was put on top of pudding layer.

Chocolate Chunk-Peanut Butter Cookies

Terry Liles
Siler City, NC

½ cup butter, softened

½ cup shortening

1 cup chunky peanut butter or creamy

1 cup granulated sugar

1 cup firmly packed brown sugar

2 large eggs

2 ½ cups all-purpose flour

1 ½ teaspoon baking soda

1 teaspoon baking powder

½ teaspoon salt

1 teaspoon ground cinnamon

1 (11.5 ounces) package chocolate chunks

Beat butter and shortening at medium speed with an electric mixer until creamy. Add peanut butter and sugars; beating well. Add eggs beating until blended. Combine flour and next 4 ingredients. Add to butter mixture, beating well. Stir in chocolate chunks. Shape dough into 2 inch balls (about 2 tablespoons each cookie) flatten slightly and place on ungreased baking sheet. Bake at 375°, until lightly brown for 12 to 15 minutes. Makes 28 cookies

Moravian Ginger Cookies

In Memory of
Mrs. Nannie Phillips

4 tablespoons butter

¼ cup packed brown sugar

2 tablespoons molasses

1 ¼ cup all-purpose flour

1 teaspoon grated lemon peel

¾ teaspoon ground ginger

½ teaspoon baking soda

½ teaspoon ground cinnamon

¼ teaspoon ground cloves

Granulated sugar

In a 2 quart saucepan, combine butter, sugar and molasses. Cook over medium heat until sugar dissolves and butter melts, stirring occasionally. Remove from heat, stir in flour and remaining ingredients except granulated sugar. Chill dough 2 hours or until firm enough to roll. Preheat oven to 350°; grease cookie sheet. On floured surface with floured rolling pin, roll half of dough. Using cookie cutter, continue to cut cookies using all the dough, placing cookies 1-inch apart on cookie sheet. Prick with fork to make design. Sprinkle with sugar. Bake about 7 minutes.

Cappuccino Cookies

Lorrie, Brooke, and Lauren Moore
Bonlee, NC

1 ¼ cups firmly packed light brown sugar

1 cup shortening

2 eggs

¼ cup light corn syrup or regular pancake syrup

1 teaspoon vanilla

1 teaspoon rum extract

2 tablespoons instant espresso or coffee powder

3 cups all-purpose flour

¾ teaspoon baking powder

½ teaspoon baking soda

½ teaspoon salt

½ teaspoon nutmeg

Chocolate 'jimmies'

Place brown sugar and shortening in large bowl. Beat at medium speed of electric mixer until well blended. Add eggs, corn syrup, vanilla, rum extract and coffee. Beat until well blended and fluffy. Combine flour, baking powder, baking soda, salt and nutmeg. Add gradually to shortening mixture, beating at low speed until blended. Divide dough in half. Roll each half into two logs approximately 2-inches in diameter. Wrap in waxed paper. Refrigerate several hours. Heat oven to 350°; place sheets of foil on countertop for cooling cookies. Cut cookies into ¼ inch-thick slices. Place 2 inches apart on ungreased baking sheet. Sprinkle center of each cookie with jimmies. Bake on baking sheet at a time at 350° for 10-12 minutes or until golden brown. DO NOT OVERBAKE. Cool 2 minutes. Remove cookies to foil to cool completely. Makes about 4 ½ dozen cookies.

Chocolate Chip Pudding Cookies

Susie, Abby & Annie Jordan
Belinda & Wayne's granddaughters and
daughter-in-law
Hoffman, NC

2 ¼ cups all-purpose flour
1 teaspoon soda
1 cup butter, room temperature
¼ cup white sugar
¾ cup packed brown sugar
1 teaspoon vanilla
1 package (4 serving size) instant vanilla pudding
2 eggs
1 (12 ounce) package chocolate chips
1 cup chopped nuts, optional

Mix flour with baking soda, combine butter, sugars, vanilla and pudding; mix in larger mixer bowl. Beat until smooth and creamy. Beat in eggs, gradually add flour mixture then stir in chocolate chips and nuts. Batter will be stiff. Drop by teaspoonful on ungreased baking sheet. Bake at 375° for 8-9 minutes. Do not over bake; will finish cooking out of oven in pan.

Chewy Butterscotch Bars

Suzie Q Jordan
Hoffman, NC

⅔ cup brown sugar
½ cup butter
2 eggs
1 teaspoon vanilla
½ cup flour
1 small package instant butterscotch pudding
¼ teaspoon salt
¾ cup quick oats

Cream sugar, butter and eggs. Stir in rest of ingredients. Spread into 9x9 baking dish or pan. Bake 15-20 minutes at 350°. Do not over bake it will finish cooking in pan after removing from oven. Cool, then sprinkle with powdered sugar.

Chocolate Macaroons

Mildred Hester
Durham NC

1 ½ cups chocolate chips

3 egg whites

Pinch of salt

¾ cup sugar

1 teaspoon vanilla

2 ¼ cups shredded coconut

½ cup chopped walnuts

Preheat oven to 325°. Lightly grease baking sheet and set aside. In double boiler over low heat, place chocolate chips. Remove from heat and let cool slightly. In a large mixing bowl, beat egg whites until foamy. Slowly add salt and sugar a little at a time, until soft peaks form. Stir in vanilla, fold in melted chocolate, shredded coconut and chopped walnuts. Drop dough by teaspoonfuls 2 inches apart onto prepared baking sheet. Bake in oven 10-12 minutes. Cookies should be soft in center. Let cookies cool slightly before removing from baking sheet. Makes 3 dozen

Sugar Cookies

In loving memory of Sue Wilson
By Lisa Scott
Co-owner
Bear Creek, NC

1 cup 'Crisco'

2 eggs

⅔ cup sugar

2 ½ cup flour

1 tsp vanilla

Mix Crisco, eggs and vanilla very well. Add to the mixture flour and sugar until all is blended. Roll out cookie dough to ¼ inch thick. Cut cookies to desired shape, sprinkle with sugar. Bake at 375° for 15 minutes.

No Bake Cookies

Lois Brady
Bennett, NC

2 cups sugar

¼ cup cocoa

½ cup milk

¼ pound butter

1 teaspoon vanilla flavoring

1 pinch salt

½ cup chunky or plain peanut butter

3 cups quick cooking oatmeal

Mix in saucepan sugar, milk, cocoa, and butter. Cook on medium heat until it starts to boil, (a rolling boil, stirring constantly). Remove from heat and cool for 1 minute. Add 1 teaspoon vanilla, salt, peanut butter, and oatmeal. Stir well and drop by teaspoonfuls onto wax paper.

Death By Chocolate Cookies

Kathryn Frazier
Liberty, NC
Showroom Employee

2 packages (16 squares) semi-sweet baking chocolate, divided

¾ cup brown sugar

¼ cup butter, softened

2 eggs

1 teaspoon vanilla

½ cup flour ¼ teaspoon baking powder

2 cups chopped nuts, optional

Heat oven to 350° coarsely chop 8 ounces (1 package) of the chocolate; set aside. In a large microwavable bowl, put in remaining 8 squares of chocolate and cook on high for 1-2 minutes. Stir until chocolate is melted and smooth. Stir in sugar, butter, eggs and vanilla. Stir in flour, baking powder, reserved chopped chocolate and nuts. Drop by ¼ cupfuls onto ungreased cookie sheet. Bake 12-13 minutes or until cookies are puffed and feel set to the touch. Cool on cookie sheet 1 minute. Transfer to wire rack to cool completely. Makes about 1 ½ dozen cookies.

Old-Fashioned Gingerbread

Linda Sheffield,
Fruitcake Kitchen Staff
Carthage, NC

½ cup butter, softened

1 cup sugar

1 cup molasses

1 large egg

2 ½ cups all-purpose flour

1 ½ teaspoon baking soda

½ teaspoon salt

1 teaspoon ground ginger

1 teaspoon ground cinnamon

1 cup hot water

Beat butter with electric mixer until creamy. Gradually add sugar; beat well. Add molasses and egg; beat well. Combine flour and next four ingredients. Add to butter mixture alternately with hot water beginning and ending with flour mixture. Mix at low speed after each addition until blended. Pour batter into lightly greased and floured 13x9" pan. Bake 350° for 35 to 40 minutes or until toothpick inserted in center comes out clean. Cool slightly in pan and on wire rack. Serve with lemon hard sauce.

Hard sauce is an old-fashioned butter and sugar topping that is chilled. It quickly melts into a sauce when spooned over a serving of hot gingerbread or fruit cobbler.

½ cup butter, softened

1 teaspoon grated lemon rind

¼ cup sifted powdered sugar

1 tablespoon fresh lemon juice

Beat butter and lemon rind in a small mixing bowl at medium speed with an electric mixer. Gradually add powdered sugar and lemon juice beating until light and fluffy. Cover and chill until ready to serve. Serve at room temperature.

269

Pies

Banana Split Pie

Marilyn Sehen
Sanford, NC

1 stick melted margarine
Graham crackers
½ cup lemon juice
1 can sweet condensed milk
Bananas
1 can crushed pineapple
1 carton 'Cool Whip'
2 cups flake coconut
1 cup chopped nuts
1 small jar maraschino cherries

Crush graham crackers and line bottom of oblong dish. Pour melted margarine over crackers. Slice bananas and cover graham crackers. Mix lemon juice and milk pour evenly over bananas. Drain pineapple and spread over bananas. Spread Cool Whip over pineapple. Cover with coconut. Sprinkle with nuts. Top with maraschino cherries. Refrigerate.

Chocolate Pie

Sara Ellis
Mt. Holly, NC

1 cup sugar
3 eggs (separated)
½ cup cocoa
½ cup butter
1 teaspoon vanilla
Pinch of salt
1 can evaporated milk (large undiluted)

Combine sugar and cocoa and mix well. Beat egg yolk, add to sugar and cocoa and mix thoroughly, then add milk, butter, salt and vanilla. Pour in large pie plate and cook slowly until mixture is thick. Top with egg whites well beaten with ⅛ teaspoon cream of tartar and 6 tablespoons of sugar. Cook at 350° for 10 minutes. Reduce to 325° and cook until firm when shaken.

Granny's Sweet Potato Pie

Marge Decker
Greensboro, NC

2 ¼ cups cooked mashed sweet potatoes

¾ cup sugar

½ cup firmly packed brown sugar

1 small package vanilla, lemon or butterscotch instant pudding

¾ cup evaporated milk

2 large eggs beaten

6 tablespoons butter or margarine melted

1 teaspoon mixed spices or use cinnamon allspice & nutmeg

1 ½ tablespoons vanilla extract

2 unbaked 9 inch deep dish pie shells

Combine all ingredients in a large bowl. Spread evenly in pie shells. Bake 450° for 10 minutes. Reduce to 350° bake for 40 minutes longer or until set.

Cool and garnish with pecans or cool whip.

You may add crushed pecans to batter if desired or coconut!

Coconut Pie

Mrs. Maggie W. Williams

1 pint sweet milk

6 eggs, separated

2 tablespoons melted butter

1 tablespoon cornstarch

¼ tablespoon salt

1 can coconut (save 3 or 4 tablespoons)

Beat egg yolks until light. Add sugar and cornstarch and beat until lemon color. Heat milk to boiling point and add butter. Add salt and coconut. Bake in a moderate oven until almost done then cover with meringue to which has been added 6 tablespoons of sugar. Sprinkle with coconut and brown.

Sweet Potato Pie

Martha Gilmore
Siler City, NC

1 can "Eagle Brand" sweetened condensed milk

2 eggs

1 cup sugar

1 stick margarine

3 medium potatoes

1 teaspoon vanilla or nutmeg

Mix and cook 350° for 40 minutes. This makes three pies. It takes 2 or 3 pie crusts.

No Crust Pumpkin Pie

Joann Wingler
(Grammy)

2 cups pumpkin
1 ½ cups sugar
1 cup evaporated milk
2 eggs
½ teaspoon salt
2 teaspoons vanilla
2 teaspoons pumpkin spice-or some
cinnamon (my preference ½ teaspoon).
½ cup "Bisquick"
2 teaspoons margarine (melted)

Mix ingredients in blender. Pour mixture
in glass pie pan. Bake at 350° for 50
minutes. Serve with whipped cream.

My seven-year old grandson (Jacob
Sykes) loves to make and eat this pie.

Blueberry Pie

Marilyn Sehen
Sanford, NC

4 cups fresh or frozen blueberries
1 cup sugar
3 tablespoons cornstarch
⅛ teaspoon salt
1 cup water
1 teaspoon lemon juice
¼ teaspoon ground cinnamon
1 tablespoon margarine
2 pie shells (baked)
1 carton 'cool whip'

Wash and drain blueberries. Mix sugar,
1 cup blueberries, water, cornstarch, salt,
cinnamon, and lemon juice in saucepan.
Cook over medium heat, stirring
constantly until thick. Remove from heat
add margarine and remaining berries.
Mix until margarine melts, and sauce is
mixed with berries. Pour into baked pie
shells. Let cool. Spread 'cool whip' over
top. Refrigerate.

Pear Pie

Marilyn Sehen
Sanford, NC

1 cup all purpose flour

¼ teaspoon salt

⅓ cup shortening

½ cup (2 ounces) shredded sharp cheddar cheese

3 or 4 tablespoons ice water

5 ½ cups peeled and sliced "Bartlett" pears (about 3 pounds)

2 teaspoons lemon juice

½ cup sugar

¼ cup all-purpose flour

¼ teaspoon ground cinnamon

¾ cup firmly packed light brown sugar

½ cup butter or margarine cut into pieces

Combine 1 cup flour and salt. Cut in shortening with pastry blender until mixture is crumbly. Add cheese, sprinkle with water one tablespoon at a time evenly over surface. Stir dry ingredients with fork until moist. Shape into a ball.

Roll pastry to ½- inch thickness on a lightly floured surface. Place in a 10 inch glass pie plate. Trim off excess pastry along edges, set aside.

Stir together pears and next four ingredients in large bowl; spoon into pastry shell.

Combine brown sugar and ½ cup flour. Cut in butter with pastry blender until mixture is crumbly. Sprinkle topping over pear filling.

Bake at 375° for one hour or until golden. Cool completely on a wire rack. Yields one, (10 inch) pie.

Strawberry Cream Pie

Chaplain Larry E Small
Asheville, NC

1 graham cracker crust
1 cup sour cream
¼ cup milk
1 pack large vanilla pudding
½ teaspoon cinnamon
1 teaspoon orange peel
1 pint strawberries, sliced

Layer ½ the sliced strawberries on bottom of the crust. Combine remaining ingredients and pour over strawberries. Top with the remaining strawberries. Chill for 2 hours.

Pineapple Ice Box Pie

Marge Decker
Greensboro, NC

1 can sweetened condensed milk
1 large can crushed pineapple-drained
6 tablespoons lemon juice
1 (8 ounce) container Cool Whip
2 graham cracker crust

Combine all ingredients. Spoon the mixture into graham cracker crust. Refrigerate for 2 to 3 hours before serving.

You may also use fruit cocktail or other canned fruit-drained.

Blueberry Pie

Reba Thomas
Pittsboro, NC

1 graham cracker crust
1 can sweetened condense milk
¼ cup lemon juice
1 teaspoon lemon flavoring
1 or 2 cups blueberries
1 (12 ounce) container whipped topping

Mix condensed milk, lemon juice, and flavoring-mixing well. Mixture will thicken. Stir in blueberries. Fold in whipped topping and pour into graham cracker crust. Refrigerate several hours or overnight.

Note: Fat free condensed milk works well. Peaches can a substitute for blueberries.

California Peach Pie

Dorothy Coates
Timberlake, NC

1 (10 ounce) package dried peaches
1 cup sugar
4 eggs beaten
1 ½ cups sugar
1 stick margarine, melted
1 teaspoon vanilla

Cook peaches in water enough to cover peaches well. When tender, mash peaches and add 1 cup sugar. Stir well. When cool, put in refrigerator overnight. Divide the peaches into 2 uncooked pie shells. Mix eggs, 1 ½ cups sugar, vanilla, and melted margarine together good. Pour over top of peaches (do not mix).

Bake at 350° until set and browned. Enjoy!

Raisin Meringue Pie

Sandra Cook
Siler City NC
Office Employee

9 inch baked pie shell
2 cups seeded raisins
2 cups water
¼ cup cornstarch
½ cup sugar
½ teaspoon salt
2 egg yolks slightly beaten
¼ cup orange juice
1 teaspoon orange zest
1 tablespoon butter
½ teaspoon vanilla

Meringue:
2 egg whites beaten with ¼ teaspoon cream of tarter and 4 tablespoons sugar until stiff and glossy

Cook raisins and water 15 minutes (There should be 2 cups when done) Add more water if necessary to make up difference. Mix together cornstarch, sugar, egg yolks, salt, orange juice, orange zest, butter and vanilla. Combine with raisins mixture. Cook over low heat, stirring constantly until thickens. Pour into pie shell; cover with meringue. Bake 8-10 minutes until brown in 400° oven.

Key Lime Pie

Betty King
Siler City, NC

Combine a 14 ounce can sweeten condensed milk with enough real lime juice to start thickening. I use 1 ½ to 2 limes (juice only). Next, add 12 ounces whipped topping and blend well. Add a few drops of green food coloring. Pour into prepared graham cracker crust; refrigerate; can be frozen for later use.

Hawaiian Pie

Dottie Josey
Employee
Bear Creek, NC

(5.1) ounce package instant vanilla pudding
20 ounces crushed pineapple in heavy syrup
8 ounces sour cream
9 inch graham cracker pie crust

In a large bowl, combine vanilla pudding mix, undrained pineapple, sour cream; stir until well blended. Pour mixture into piecrust. Cover and chill 2 hours before serving.

Mud Pie

Holly Reynolds
Granddaughter of Ethelda

1 box (18 ¼ ounces) 'German Chocolate' cake mix
1 stick margarine or butter, cut into pieces (4 ounces)
1 package (8 ounces) cream cheese, cut into pieces
1 cup brown sugar, packed
2 cups chopped walnuts
1 can (3 ½ ounces) flake coconut

Grease two 9 inch pie pans. Prepare the cake batter according to package directions and spread evenly in the pans. In a saucepan over low heat, soften the cream cheese and margarine and combine well. Remove from heat and add the brown sugar, mixing well. Add the walnuts and coconut, stirring to mix. Using a spoon, place the cream cheese mixture evenly over the cake batter. Bake 350° for 30-35 minutes.

Cherry Cheese Cake

Evelyn Cheek
Asheboro, NC

2 cans crescent rolls
2 (8 ounce) package cream cheese
1 ½ cups powdered sugar
1 egg white
1 teaspoon vanilla
3 tablespoons milk
2 cans cherry pie filling

Layer 1 can of crescent rolls on bottom of 12x9 pan. Mix well cream cheese, sugar, egg white, vanilla. Mix with 3 teaspoons milk. Pour over layer: 2 cans cherry pie filling. Place other can crescent roll on top. Bake 350° for 25 minutes. Mix ¾ cup powdered sugar and 3 tablespoons milk. Pour over cooled cheesecake.

Apricot Chiffon Pie

Peggy Fox
Asheboro, NC

1 cup stewed apricots
¼ teaspoon salt
½ cup water
3 egg whites, beaten
½ cup sugar
2 teaspoon lemon juice
1 cup whipped cream
1 envelope gelatin, dissolved in ¼ cup cold water.

Stew apricots; add sugar, water, salt, and lemon juice. Dissolve gelatin in this mixture and cool. Add to beaten egg whites, and then fold in whipped cream. Pour into a cooked pastry shell and refrigerate until ready to serve.

Southern Pecan Pie

Shirley Mabe
Stoneville, NC

3 eggs
1 cup sugar
1 cup light or dark syrup
1 tablespoon margarine
1 teaspoon vanilla flavoring

1 cup pecans
1 pie shell

Mix ingredients together, pour in pie shell, and bake on 350° for 55 minutes.

Strawberry Cobbler Pie

Sandy Brown
Bear Creek, NC

3 cups sliced strawberries
5 tablespoons butter
2 eggs
¾ to 1 cup sugar (depending on sweetness of berries)
⅛ teaspoon salt
1 prepared pie pastry

Line a 9 or 10 inch pie plate with pastry. Place sliced strawberries in bottom. Cream sugar and butter; add beaten eggs and salt. Blend well. Pour batter evenly over berries. Bake in preheated 425° oven for 10 minutes. Reduce heat to 325° and bake 25 to 30 minutes. Serve hot.

Rhubarb Pie

Carson Wise
St. Paul, VA

4 cups fresh or frozen rhubarb
1 ½ to 2 cups sugar
¾ cup plain flour
½ teaspoon salt
If desired, add cinnamon and or raisins.

Mix well all ingredients. Put into piecrust, top with sugar. Cut slits in top. Bake at 350°, for 1 hour until brown. Depending on how sweet you want your pie use 2 cups sugar.

This 'Rhubarb Pie' recipe; has been passed through the Wise Family since who knows when.

Southern Chess Pie

Aunt Lois Brady
Bennett, NC

1 cup brown sugar
½ cup granulated sugar
1 tablespoon flour
2 eggs
2 tablespoons milk
1 teaspoon vanilla
½ cup butter (melted)
1 cup pecans

Preheat oven to 350°. Mix together sugar and flour. Thoroughly beat in eggs, milk, vanilla and butter. Fold in nuts and pour into a regular size piecrust. Bake for 40-50 minutes.

This pie will freeze well. I double the recipe and freeze one for later.

Derby Pie

Lisa Scott
Bear Creek, NC

1 stick butter, melted
2 eggs
1 teaspoon vanilla flavoring
¾ cup walnuts
3 ounces coconut
1 cup sugar
½ cup self-rising flour
6 ounces chocolate chips

Mix first five ingredients. Stir in chips, walnuts, and coconut. Pour into unbaked pie shell. Bake at 350° for 35-45 minutes.

Key Lime Pie

Hazel McMath
Employee
Goldston, NC

1 package cream cheese, thawed
1 can sweetened condensed milk
⅓ cups lime juice
1 ½ teaspoons vanilla
Drop of green food coloring

Mix the above ingredients and pour into graham cracker crust.

Fudge Pecan Pie

Denise Holt
Bear Creek, NC
Showroom Staff

2 large eggs
3 ounces semisweet chocolate
1 stick (½ cup) salted butter
1 cup sugar
3 tablespoons all-purpose flour
1 tablespoons vanilla
1 cup pecan halves
9 inch frozen unbaked pie shell

Preheat oven to 325°. Whisk together eggs until just combined. Coarsely chop chocolate and cut butter to small pieces. In top of double boiler, melt chocolate and butter stirring until smooth. Remove top of boiler from heat. Whisk in sugar, flour, vanilla and eggs. Stir in the pecans and pour into pie shell. Bake on cookie sheet in oven until set and puffy 55-60 minutes. Very Delicious!

Peach Pie Supreme

Rae Scott
Bear Creek, NC
Lisa and Randy's daughter

Sliced fresh peaches
2 eggs
1 cup sugar
2 tablespoons flour
9 inch unbaked pie shell

Peel and slice peaches to fill shell 1 inch from top of crust. Beat egg, sugar and flour together. Pour mixture over peaches. Bake 1 hour in 325° oven.

Dang Good Pie

Nellie Brewer
Bennett, NC
Sample Bar Employee

½ stick of butter (melted)
2 eggs
1 cup coconut
1 tablespoon flour
1 ½ cup sugar
1 cup drained crushed pineapple

Mix all ingredients together and pour into a 9 inch pie crust. Bake for 1 hour at 350°.

Strawberry Cream Pie

Gail Scott
Bear Creek, NC
Co-owner

1 can sweetened condensed milk
1 large container Cool Whip
1 ½ cups sliced or chopped strawberries
3 tablespoons lemon juice

Mix milk, cool whip and lemon juice; fold in berries. Pour into graham cracker crust. Let chill and serve. Makes 2 pies.

Coconut Pie

Wyanne L. Caviness
Bennett, NC
First Bank

4 eggs
2 ¼ cups sugar
¼ cup flour
½ cup melted margarine
¾ cup milk
3 cups grated coconut
1 teaspoon coconut flavoring

Mix well. Pour into 9 inch unbaked pie shell. Bake at 350° for 45 minutes or until brown. Makes 2 pies.

Key Lime Pie

Lorrie Moore
Showroom Staff

Graham cracker crust:

1 ½ cup graham cracker crumbs

⅓ cup sugar

6 tablespoons unsalted butter melted and cooled

Filling:

2 cups heavy cream

1 teaspoon freshly grated lime to eat

½ cup fresh lime juice —about 4 large limes

1 (14 ounce) can sweetened condensed milk

To make the crust: preheat oven to 350°. Combine graham cracker crumbs, sugar and butter. Turn into 9 inch pie pan and press ingredients firmly on bottom and up the sides of the pan covering entire surface. Bake for 7-10 minutes. Remove from oven and cool completely.

To make fillings: whip heavy cream to soft peaks and set aside. In a large mixing bowl combine lime zest, juice and sweetened condensed milk. Whisk together until mixture is slightly thickened and well combined. Add ⅔ of the whipped cream to the lime mixture and gently fold to combine. Refrigerate remaining ⅓ of whipped cream. Pour pie filling into prepared crust and place in refrigerator for at least 2 hours so that it will be firm enough to cut when ready to serve. Remove from refrigerator and top with remaining ⅓ of whipped cream.

French Silk Pie

Bonnie Reynolds
Daughter of Ethelda Co-owner
Carthage, NC

2 (1 ounce) squares unsweetened chocolate
⅓ cup butter or margarine
¾ cup sugar
⅓ cup all-purpose flour
3 cups whipping cream, divided
2 egg yolks slightly beaten
1 baked 9 inch pastry shell
2 tablespoons powdered sugar
Garnish chocolate shavings

Place chocolate and butter in top of double boiler; bring water to a boil. Reduce heat to low. Cook until chocolate and butter melt. Add sugar and flour; stir well. Gradually stir in 2 cups whipping cream. Cook, stirring constantly 20 minutes or until mixture thickens. Gradually add ¼ of hot mixture to egg yolks. Add to remaining hot mixture; stirring constantly. Cook until mixture thickens and reaches 160°. Remove from heat, cover tightly with plastic wrap, cool to room temperature then spoon mixture into pastry shell, cover and chill 2 hours. Beat remaining 1 cup whipping cream at medium speed with electric mixer until foamy; gradually add powdered sugar, beating until soft peak forms. Spread whipped cream on pie, garnish with chocolate shavings if desired.

Egg Custard Or Coconut Pie

Hazel McMath
Goldston, NC
Employee

2 cups sugar
4 eggs
1 teaspoon vanilla
1 stick butter
1 can coconut
1 cup milk
2 tablespoons flour

Beat eggs lightly. Mix flour and sugar together; add eggs. Melt butter and add to mixture; then vanilla, coconut and milk. Pour into two unbaked pie shells and bake at 350° until lightly browned. If you want to make plain egg custard just leave out the coconut.
***Personal notes: I use Mrs. Filbert's margarine instead of butter.

I think a can of coconut says it contains 1 ⅓ cups of coconut loosely packed. So if I am using coconut from a bag or package, I use maybe a little more than 1 ⅓ cups.

Tarts, placed on a cookie sheet, will usually cook in about 30 minutes. Depending on your oven, 30-45 minutes of cooking time is required.

Will make 16 tarts or 1 deep-dish pie. Happy Cooking! Call me when they are ready.

Streusel Topped Creamy Pumpkin Pie

Karen King
Sanford, NC

1 ¼ cups cold milk

2 packages (4 serving size) cheesecake flavor instant pudding & pie filling

1 teaspoon pumpkin pie spice

1 cup canned pumpkin

1 tub (8 ounces) frozen non-dairy whipped topping, thawed, divided

1 Graham pie crust

Streusel Topping:

½ cup chopped walnuts

2 tablespoons brown sugar

1 tablespoon margarine or butter

In large bowl beat milk, pudding mix and spice with wire whisk for 1 minute. Whisk in pumpkin. (Mixture will be thick.) Fold in half of whipped topping.

Spread in crust. Refrigerate at least 4 hours or until set.

In small microwaveable bowl, combine walnuts, brown sugar, and margarine. For 1 ½ to 2 ½ minutes, microwave on high until bubbly, stirring once. Spread on foil to cool.

Crumble walnut mixture over pie. Serve with remaining whipped topping. Store in refrigerator. Yield: 8 servings

Helpful Hint

To prevent crust from becoming soggy with cream pie, sprinkle crust with powdered sugar.

Pecan Pie

In loving memory of Sue Wilson
Lisa Scott
Bear Creek, NC
Co-owner

½ cup brown or white sugar

4 tablespoons butter

1 cup 'Karo' syrup

3 eggs

1 teaspoon vanilla

⅛ teaspoon salt

1 cup pecans

1 (9 inch) unbaked pie shell

Combine sugar, butter and 'Karo' syrup; cook over low heat until sugar melts. Add eggs, vanilla flavoring and salt; blend well. Add pecans and pour into 9 inch unbaked pie shell. Bake at 350° for 45 to 50 minutes.

French Coconut Pie

In loving memory of Sue Wilson
Lisa Scott
Bear Creek, NC
Co-owner

1 stick butter

1 ½ cups sugar

3 eggs

1 (7 ounce) can shredded coconut

1 teaspoon vinegar

1 teaspoon vanilla

1 (9 inch) unbaked pie shell

Melt 1 stick butter, combine sugar, eggs, coconut, vinegar and vanilla flavoring. Pour into unbaked pie shell and bake at 350° for 45 minutes.

Apple Pie

Wyanne L. Caviness
Bennett, NC
First Bank

6 Apples (sliced thin)

1 ½ cups sugar

¼ teaspoon cinnamon

6 slices bread (each cut into 4 strips)

1 egg

1 stick melted margarine

2 tablespoon flour

¼ teaspoon cinnamon

Cook apples in small amount of water to steam with ½ cup sugar and cinnamon. Place in 9x13 dish. Cover with bread strips. Mix egg, add remaining sugar, margarine, flour and cinnamon. Spread on top of bread. Bake at 350° for 35 minutes or until brown.

Granny's Apple Pie

Rae Scott
Bear Creek, NC
Daughter of Randy and Lisa Scott

Crust:
2 cups plain flour
¾ cup Crisco
1 teaspoon salt
5 tablespoons ice cold water

In large bowl mix flour, Crisco and salt, stir together until flour forms into pea shapes. Add water. Stir until everything sticks together. Break dough in half. Roll out both pieces to form top and bottom of crust (must be very thin).

Filling: 4 or 5 apples, sliced thin
Water for boiling
1 cup sugar
2 tablespoons cinnamon

Put apples in pot and pour water over to cover halfway up the apples. Boil until the apples are just mushy. Add sugar and cinnamon. Pour filling in piecrust, dot with 5 teaspoons of butter and top with remaining crust. Press top crust with fork around edges to seal. Poke holes in top with fork. Bake at 400° for 30 minutes or until golden brown.

Strawberry Pie

Olga Phillips
Bear Creek NC

Cook until brown one pie crust in oven at 400°.

Slice strawberries and pour a little sugar over them.

Let strawberries stand. Drain off juice and place them in the pie crust. Mix (for one pie)

10 ounces of 7-up
1 tablespoon cornstarch
1 cup sugar

Cook on medium heat until mixture starts to boil. Remove from heat, add red food coloring, stir and pour over strawberries that are in the pie shell.

Let cool in refrigerator and top with Cool Whip when ready to serve.

Jams

Zucchini Jam

Jeanne Belford
Camp Hill, PA

6 cups zucchini, peeled and shredded
6 cups sugar
½ cup lemon juice
1 cup crushed pineapple
1 (6 ounce) package orange jell-o

Puree zucchini. Place in large pot and cook slowly for 6 minutes stirring constantly. Add sugar, lemon, and pineapple. Boil for 15 minutes. Stir often. Remove from heat. Add jell-o; stir until dissolved. Pour into jelly jars and seal. (Also works with pumpkin instead of zucchini).

Strawberry Freezer Jam

Elizabeth Rea
Employee
Robbins, NC

1 quart strawberries
4 cups sugar
1 box Sure-Jell

Use 1 to 2 cup glass containers with tight-fitting lids. Wash and scald containers and lids. Have fruit at room temperature and remove caps from strawberries. Crush fruit and measure out 2 cups. Add sugar to fruit and stir thoroughly. Let stand 10 minutes. Mix ¾ cup water and Sure-Jell in a small saucepan. Bring to a full boil and boil 1 minute, stirring constantly. Immediately stir into fruit. Continue stirring for 3 minutes. Immediately ladle into containers, leaving ½ inch space at top. With damp cloth, wipe any spills from containers. Cover at once with lids. Let stand at room temperature 24 hours. Store jam in freezer.

Pickles & Relishes

Fig Pickle

Marilyn Sehen
Sanford, NC

3 quarts of figs-firm not too ripe-leave stem on
2 quarts boiling water-pour over figs (let stand 5 minutes)

Make syrup:
1 cup water
1 cup vinegar
1 tablespoon whole cloves
5 ½ cups sugar
1 stick cinnamon

Put cloves and cinnamon in cheesecloth and tie. Drain figs and pour syrup mixture over figs. Bring to a boil. Let simmer for 10 minutes. Leave figs in syrup in pot. Set aside.

Day 2: Bring figs to a boil for 10 minutes, set aside.

Day 3: Bring figs to a boil for 10 minutes, set aside. Put figs and syrup into pint jars. Place in water bath for 15-20 minutes.

Pear Relish

Nannie Williams
Yadkinville, NC

14 pears
12 green sweet peppers
1 hot pepper
1 quart vinegar
1 quart sugar
1 teaspoon celery seed
1 teaspoon mustard
1 teaspoon turmeric
8 onions peeled

Cut pears and onions in large pieces. Grind this with pepper in food chopper. Add vinegar, sugar and spices. Add salt to taste. Cook for 20 minutes-seal in jars.

This is wonderful with pinto beans-potatoes and corn bread. Sometimes I use some red-yellow & orange pepper to give more color.

Raw Cranberry Relish

Lena Hollifield
Morganton, NC

1 bag cranberries (1 qt)
1 apple
2 pears
2 ½ cups sugar
2 oranges

Put the cranberries and the fruit including the peelings through the food grater. Add sugar and allow setting for 3 hours.

This relish is delicious with chicken and turkey. It can also be used with celery in a jellied cranberry salad. Yield 6 cups.

Cucumber Relish

Martha Gilmore
Siler City, NC

7 cups cucumbers-sliced
1 medium bell pepper, chopped
1 cup onions, sliced

Mix: 2 cups sugar, 1 cup vinegar and 1 teaspoon celery seed. Pour mixture over relish. Mix and let set 30 minutes at room temperature. Refrigerate, will keep one week

Chow-Chow

Marilyn Sehen
Sanford, NC

8 red peppers
8 green peppers
2 medium onions
1 stalk celery
8 carrots
1 medium cabbage

Grind all together in food processor. Add ½ cup of salt and cover with ice water. Let stand 3 hours.

Mix:
1 ½ pints vinegar
4 ½ cups sugar
1 teaspoon ground cloves

Bring to a boil and boil 10 minutes. Put into sterilized jars. Place in water bath for 20 minutes.

Helpful Hint

Flat bottom ice cream cones filled with cake batter and baked may be topped with icing and decorating confections.

Icicle Pickles

Martha Gilmore
Siler City, NC

2 gallons cucumbers cut lengthwise.

Pour one gallon of boiling water with 1 pint of salt dissolved in it. Let stand one week. It may be smelly but it is all right, stir everyday. Drain this off and pour one gallon of clear boiling water. Let stand 24 hours. Drain this off and pour one gallon boiling water with 2 tablespoons alum, let stand 24 hours. Drain this off and pour hot over pickles:

2 quarts vinegar
8 pints white sugar
Handful mixed spices.

Reheat vinegar and pour over pickles 4 mornings in tight succession. Last morning can in airtight jars.

Canned Hot Peppers

Sara Scott
Employee
Bear Creek, NC

2 quarts white vinegar
1 quart water
2 cups sugar
1 tablespoon pickling salt
1 tablespoon oil per quart

Mix vinegar and water, sugar and pickling salt; bring to a boil. Fill hot quart jars with peppers. Add oil to each jar (quart jar). Pour boiling syrup into hot jars so they will seal. Do not cold pack. These are good on pizza or sandwiches!

Helpful Hint

There are two days we should worry about, yesterday and tomorrow.

Preserves

Fig Preserves

Mae Maness
Snow Camp, NC

6 quarts figs
8 cups sugar
6 quarts boiling water
3 quarts water

Pour boiling water over figs. Let stand 15 minutes-drain. Rinse figs in cold water. Prepare syrup by mixing sugar and water. Boil rapidly 10 minutes, drop figs into syrup a few at a time. Cook rapidly until figs are transparent. Lift out and place them in shallow pans. Boil syrup down until thick. Pour over figs and let stand until morning. Pour into clean jars, put on cap screwing band tight. Process in water bath for 20 minutes at simmering temperature (180°) or bring to boil and then pour into sterilized jar and seal each jar as filled.

Watermelon Preserves

In Memory of
Mrs. Iola Jordan
Wayne Jordan's Mother

2 pounds watermelon rind
2 tablespoons lime
1 tablespoon ground ginger
2 pounds sugar
2 lemons

Leave a little red for a pretty product. Prepare ring by peeling and cutting away all red portion. Cut into 1 ½ inch squares-add lime to 8 cups water; soak rind about 3 hours in mixture, rinse rind, let stand for 30 minutes in fresh water. Drain; sprinkle ginger over rind-cover with water. Boil until tender, drain. Add sugar and juice of 1 lemon to 7 cups water. Boil 5 minutes, cool, add rind. Boil 30 minutes, add remaining lemon thinly sliced, cook until ring is clear. Pack into hot jars, process 10 minutes in hot water bath.

To the ones who have purchased or read this book....

I would like to say what a wonderful thing it is to share the memories with you.

Who knows! There could be another book down the road, if Ethelda, Deborah and my daughter Belinda ever get over this one.

I guess some of you were looking for my Fruitcake recipe or ones for other foods we carry in the store. I must admit the book does not contain them, but I assure you that there is at least one recipe in this book to suit your taste buds.

My family, friends and customers that have shared their recipes are splendid cooks.

I feel Blessed in many ways. I am grateful to God for all that he has allowed in my life.

I wish to you God's Blessings as well.

Berta Lou Scott

> I believe in the sun
> Even if it does not shine.
> I believe in love
> Even if I do not feel it.
> I believe in God
> Even when he is silent.
>
> --- Author unknown

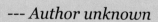

Index